The Bite in the Apple

The Bite in the Apple

A MEMOIR OF MY LIFE WITH STEVE JOBS

CHRISANN BRENNAN

St. Martin's Press
New York

www.stmartins.com

Design by Omar Chapa

Library of Congress Cataloging-in-Publication Data

Brennan, Chrisann.
    The bite in the apple : a memoir of my life with Steve Jobs / Chrisann Brennan.
        pp. cm.
    Includes bibliographical references and index.
    ISBN 978-1-250-03876-0 (hardcover)
    ISBN 978-1-250-04854-7 (trade paperback)
    ISBN 978-1-250-03877-7 (e-book)
    1. Jobs, Steve, 1955–2011.   2. Jobs, Steve, 1955–2011—Relations with women.
3. Brennan, Chrisann.   4. Jobs, Steve, 1955–2011—Psychology.   5. Jobs, Steve,
1955–2011—Family.   6. Computer engineers—United States—Biography.
7. Businessmen—United States—Biography.   8. Apple Computer, Inc.—
History.   I. Title.
    QA76.2.J63B74 2013
    338.7'6100416092—dc23
    [B]

                                                                    2013023758

First Edition: November 2013

10 9 8 7 6 5 4 3 2 1

To Lisa, who is the whale rider

CONTENTS

CONTENTS

NOTE TO THE READER

There are three things I never thought I would do in this life: study history (history gives me migraines); play the drums (I'm just not very good at it); and write a book. And here I am writing a note to the reader . . . of my book.

Over the years, a number of people have encouraged me to write my story. And many more have warned me off it, even going so far as to say that I didn't have the right. This *right* that they were talking about was the right to tell the story of my history with Steve Jobs. I met Steve when I was just seventeen. I became his first love and the mother of his first child and, as such, I have a unique perceptive to share on this man who has fascinated the world. I've always been reluctant to share my story. For one thing, most of my time and attention has been devoted to my daughter, Lisa, and to my life and work as an artist. For another, my relationship with Steve was nuanced and difficult; I never wanted to revisit that history, much less go public about it.

Never say never.

In July of 2006, I became sick. Doctors were unable to diagnose the problem. I wasn't able to work—the fumes from my painting exacerbated my illness—and within five months I was virtually homeless. My illness slowed me down and left me bored and scared. So I found myself reaching for something meaningful on which to focus. I put my things into storage, packed up my car, and traveled around the Bay Area—from Marin to Santa Cruz counties—staying with friends while trying to heal. I drove up to visit my father in Sacramento and it was then, while I was alone in my car, that I had the first spark of an idea to write this book. The words came to me: *It's time.*

My circumstances were dire and I can say now that nothing short of these dire circumstances would have led me to do the painstaking work of looking back into that history with Steve, much less write about it. But as I had nothing left to lose, I began.

Writing a memoir is a lot like spelunking. Headlamp on, I felt as if I were dropping down into deeper and darker caverns, negotiating vast and tight spaces to discover the great and terrible beauty that had been sustained in the cool dark places under the surface. Once I started putting it all together, my only thought was to keep going.

I found the process rich and revelatory. Revisiting the past and working to define my own place in it gave rise to life-altering insight and freedom. What I didn't know then is that it would take me nearly seven years to write my memoir, and that in the writing I would experience something of a rebirth. That's what it was for me to finally tell my story—first to myself and now, here, to you, the reader.

I'm fortunate: Few people can afford to review a whole life and find an outlet for their endeavor. I've long had a feeling—right or wrong—that I have a unique responsibility to share my experience of the pre-Apple Steve Jobs and to add my perspective to the record. Little is known about Steve as a teenager and young adult. But I knew the young man who was funny and thoughtful. The intellectually honest one who was searching for his place in the world and for what he believed was his big destiny. And I saw firsthand how he changed and changed and changed again as he learned to make use of and misuse power. As such I believe that I have something to say about Steve, also I believe that my reflections as a young woman dealing with systems of power are valuable, too. I suspect that many people will recognize their own stories in some of the details of this book. This and more kept me going, purposeful and inspired.

In the end, what I have written is my story. This is not a tell-all or an exposé, nor is it journalism. This is my own narrative and like all personal narratives, it takes its shape from experience, memory, and insight. I have tried to paint a thoughtful portrait of Steve, of myself, of the time, and of our relationship, and to gain an awareness of things that neither Steve nor I understood when they were happening.

I can say for sure that were it not for the computer, I would never have been able to write this story. But if it weren't for the computer, I may not have needed to. Such are the simple ironies that have kept me amused throughout the past seven years. (And yes, I did write this on a Mac.)

ONE

THE CREATIVES

I first noticed him in early January of my junior year of high school. It was 1972. He wore thin blue jeans that were full of big holes, the torn material hanging in loops around his legs. He was dressed in a nice pressed shirt and tennis shoes and walked then, as he did as an adult, in a forward-falling gait, arms swinging with a contained reserve in his hands. It was a sunny California afternoon in early spring and he was standing in the quad with a small book in his hand. I don't know why I hadn't seen him before, since, as I would find out later, many of my friends knew him. I was drawn to him immediately, and when he walked off campus I followed him, wanting to say something but having no idea what or how. I surprised myself, because I ended up following him out to the edge of the campus three times over the next week. I finally gave up because it was too big a leap for me to introduce myself out of the blue to a boy I thought was cute. I never even learned his name.

A month later my friend and classmate, Mark Izu, started a film project and invited me to do the animation for it. Mark wanted to make a film, combining 2-D animation, Claymation, and actors about how the students at our high school were struggling against forces that we believed wanted to stamp out our individuality. Mark's parents had been interned in a concentration camp for Japanese in the United States during World War II, and even though he didn't know this at the time we were making the movie, he was deeply motivated to speak about what it was to be made invisible. We all had our stories. In the course of the project many people would be invited to contribute, but in the beginning it was just three of us: Mark, myself, and a guy named Steve Eckstein, the cameraman.

We worked on the film at least one Friday or Saturday night a week for about three months, starting at 11:00 p.m. and going until dawn. Mark called the film "Hampstead." A nod to the name of our school—Homestead High School—it was also the name of the stumpy little clay character he made to represent the everyman in the film. Our stage was a raised cement section in the central quad on campus where I usually sat and ate my lunch during the school day. But this was night and we were there without permission, risking God-knows-what if we were caught.

The nights were cold. I was awed by the stars, and I loved that we were out there on our own, making something happen. Our tiny sounds were lost in the expanse of the cavernous, cinder block campus, and it felt like joy to be so focused and quiet, creating something from the margins with that sense of *just we few*. We worked continuously: Mark and Eckstein behind the camera, exchanging quiet words as they filmed; me under a single, brilliant low-angled spotlight. From a semi-prone position I drew my designs frame by frame, careful not to draw too little or too much before getting up and stepping back to pause for the frame to be shot, and then returning. This would go on for hours.

On one night, Mark instructed me to build his clay man out of the ground piece by piece so that it looked like Hampstead was emerging from the cement. He then handed me a second Hampstead that he had cut in half, from which I was to start the emergence scene. Once the little guy was fully out of the cement, I made his arms flail in painful insanity from having been buried alive. Another evening I was to draw a pathway for the little figure to walk down. Using cheap colored chalk, I started by illustrating a soft, morphing pattern that enfolded a mutated shape like a flickering fire. It looked psychedelic, but in truth it was drawn from the memory of my parents' curling cigarette smoke, which I had loved watching as a child in Ohio, just tall enough for my eyes to follow during their monthly poker games with my grandparents.

These were wonderful nights on the Homestead campus and they created a sense of independence and spaciousness in me. If the film was about losing our authenticity, then making it was the antidote. Over time, word got out and people started showing up in twos and threes to see what we were doing. Musicians, cartoonists, late-night stoners, and others joined in, the "Creatives" who represented the gifted and curious Homestead student body. I would look up from my work to see a surprising riot of quiet activity as more and more familiar faces appeared. There was some kind of rare nutrient happiness in all this, and I felt my life filling in around me. By the time the lavender dawn came to end the night, I went home spent, profoundly grateful, and achingly relieved that once again we had not been caught trespassing.

It was maybe a little more than a month into the project when Steve emerged through the darkness and walked straight over to me. I wondered if he'd known that I was interested in him because his path to me was so unerringly direct. But I had told no one. He was tall and beautiful and intentional, a study in contrasts, something like a fine prince in shabby jeans, a little awkward and vulnerable but courageous, too. Behind the small talk we sought out a connection. Then he reached into his pocket and gave me a copy of Bob Dylan's song "Sad Eyed Lady of the Lowlands." I could feel the indent of the letters as I opened the paper, and I wondered if it was typed for me or if he just happened to have it on him and wanted to share it. I never asked. Later I would come to understand that there was a kind of morphic field around Steve. Things happened; they were uncanny, not particularly planned, but perfect.

We talked for about twenty minutes, long enough for me to observe every minuscule detail about him—the power of his intense eyes and his young sensitivity, the sense that he was just passing through. At the end of our conversation I saw him retreat back into himself, and then with an inexplicably harsh scan of me and the quad—a look that seemed to come from nowhere—he disappeared back into the night.

Over the months of working on the film I had plenty of downtime. I found it hard to wait around when I wasn't useful to a scene, so I filled my time by painting a picture copied from the photography book put together by Edward Steichen, called *The Family of Man*. This book, which I had furtively removed from my mother's bookshelves, was dated and signed by an old boyfriend of hers who had apparently given it to her as a gift. I looked at this book often, and had considered this signature as the limited window into my mother's world before me. It was all so frustrating. Who was this man? Did he and my mother love each other? Many times my mother had told us that she hoped my sisters and I would be undressed by a poet once in our lives. Was he her poet? And why, for God's sake, *only once*?

The Family of Man is a beautifully conceived book with images from hundreds of contributing photographers from all over the world. It's a treasure that captures the breadth of shared human experience, not just in the photographs, but in the very poetry of the captions.

"The world of man dances in laughter and tears."—Kabir
"Clasp hands and know the thoughts of men from other
     lands."—John Masefield
"Eat bread and salt and speak the truth."—old Russian proverb
"If I did not work, these worlds would perish."—*Bhagavad Gita*
"With all beings and all things, we shall be as relatives."—Sioux
     Indian

I'd pored over this book so many times that it taught me to love the world, to love life, and know myself by way of word and image. I had both drawn and painted from it, and this time I wanted to paint a photograph taken by Homer Page of a South African black man who had been captured with the camera looking directly into his powerful, searching face. The one line under his image is *Who is on my side? Who?* The book has imprinted my life so profoundly I feel my cells could give an account of it.

I had always liked this photograph; it spoke to me. My great-uncle was Branch Rickey, the man who had the heart and the vision, the power and position to bring Jackie Robinson into the major leagues. They were both heroes of mine and I was proud to be associated with that history. These men embodied the kind of aspirations I had for myself: to be a leader and do something for others, to make a difference. So this painting was, for me, a form of guerilla art. I cared about getting it right. And I cared about making a statement from the margins.

I worked in oils and painted directly on cement at the edge of the quad, in a relatively dark location near the filming. Steve must have seen me working on the painting because he appeared one night happily fumbling with a candle and some matches so that I could see better. That spring, as the film progressed and I painted, Steve would show up to sit next to me while I worked. I was always unspeakably thrilled to see him, and yet I never could stand having someone hover while I worked. My painting was always deeply private and I never painted when people were around. But because I had no idea how to ask him to leave, and because he sat so quietly, barely perched on the seat next to me as if in some kind of transcendent state, I let it be. I pushed the paint around—distracted and noncommittal—and saved the real painting for the nights he didn't come.

In mid-April, more than a month after our first meeting, Steve and I excitedly decided to meet at his house so that we could spend some time together, just the two of us. He said his parents worked and that we would have the house to ourselves. I agreed that it would be nice to see each other alone in the daytime for once. Since he left school at 1:00 and I got out at 3:30, he drew me a map to his house on Crist Drive, a mile and a half away.

When I arrived at the Jobses' front door Steve motioned to me from his bedroom window—*come in*. I remember being a little taken aback by his not coming to meet me at the front door. No grand gestures of chivalry on this day. My guess is that he was so nervous he had decided to play it cool. Maybe he had even staged the scene to look casual. I entered the house and turned the corner into his bedroom.

Steve's room was small and almost barrackslike. Everything in it was plain and organized. He had a single bed, a dark-stained wooden bookcase, a chest of drawers, and a small desk under the window that looked out onto the front yard. I noticed a typewriter on his desk, a huge IBM Selectric in a bright shade of red. I was impressed that Steve owned such high-end technology. Etched in my memory from that time is the quality of his hands on that typewriter. He had beautiful, quiet, intelligent hands, with long elegant fingers. When he was typing, the machine would pound out individual letters with such shocking force and velocity that it belied the casual touch of his fingertips. Steve's hands were made for technology. There was a sublime compatibility with the machine in them, natural and unaffected from the beginning.

Other than that typewriter, Steve's room was reminiscent of the boys' rooms I had played in as a child, especially the colors: dull beiges, browns, army greens; harsh, garish oranges, and reds. I didn't like them, but the room felt good because it was bright with some ineffable sense of light and order. I could feel and smell the air of it in Steve's room and near him, and I liked this very much.

Over a year later, he would show me the inside of his closet after he had apparently spent the day cleaning. It was a thing of beauty for its organization. The closet was small but deep, and everything was arranged for the best use of space. Steve's clothes were hung neatly and his backpack, tent, and other camping equipment were looped over hooks in the back. His shoes were arranged on some floor shelving, his tapes were nicely boxed, and his books and other belongings were organized on the top shelf overhead. Sweeping his hand as if performing he said, "Look at this!" I had never seen him proud of cleaning. I didn't really care, but he was positively glowing. It's not too big a stretch to consider this the precursor to his sense for aesthetics—perhaps even his showman's flourish.

Smiling, Steve told me he threw anything away if (a) he wasn't using it and (b) it cost less than $25. Twenty-five dollars was his tipping point, apparently, and it wasn't worth taking up space if he could replace it for that amount or less. He had put real thought into this—weighing the relationship of money, organization, and serviceability (both present and future). It was like child's play showing the mind he would apply later to computer design.

Steve was sitting on the floor when I walked in that first day. His knees were bent and he was leaning against his bed. He had super plush headphones over his ears that plugged into a three-foot-high reel-to-reel tape player. We were both nervous and he made gruff references to his collection of Bob Dylan bootlegs from this or that concert. The importance of all of this was completely lost on me. I was clueless about bootlegs of anything, thinking bootlegging had something to do with alcohol during Prohibition, though I got the drift they were some kind of contraband. It was the beginning of my fragile girl-window into his tender boy-world.

I don't recall the conversation that first spring afternoon. I just remember that it was a little work to get beyond the awkwardness of a new friendship to find out who the other was, who we were together, and how much might be possible. There was that excited feeling in the air. Since he had invited me there and I had accepted, I think both of us knew that doors were opening and love was coming.

Mark's project was finishing by mid-May and most everyone who had been a part of the weekly events came to celebrate. We threw a formal dinner party in the middle of the night in the central campus, the motherboard of our communal lives. Converging in the freedom of the night air one last time, we, a band of bright happy creatures dressed in gowns and tuxedos (Steve had managed to score a top hat), toasted, ate, and laughed around a long candle-lit table in full Felliniesque style. A quartet and a strobe light made us all feel as if we were in some elegant silent film.

During that spring, with the film and some Saturday afternoon baseball games as backdrop, Steve and I got to know each other better. He didn't talk a lot but he was funny and vibrant and really good at making me laugh. But he was shy. So shy, in fact, that he couldn't give me our first kiss. I was so embarrassed by his trying that *I* finally kissed *him*.

After we were together for a while, Steve ventured to tell me that I was his "North Country Girl," the one from the Dylan song who was a true love, the one he would know before fame and wealth came, the one hit by heavy winds. Even then he had placed me in his "life-as-Bob-Dylan" timeline. I didn't understand that I was somehow being set up to play a part in some mythic script he was designing for himself.

I was a small-boned, petite girl—just five feet two. I had long, light brown hair turned gold on the outer layers by the sun. I have a high forehead and slightly elongated face, refined, expressive hands, and green eyes. I am dyslexic, which has had the effect of making me differently wired, creative, and a voracious problem solver—bright, but more than slightly clueless to convention. I suppose Steve would have intuited that I had a perceptive mind with a sense-oriented awareness of the world around me.

What did I see in Steve?

I knew he was a genius when I first saw him because his eyes shone with brilliant, complicated cartwheels of light. In time I came to understand how fully off-the-charts intuitive and mature beyond his years he was, like an old soul with quiet knowledge. He had deep brown hair and marble-white skin—skin that was supersensitive and yet also thick, which I would later realize was not unlike his personality. He had a slight lisp and his upper and lower teeth met perfectly, giving his Middle Eastern lips and nose an even more distinctive look. His smile had the glint of a pirate with treasure in the hull. There was a profound sadness about him that drew me in, but there was also an unspoken fullness in his stature that gave the impression he had the humility and strength to walk through the world as he truly was. I admired this right from the start. I know humility might sound unlikely to some, but it's like the salt in chocolate, the small contrasting flavor that makes you know that the strength is real and true. The mix of all of this came to life in a personality that was irreverent, bright, offbeat, awkward, funny, and full of mystery. I adored him beyond everything, pure and simple.

We were different from each other in many ways. I was sense- and soul-oriented and he was logical and intuitive. Yet we shared basic creative values and were both fiercely experimental. Steve and I wanted to find the pathways through any and all limitations, and that impulse was stronger than the fear of making mistakes. Neither of us placed great importance on the need to be right. The notion that we were a true yin and yang still resonates for me, even though in time this same quality would become polarized—destructive, even.

In those days, I considered Steve a guide for me because I saw an intellectual honesty in him. He was tall and had the sophisticated, unadorned presence I imagined Abraham Lincoln to have had: self-effacing and honest, funny, nothing extra. I was dealing with a corrosive home life, which was shattering my ability to build the next stages of my life, but Steve was further along in thinking about the shape of his adulthood and the road that would take him there. He had an aerial view of things and I could see he was cataloging information that implied scope and goal. He spoke in cloaked metaphors and had a big conversation going on inside. I wanted to know more about that conversation. I needed to know more and found myself quick to pay attention to his young stores of knowledge to get the sense of how he saw things. I believe that he was equally delighted and interested to see the world through my impulses, perceptions, and creativity.

Steve would play with words that were quirky and obscure to me, often saying that he was "The Imposter," or mysteriously repeating that something was going to last "for forty days and forty nights," or that it was "thirty-nine past the hour." Then there were the numerous rounds of *The Fool is the highest card,* a reference that indicated an archetype and more, because The Fool—marked by the zero in the tarot—is about nothing and everything. It's all about potential. Placing himself in this starring role and winking at me with a shiny smile, Steve was *The Fool,* the one who would walk over the edge of the known world and willy-nilly take the consequences. Oh yes, he was the courageous fool who knew from a very early age that he had something to do in the world. But this all contrasted with the darker warning he would give that he was a "no good boyo" from Dylan Thomas's *Under Milk Wood,* which I wondered at each time he said it. Finally there was the "I'm living on borrowed time" refrain. I never knew what he was talking about, but I would tilt my head to listen as if from an inner ear, searching for clues in the mix of it all.

We had both been hit by the winds of the sixties and had developed a core distrust of convention and an unbounded excitement for the amazing possibilities that lay ahead. Whatever we were to become, we shared this teenage stage of hunting and gathering that would keep us delighted and unfolding. From this shared ground and atmosphere we were willing, indeed bursting, to be experimental. We might have been called visionaries, except back then I never would have connected this word to the urgent need to expand beyond the known. It was just what was.

TWO

AN ABSOLUTE AUTHORITY

For the first six weeks of our friendship, Steve and I existed almost exclusively in our teenage world: high school, the nighttime movie set, baseball games on the Cupertino middle school lawn. But it would be some time before we would meet each other's parents.

It was a late Saturday morning when I first met Paul and Clara Jobs. They were painting his sister Patty's bedroom, and in the background hum of introductions I noticed the most beautiful yellow I had ever seen. The tone caught me off guard and made me wonder who these people were to have chosen it. My mind raced: no one in all of my extended family had ever used such a color, or even come close. Its soft warmth aroused in me a spirit of awe. Harder to understand were the other feelings it provoked—a sense of having missed something, of disappointment in my own family.

But I soon understood that this yellow was an exception. Everything else in the Jobses' house was predictable and austere: the beige couch; the big brown La-Z-Boy and ottoman; the blond wood dining and coffee tables. A large TV took center stage in the living room, and above it a bookshelf that displayed the family's entire collection of about fifteen books (including the Book of Job), along with school photographs of Steve and his sister Patty. Steve's photograph showed a chubby fifth grader with that one eye half-closed, and whose beautiful face was mischievous and sweet, but inscrutable nonetheless.

The Jobses' home had economy-size bags of candy lying around the living room and grocery-store jelly rolls in their '40s-style kitchen. They had a big boat in the driveway (Steve and Patty water-skied), and a pet rabbit that roamed freely around the house and backyard, which surprised me no end. I mean, no end. And when I glanced into the master bedroom I saw twin beds. Steve's parents slept separately like a 1950s TV couple. There was no romance here. This was a home filled with things well considered for practicality, a home without nuanced beauty. It was the kind of place I imagined would have belonged to someone's grandparents.

Paul Jobs was a thin man, just shy of six feet tall. He had a military haircut, which was a little unusual in those days, even on fathers, when sideburns were the norm. He had elongated lines in his pinched cheeks, and watery gray eyes. His nerves were close to the surface and he was given to small bursts of exasperation. His voice ran to a rattling high pitch when he was stressed, and he would often talk about giving someone a *knuckle sandwich*. There were times he reminded me of a Popeye cartoon and the first time I heard him use the phrase *knuckle sandwich* I looked around to see if I was supposed to laugh. I definitely wasn't.

Paul was hard on Steve, often fretting that Steve was doing everything wrong. I mainly remember Steve lumbering under what seemed like a constant flow of disapproval. Years later, one of Steve's other girlfriends, Tina Redse, told me that she thought Paul Jobs had been beaten as a child, and though I have no idea if that was true, it makes sense from the way he sometimes behaved. Steve would respond to his father with sad smiles and a painstaking patience. I believe that Steve was an empath and I imagine that highly empathic people can flip and become cruel, as was the case with Steve. That Steve's life was compelled in part to rectifying the wrongs done to Paul was something that has always had the feel of truth to me. Sometimes I think that Steve's profound sense of empathy got scrambled and used up in response to Paul.

Paul Jobs wasn't an easy man to be around. Quite apart from his *knuckle sandwich* routine, that first day I met him he kept repeating "Pretty is as pretty does." I didn't really understand what he meant, but since this was my new boyfriend's father and I was trying to be agreeable (and since Steve had left me to handle this by myself), I just kept responding to him very conscientiously, saying, "Oh." It took me a while to understand that not only was Paul referring to me, but he regarded me as a problem. On another occasion, I remember his barking with irritation that teachers were lazy, and that they shouldn't be paid in the summer months. I disagreed with him—politely—but he repeated his opinion four times over the next fifteen minutes. Steve let me handle this by myself, too. At the time I wondered if perhaps Paul thought I was going to be a teacher.

Paul was an industrious man who made his two-car garage into a well-equipped workshop. It was an impressive space filled with tools, machinery, workbenches, and stored household and vacation items. A large sheet of pegboard served as home for hundreds of tools—some with shapes I'd never seen before—and each tool had been outlined by a black marker so it could be put back in its proper place. The garage was so well organized—so filled with interesting things—that it was wonderful to see.

I don't know what Paul did in his normal workday, but his garage was the place of a second job and source of income. On weekends, he fixed up older American cars he'd bought through newspaper ads, reselling them at fair prices. I'd often see him bending over engines and sliding beneath cars, sweeping and hosing the driveway in his coveralls, with an oily red rag hanging out of his back pocket. He was purposeful, always working, and often irritated and vocal about what griped him, except when he was focused. A business magazine once described Paul Jobs as a "used car salesman," but this leaves a completely inaccurate impression. Paul's work on cars was a hobby and, I felt, a public service. He was really competent at what he did and cared about doing a good job. I bought my first car from Paul, a four-door Chevy, for $250. I bought my second car from him, too, and each time he took great care to explain everything about the vehicle to me.

I learned early on not to take him too seriously. I felt that he had a deep sense of powerlessness that made him combative. And I always cared about him; it never occurred to me not to. After all, he was Steve's dad.

Clara Jobs was a sensible-looking woman who seemed both youthful and mature at the same time. Her eyes were shy and sweet, and her voice had a caramel tone. Like many women of her generation, she smoked. Clara Jobs had slightly dark skin and warm, brown hair. She had wide cheekbones and a wide smile. Steve may not have been Clara's natural child, but they shared a strong resemblance. I mentioned this once to Clara, and she turned red. Some years later I met Steve's biological mother, Joanne Simpson, and saw that she and Clara did indeed have similar features and coloring: broad cheekbones and warm-toned skin and brown eyes.

Through the years Clara told Steve that his birth mother was one of the most beautiful women she and Paul had ever seen. Steve repeatedly told me in a self-assured way, that *his* mother was *beautiful*. The ideal of her beauty became an untouchable, personal triumph for him, remarkable and perfected in the gap of her absence. When he talked about her, I felt my heart move toward something like pity. Not because Steve was pitiful, but because not knowing where he came from mattered so much to him, and for so many unnamable reasons.

The value Steve attached to beauty was peculiar to me. Once he showed me a professional glam photo of the younger Clara. His enthusiasm for it was way over the top and made me wonder if Clara had built up an image of his birth mother's beauty not only because of his longing to know where he came from, but because she could see how much glamour and beauty meant to him.

Not long after I met the Jobses, I was standing alone in their living room waiting for Steve, when Clara came in and made a startling admission. With no real lead-in, she told me that she and Paul had adopted Steve at birth, but that soon after, Steve's biological mother had taken them to court in an effort to place him in a different home. Steve's biological mother had felt that the Jobses didn't have the profile she wanted for her baby. In fact, she had originally chosen a different home for her son: Catholic, well-educated, and wealthy. But at the last minute that family had opted out because they wanted a girl. So the Jobses got Steve and Steve got the Jobses. But it wasn't to be easy. She and Paul had to go to court and fight to keep their infant son as his birth mother decided that she wanted him placed with a different—some might say *better*—family.

"I was too frightened to love him for the first six months of his life," Clara told me. "I was scared they were going to take him away from me. Even after we won the case, Steve was so difficult a child that by the time he was two I felt we had made a mistake. I wanted to return him." Her eyes widened as if she was telling me the deep, broken truth of their lives. I could see how she blamed herself and felt guilty, but there was more to it. When I think back on it now, I wonder if she had been trying to warn me off or simply explain.

I was very young when I met Clara; I don't think she understood how young. I just nodded with as deep an appreciation as I could, to comfort her and acknowledge that she had told me something profound. But I was also embarrassed because I knew that I was ill equipped to speak to an adult's reality. Up to that time I had, at most, met Clara on only three occasions. She was my new boyfriend's mother, and in an era when most young people didn't trust adults, Clara's confession seemed utterly remarkable to me. I felt sad and way out of my depth. I remember scanning the floor wondering if they loved him now.

Steve nodded his head thoughtfully when I recounted what his mom had told me. He said that the case had gotten settled when his parents legally committed to sending him to college. By the time I met Steve, he had already been accepted by Reed College, so that agreement had been honored. Steve repeated a number of times, "I just shut my eyes, and pointed at the book with the names of all the colleges and when I opened them, my finger was pointing to Reed College. That's how I picked Reed."

Steve told me that the kids in his grade school had taunted him about his adoption. "What happened?" they would ask. "Didn't your mother love you?" It must have been ten years after the fact when Steve recounted this episode to me, but still his mouth twisted with bitterness. This grade school bullying was so damaging to Steve that he came home one day and told his parents he would no longer tolerate it. He wasn't going back to that school.

Steve always had a sense of authority about himself. An absolute authority.

I can imagine that Paul and Clara recognized this and knew that they had to do something to protect their son. And they did, moving to Los Altos and another school district. I've always been in awe that the Jobses actually moved houses to protect Steve. At that time most parents I knew of would have sent their kid back into the bullying, telling him to "fight back." Oddly, though this response wasn't enough, as Steve would grow up to express very sophisticated levels of emotional and psychological bullying himself.

I was impressed by how much freedom Steve had to be himself and how much his parents seemed to respect him. Steve had a poetic streak and an intuitive turn of mind. He would often say things that seemed to come from the high winds of a vast plain. I never failed to be struck by how these hard-working, blue-collar parents, these people with common sense but so few books, gave him the space to be completely other-worldly. To be extraordinary, in fact.

To me, it was like the creamy, yellow paint in Patty's room; there was a strain of something very sophisticated about Paul and Clara, despite their lack of education. And when Steve showed signs of his prosody, everyone seemed to breathe more deeply, look down, and move in a different direction, as if they were dancers responding to a new choreography.

I wasn't very conscious during those early years about how Steve's subterranean world of loss and worry must have focused him. But the tension was there, like an arrow pulled back in the bow, taut and concentrated by the terrible losses he'd endured. But when he let that arrow fly—wow! It would move him and by extension me, forward in delight and discovery. Inspiration is always a response to what's missing. The creative process is about filling the gap. That's why, for example, Picasso never painted another guitar after he bought one for himself.

Steve could always surprise me. One day he expressed a sentiment that let me glimpse the man in the child—and the child in the man. He said something about bombing the Communists and it struck me as revealing a kind of a Cold War mentality. At the time I was idealistic in my belief that peace was the goal and, as the Beatles sang, *love is all you need*. I thought that polarizing comments about U.S. and Soviet relations were a ploy by the lesser gods of the media to keep people unthinkingly nationalistic. I rejected nationalism because I thought ours was a new generation meant to look beyond for more enlightened answers to the problems of our day, but Steve's comment made me stop and recognize that he had an older political context. It jarred me.

In truth a Cold War mentality was very much a part of my own life, although sub rosa. My father was employed by Sylvania, a company that did a lot of work for the Department of Defense. Due to the constraints around his work with classified information (he operated within layers of security clearances), we simply did not talk about politics or U.S. relations around the dinner table, even though it was what provided us with our upper-middle-class life. In every state we lived in, all of our neighbors would be interviewed by government authorities so my father could keep or increase his security clearances. I was blithely unconscious of the implications of all this in my own life; nevertheless, I felt Steve's Cold War outlook marked him as naïve.

Still, it was Steve's boy-ness that I loved. His mind and his silliness fed me like nothing else. At seventeen, he would do imitations of '50s robots where he would burst out laughing like a wiggly child and then pull himself into a structured metallic being, acting in response to an imagined control center outside of his brain. Arms outstretched like Frankenstein, he would walk forward stiffly, tilting on one foot then the other, droning out commands from a higher office. And running into the kitchen one day, he took the phone off the hook, pressed the pound key, and told me he had just blown up the world.

Steve was in a kind of child's dialogue with the issues of the day, but he was also bitter like an adult when, of all things, he told me of the time he'd learned that Santa Claus didn't exist. "I was mad that they had lied to me." He repeated this on several occasions and each time I could see that he was still unforgiving, still angered by the humiliation. For Steve, the vulnerability of childhood wasn't about suspending disbelief with enchanted narratives; it was about getting the facts straight and knowing how things really worked. Here again we were the opposite because I always loved and yearned for enchantment. It's why I loved him.

THREE

EXPERIMENTAL FLOWERING
IN FULL TILT BOOGIE

The high school grounds must have felt like home away from home to Steve and me; that's the only reason I can think of to explain our decision to take LSD on the Homestead campus. We must have been innocent and arrogant to believe it was a good idea, but to our credit, the grounds were large, hidden from the main street, and blessedly deserted on a Saturday.

I don't remember how we got the LSD, but I'm pretty sure that I would have been the one to get it because Steve had never tried it before. I have a slight memory of pulling the two wrapped hits out of my pocket to show Steve, thinking that we might split one by just ripping it in half. But that's not what either of us wanted, so we swallowed the little pieces of paper whole. And then we waited.

We sat in the stairwell under the covered enclosure of the two-story humanities building in thrilling expectation. At least I was thrilled. This was Steve's first time and though he had a lot of bold theories, he seemed frightened as we waited for things to take effect. And then, out of the blue, he started to tell me that I would need to tell him "not to put on airs" should he "act out." The word "airs" was so Shakespearean, I thought it was exaggerated but also magnificent. But then he said he actually wanted me to practice saying, "Don't put on airs," so I would be prepared to handle "it." *Prepared for what?* I had no idea what he was talking about. It was strange and embarrassing, but he was so earnest that I went along.

"*Don't* put on airs!" I said.

"No! You've got to say it with more conviction." He was serious.

"Okay," I said. Hem-hem . . . "DON'T put on airs!"

But, no, this still wasn't strong enough for him.

"NO!" He raised his voice. He was getting impatient with me but trying to be polite. "Try it again. This is important. You won't be able to stop me if you're not stronger."

Stop what? I laughed with alarm. It was all coming out of left field.

After my third attempt he stood up and repeated himself, taking great pains to explain. "No! You have to do it like *this,* you have to *DO* it with more force!" Then with his arm outstretched, he yelled, like this, "DON'T PUT ON AIRS!"

Lordy. I was doing my best, but the whole thing seemed so hilarious that I started laughing. But Steve wasn't laughing, just looking at me and repeating, "Speak like you MEAN it!" His brows furrowed. "Do it, say it!!!" Try as I might, I was soon laughing so hard that I couldn't form a single word with any conviction. And I wasn't improving with practice. I was getting worse.

Steve's sweetness was unspeakable to me, made more so by the seriousness with which he perceived a problem that I apparently wasn't grasping. I wondered how we were going to get beyond this when I realized that the LSD was already taking effect.

"Hey, it's started!" I yelled. "You're fine!"

A lifetime later, I visited Steve after he was married. Our daughter Lisa was about thirteen and Steve's son, Reed, was a tiny baby in a stroller. We were all outside his house in Palo Alto and about to go for a walk when, without warning, Steve blurted out the meanest, most ridiculous, terrible comments at me, like a machine gun spraying bullets across me. It was so unexpected and awful, something about why I was such a total failure of a human being that I gasped. You can't prepare for this sort of behavior, no matter how many times it happens. I fell silent, but Steve's wife, Laurene, yelled at him to stop. Even she was indignant on my behalf. Thinking back to Steve's first day on LSD—was it this he was scared of? He must have known he was capable of this Tourette's-like behavior. It sort of breaks my heart now to grasp how much he understood and tried to keep hidden back then.

But on that day many years earlier, when Steve realized that nothing terrible was going to happen, he relaxed into a kind of awe and dropped the worry without any residue. We spent the next nine hours playing, talking, peering into each other's faces, and laughing and serious in turns. Him making jokes about himself and me. Making me laugh. Making me think. It was very rich. Everything shimmered and vibrated with the LSD and the state of being so in love. Our kissing each other felt wet and bizarre and then instantaneously we merged into each other and everything floated pink and we touched our eyelashes to see what it felt like. There was nothing to hide. No fear, no barriers, no sense even of time as the sun slowly trekked across the sky until our stomachs were growling in the late afternoon when we realized that we hadn't eaten all day and were famished. Then we took just one adventure from our humanities base camp, to a nearby orchard at the corner of Stelling and Homestead (sadly not there anymore), for some apricots, the only food we would eat that whole trip. And it was enough.

That day we did the kinds of nothing that new lovers do and it was everything. In the evening, after the intensity had started to wear off, we parted and went to our homes. The next Monday at school Steve told me with great excitement that he could feel the lining of his stomach as a result of the LSD experience. He was so excited. I could tell it meant more to him than I could make sense of.

After that first time we took acid, Steve dropped with some of his friends at the Santa Cruz boardwalk. He told me that it was so much fun for him that he wanted to do it again with me. I think he loved riding the Ferris wheel in an altered state, something about looking at the people below and the huge expanse of ocean under the moonlit sky.

It never sounded like a good idea to me though, and now I can say with certainty that there's nothing more terrible than taking LSD at an amusement park. I was freaked as I looked into the gross faces of the crowd, left unhinged by the loud noises and flashing lights. All I wanted to do was crawl under a rock and wait it out until it was all over. We did ride the Ferris wheel but I was so terrified that I gripped the side and held onto Steve praying for it to be over. It was the longest Ferris wheel ride of my life.

Steve and I decided to leave the boardwalk, but he was oblivious to his condition and to the fact that he couldn't handle driving, so my body literally got sick at the car door to stop him from trying. After that we huddled at the edge of the Santa Cruz boardwalk, sitting on the sand for hours looking at each other, laughing and waiting late into the evening until the acid had worn off enough that it was safe to drive.

It was there, with nothing to do and all the layers of personality peeling away, looking into the sweetness of his smiling face that I understood how purely and profoundly in love I was with Steve, and he with me. This was a love unlike anything I had ever known. The hours went by like a flipbook. I could barely talk, the river of life was moving through us so fast that I could not find the vocabulary to speak and so we just looked into each other's eyes and Steve made jokes until I told him I felt better. We headed north up the coast and found a beach with a huge shore. There we laid our sleeping bags, far enough from the water to make sure we didn't wake up in the waves. Snuggling in together, Steve soon fell asleep curled up next to me. I couldn't sleep, but lay awake for hours, soothed by his breathing and the waves.

During this time I had one of the most profound and lasting visions of my life. In the vestigial effects of the LSD (which is the best part of LSD because all stress is gone and simply breathing is pure wondrous joy), I experienced a form of lucid dreaming in which I saw transparent, light-filled chimes that were billions of miles high clanging together into the universe. Watching and listening for hours to these bell towers of the sky that rang through my body every time the waves crashed, I saw that color and sound were one great continuum. Where before I had divided my perceptions between the senses, after that night there has never been a time when I didn't see sound, hear color, and sense color, form, and sound as one big connectedness. I believed then that that vision of the bells had come from our merged consciousness. I still do.

LSD is like going to the mountaintop and getting a life-altering vision. And once you have it, it never leaves. (Or if it does, it's only because you go beyond it or something more mind-blowing subsumes it.) After taking LSD, you don't even know that your whole life has reorganized itself around those moments of blasting insight. This is always the case with insight. It takes years to know. It can be a reckless ride if you don't use it with some kind of sacred intent, but use it with reverence and you can access realms of potential not yet in the world. It's a fire-of-the-gods kind of stuff, a game changer that opens doors to vital perceptions that never close again. Not to put too fine a point on it, it can change a person's destiny.

What did Steve take from it? I don't know. Can it turn muggles into Jedi? I don't know that, either. I think it can offer a good religious experience, but it's not a substitute for a spiritual practice. Steve would later publicly talk about the glories of LSD, which gives me the impression that he thought it made an important difference for him. But I don't think either of us used it past the age of nineteen or twenty when adult responsibilities began.

More than anything, I think that the wide use of LSD was part of the response to the nuclear bomb. While Ram Dass would later say that we could access much higher states with meditation (and that it would be more stable and longer lasting than drugs), I consider LSD very much in step with the time, part of a profound urge to open the world up to a new vision based on life, not death. And even though the movements of the sixties and seventies might seem naïve by today's standards, they informed the complex and sophisticated country we know today.

Encounter groups worked to get men to cry, and to get men and women to exchange role-playing for more authenticity in their lives and relationships. All kinds of grassroots groups organized for a more humane world. It was an iterative process that breathed through people and gathered momentum. And it created new systems of thought, vision, art, and technology meant to develop a better world: feminism; the Black Panthers; the Human Potential Movement; The Hunger Project; and the musical *Hair* all lit up for a new horizon. Hunter Thompson famously coined the rallying cry, "When the going gets weird, the weird turn pro!" saying *anyone* was qualified to make a difference if they had the heart, mind, and will to do so. Many did.

Steve had read Arthur Janov's book *The Primal Scream,* and he explained to me how both LSD and primal screaming opened up and released the stored trauma of childhood. "If we experience the feelings of our deepest unmet needs," he told me, "we can release blocked emotions and live life more fully. Anyone can do it." He said that Janov had developed the primal screaming methodology because one of his patients had been haunted by a theater performance of a guy walking around in diapers yelling, "Daddy come home! Mommy, don't leave!" The performance artist had cried out again and again, until he actually threw up on stage.

Slowly, the logic behind releasing trauma made sense to me and I saw the picture Steve was deciphering. He said, à la Janov, that the flood of hallucinations that come from LSD are the result of the speed of trauma being released from the body through some kind of biopsychological mechanism in the medulla at the back of the skull. I imagined steam from a boiling teapot streaming through the medulla, first creating a tiny hole, then a bigger one that released and transformed neurosis into images that would then dissolve in thin air. "Except with LSD," Steve said, "neurosis will always return, whereas with primal therapy, it would be fully felt and resolved."

Steve would repeatedly talk over Janov's ideas about how mothers and fathers who failed to love their children—who had walked out on them in any number of ways—would create and perpetuate patterns of trauma. I followed him in these conversations many times over. It was as if they were the liturgy and he was the shaman drumming, building and amplifying a powerful idea through repetition. Eventually, the idea that it was actually possible to reclaim sacred innocence, that everything could be recovered and made wholly new again, slipped into my awareness and changed my foundational concepts forever. I think it must have been Steve's greatest hope for himself to recover what was lost due to the adoption, but it was also a joyfully infectious idea that gave me access to my own wide vistas of potential. "Potential" itself was the aesthetic of our time.

Steve was aware earlier than most that food could be used as a way to tap into potential, to clear neurosis, and develop consciousness. Arnold Ehret's book, *Mucusless Diet Healing System,* tipped him off to practices that he used to have superior health for years. Ehret's book is one of these quirky gems written earlier in the twentieth century by an odd guy who still has a relatively large following today. In fact, Ehret might well be considered one of the godfathers of today's raw and super foods movements. Ehret proposed that by eating a mucusless diet, people could clear up emotional blocks trapped in their bodies and open themselves into greater levels of physical, emotional, mental, and spiritual clarity and integration. Steve would recount Ehret's notion of how to heal, which was to stop eating meat and cheese and sugar. He would explain that healing was innate to the body; you just had to stop eating the "bad" foods. Steve told me that "With real foods like apples or salad, your body knows when it's full. But with junk food, the body's intelligence can't get a read on the nutrients and so can't tell you when to stop eating." I loved this understanding and recognized it as a higher level of information.

Steve explained other body chemistry, too. I had discovered coffee the year before I met him, and it had literally changed my life because the focus I gained from the caffeine helped me overcome childhood ADHD and the dyslexia that had always interfered with my reading for more than twenty minutes in one sitting. Without my having told

Steve my history, he explained to me that doctors gave amphetamines to hyperactive children in order to overload their nervous systems so they could calm down. *So,* I thought to myself, *this is why the coffee made the difference in my reading.* I was too embarrassed to tell him I couldn't read well before caffeine, but once again marveled at how he'd answered the question. Later I asked a doctor if he'd gotten it right. The doctor sort of winced at me, as doctors can, but he told me Steve had, at least partially.

Steve was a problem solver. He would often explain a problem and then show me the way through it. Not intentionally, it was more like his habit. I admired how he could work pathways through things and how deftly he related them to my world. Back then he seemed to have a list of ideas about foods, medical cures, learning disabilities, and therapies, ideas that would help him unlock the possibilities of the universe. Now, it seems like he was coming close to a philosophical system known as natural law. At the time, however, I wondered if he was just a bit of a blazing fool and questioned if the answers weren't more layered and complex than he acknowledged. But Steve was looking for elegant simplicity.

I remember once how he explained the way a Dylan song spoke out on issues of power abuse at a global level. He talked about how the powerful and wealthy would create circumstances to keep people overwhelmed, working too hard, poor, and in chaotic wars, so they would be distracted from what was really sabotaging their lives. I recall how quiet Steve was when he told me that the elite leverage wealth-building tactics on the backs of people who can least afford it. This statement had a profound effect on me, not just because I had always wanted to understand how power abuse worked, but because he was so seriously clear and honest when he said it.

However profound Steve's insights were, they could also be alarmingly negative. One day I met him in the exact place I had first set eyes on him a few months before. He had just come from a science class and was describing experiments with lab rats that he was learning about in behavioral studies. "If you give a rat only positive feedback," he said, "the rat can learn a trick. And if you give him only negative feedback, he can learn a trick. But if you give a rat both positive and negative feedback he'll go crazy!" He had a shadowy smirk on his face. It was like this was information that he was pocketing for later use.

Steve's world was different from mine. His was a mix of Bob Dylan, John Lennon, and Shakespeare, science, math, and different kinds of psychology than I was familiar with. I couldn't get enough of science fiction and magic realism. I pored over the bright scenes of floating people, weddings, villages, rabbis, and animals within Chagall's paintings. I loved the deep golden resonance and earthy social realism of Rembrandt's works, and the soulful honesty in nineteenth-century Russian painting. I listened to Jefferson Starship, Jethro Tull, Leonard Cohen, Joni Mitchell, the electric violin in the Mahavishnu Orchestra, and—like Steve—John Lennon.

Steve also introduced me to the Beat Poets. He studied their literature and their cool. There was some wedge of light from that former time in him, too—the clear, hip sophistication of a handsome nerd/poet/shaman. It was a thin wire that vibrated through the center of his being, a particular rhythm in his words, humor, and ideas. I'm sure that through Steve the Beat aesthetic helped shape the future of the Apple aesthetic.

I was no blank slate when we started our relationship, that's for sure, but Steve planted many seeds that enlarged my considerations. He once shared with me the notion that Shakespeare was thought to have been enlightened. *Enlightened?* A word from the East applied to a Western European literary genius? I laughed; the idea seemed preposterous. But Steve believed it to be true. Some of his ideas would loop in my brain and never let go until I understood many years later what he had been talking about. Now I agree.

An idea of enlightenment was fueling many, consciously and unconsciously. Our whole high school was a little petri dish growing creative students and teachers, many of whom struggled to bring about a bright new conversation based on bright new values. Seven years after graduating from high school, I would talk with *Time* reporter Michael Moritz, who told me that he interviewed teachers at Homestead about Steve and Woz, many of whom had independently commented that the years between 1967 and 1974 were a creative anomaly at the school, a true experimental flowering in full tilt boogie. And then one day, without warning, it was gone. Done. Kaput. Over. According to Moritz, the teachers were left stunned, asking each other: "What just happened?" "Where did it all go?"

From my current view, I am hard pressed not to consider that all of that explosive cultural magma came to distill itself into the cool circuitry of the infinitesimally small computer chip—a rational response for the building of social complexity, organization, and *connection*. The world was demanding change and a higher level of functioning. It called out not just for a new science and technology, but for new laws to handle it, and new types of art and music to express it. Honestly new kinds of everything to integrate new levels of responsibility and love. And we were a part of that new stage.

At the end of my junior year, Homestead had started to make physical changes to the campus that seemed designed to stamp out the kind of creativity we represented. Small grassy areas were, one by one, covered with cement. As I recall, they were painted pale green. Surveillance floodlights were put into the quad, and an eight-foot fence was erected around the entire campus. A year after I left, the cinder blocks were painted a suffocating, off-white enamel. Maybe it was done in the interest of preservation, protection, and cost cutting, but it seemed that the school was being redesigned for control. Our time came and went, and with it, a unique culture. Now, however, thirty years later I have to say, the school is stupendously beautiful. Things change. And there are different purposes growing inside a new generation of children at Homestead now. I can see and feel it. And these children are softer and kinder than we were, too.

Looking back on everything now, I recall how close Steve and I

were, how much time we spent together. Like young couples everywhere, we went to the movies. We saw films by François Truffaut, Fell-
ini, Charlie Chaplin, Woody Allen, and others—films about Bob Dylan,
John Lennon, Lenny Bruce, and Woody Guthrie, all of which we
would see at Steve's behest. The romantic in Steve particularly loved
Truffaut's film *Jules and Jim* and Marcel Carné's *Children of Paradise*.
And though I loved and was captivated by the textures in these movies,
I'm afraid I just didn't get the depth of the drama. Both films had a terrible sense of devastating romantic loss that escaped my understanding.
Not until much later, when I saw *The Enigma of Kasper Hauser* in 1988,
did I experience the truth of my own devastating emotional theater for
the first time. Leaving the movie house that day I felt as if I were walking on the bottom of the ocean. *So this is what that was for him,* I thought.
Sadly, there were many instances back then when my full appreciation
for Steve's emotional life would be subject to great time delays.

The extent to which Steve could be affected by a film was made
clear to me one night we went to Camera One in San Jose. The 1967
Dylan documentary *Don't Look Back* was playing, and I recall at one
point I turned away from the movie to look at Steve because his energy
was so intense it was as if terrible electricity moved through his body.
The movie had made a point of comparing Dylan with another contemporary folk singer, Donovan. Identified as he was with Dylan's musical superiority and success, I saw in Steve how personal it was to him
to be on the winning side of this competition as his dark, seething expression revealed a ruthless contempt toward Donovan's "lesser talent"
that took my breath away.

FOUR

THE IMPOSTER

Homestead in the seventies was a vibrant mix. We had musicians and actors, smart people, and stoners. There were photographers, English lit kids, and various artistic types—those into fine art like me, but also cartoonists and ceramicists. Homestead had its scientists and its nerds, of course, as well as a group of boys who rode motorcycles and wore Harley-Davidson jackets, but whom we called the "Hardly Hards" because they were such sweet guys. Then there were the kids who were just themselves, with no group association you could pin on them.

Students at Homestead overlapped in their associations. Steve and I did; we bridged different worlds. His friends were odd and smart, with a shared a sense of mischief and a bright individuality. They were always finding ways to cut through the rules that others lived by. And they were loyal, like an elite band of thieves. (My friends weren't this way. We didn't need the double vision that clever insincerities call for.)

Steve had the kind of intellectual honesty that you find in very bright people who are used to tolerating a less-than-brilliant world. That Honest Abe quality again. Yet while he stayed true to himself in so many remarkable ways, he was also disconnected and awkward. Steve's baseline was a mix of genius, authenticity, and emotional woodenness. Wooden like Pinocchio, but not a Disneyfied version of that story: something ancient, about the tale of the motherless, enchanted boy. Real boys knew things that he didn't. His birth mother's love, for example. His birth father's pride. And just what did this father do for a living? Stuff most people take for granted.

Some of his qualities derailed me and made me uneasy. At seventeen, I didn't have the intellectual sophistication to know that false sentimentality can have an underbelly of indifference and brutality to offset the numbness. But I could feel it. His oft-quoted refrain that he was "The Imposter" indicated that somewhere he grasped the nature of the problem. My feelings in response to him ranged from being deeply moved to being totally removed. Not knowing better then, I questioned whether there was something wrong with me, and I observed our friendship for clues about what was present and missing in both of us—because that's what teenagers do.

This was the age of splitting the atom, an aspect of science that contributed to the development of the computer. And Steve was a child of his time, an extraordinary child who would learn to create in spite of—or perhaps even because of—the great gulf of his interior life. Of course I didn't think in these terms then.

Steve invented the name "Oaf Toabar" for himself. Oaf was a secret name, he said, and I wasn't to tell anyone about it. It seemed a tender expression of vulnerability and self-confessed awkwardness, although his oafishness wasn't such an attractive quality to me. He signed love letters with "Love, Oaf." And like a note slipped under a door, this name made me wonder about his hidden sense of identity. Steve often made a big deal about being an oaf and laughing at himself; it's why he loved the psychological complexes of Woody Allen's characters. Yet the nature of Steve's feelings of awkwardness would give way to another layer of insight. Steve was a magician, and it was as if from within the secret logic of fairy tales that he leveraged his shyness and low self-esteem into its opposite expression, to become a man of exceeding self-confidence and invulnerability. It was a deft sleight of hand, but it felt slightly sketchy to me. I was aware of feeling uncomfortable with a false intimacy when he told me not to tell anyone about this secret name. (Much later I would discover that it was the code name he used to identify himself in the underground business of selling blue boxes with Woz.)

One day early in our relationship I saw Steve standing by himself, holding his body in a way that I found so disturbing that it made me question if I was seeing right. It was an aspect of him that never appeared when he was animated and talking, but after observing it several times in the months that followed I knew for sure I was seeing a different side of him. When he was by himself, Steve's posture sometimes took on the quality of a mad cripple. Whether he was standing or leaning against a wall, he would hold himself frail and stooped, with a bony knee bent and torqued inward. His head would be dropped and he'd peer out with one eye under his forward falling hair. Steve could be standing in the brightest sunshine, but his angled posture would create sharp shadows. A buzz of mean darkness would gather around him at these times, leaving the unmistakable impression of a devastating loneliness. The emotional starvation in him pierced right through me.

I remember one of his friends at that time was a girl who was solid and witty, not especially pretty, but so self-possessed that she was beautiful and impressive. This girl would challenge Steve in ways that seemed beyond me, ways that made me sit up and take note. I think she saw something in him that she felt called to engage. She had a pinch of the dominatrix in her and she was getting him to be brave by doing things that were socially undesirable.

This girl's strange requests made me uncomfortable. You could almost hear her say, "Now my puppet . . ." I remember how she would sidle up close to him and whisper some new idea: "This is what I want you to do." She'd always begin that way. "Now this is what I want you to do." Steve would come under her spell. And a rhythm would move through his body as he readied himself for the challenge. Any chance to win the prize of her approval.

Steve couldn't back out; she wouldn't allow it. He tried once, and I watched how she stood her ground, how she confronted him and repeated her challenge. I suspect now that he was attracted to her strength. I wasn't jealous of her, but I was uneasy with the way she spoke to him and the things she got him to do. They were funny, these challenges, and at the same time not funny at all. I wish I could remember the many examples, but I can recall one time when she had him cut in front of about fifty people to get tickets for a theater performance in San Francisco. She asked and he did it. That cleared it all up for me: these requests were designed to get the awkward boy to stand up to his own outrageous potential. I must have looked like a gnat to her and all her power.

Another of his friends, whom I'll call "Lew," was a tall, thin Eurasian guy. He looked slightly tipped, as if he had fallen out of a Paul Klee painting. There was something lyrically off balance about the two tall friends, something idiosyncratic in their sweetness and respect for each other, too. Steve told me that Lew wanted to become a San Francisco cab driver after high school, so he could learn the streets of the city. I was fascinated by this idea and the way he intended to, as I thought of it then, stack his purposes one on top of the other. For him it was simple: make an income while learning the city streets as if he were both a cab driver and an undercover agent. Lew's plan tipped me off to a creative principle about organizing complexity. I had never considered achieving multiple outcomes in one action like this. Silly as it might sound— because this is all anyone ever does now—the way Lew stacked his purposes indicated the creation of a multiuse device. Like a smartphone that's also a camera and an address book and everything else under the sun. This idea seemed exciting and generative to me as an artist. And it was a glimpse into their conversations that I was otherwise never in on. I am sure that Steve told me about it because he was musing over it, too.

One day Steve told me that Lew's father drank and beat Lew. Steve had always made a big deal out of the fact that he never had been spanked or hit by his parents in any way; once again, I believe this was important to him because something similar may have happened to his father, Paul.

Lew's situation seemed to have a tremendous impact on Steve. It turned him into something of a healer. In all the time I knew Steve this was a role I rarely saw him take on. But he had a huge capacity for empathy when it came to men's stories. I think that Lew and Steve recognized the reality of male brutality together, bonding in the brotherhood of a terrible shared knowledge.

My best friend in high school was Laura Schylur. A dancer, musician, and poet, she had a beautiful childlike face. Laura also had a quality of being different—perhaps because she, like me, was dyslexic. Laura and I would hang out together in nature, in the apricot orchards that were so abundant in our area back then, and in the hills behind St. Joseph's Seminary close to her home. Together we learned to play music on recorders, later on flutes: folk songs, ballads, Beethoven, Bach, and John Lennon's "Oh My Love," which was the song that Lennon wrote after going through primal therapy with Yoko Ono. The tenderness of this simple song touched something important in me; it offered a vision of the kind of emotional intimacy I yearned to know with a man.

Laura wasn't happy about my relationship with Steve, and not just because he took up so much of my time. Steve was dismissive of her and she resented it. Laura remembers the way I once ran up and told her that Steve and his friend, Woz, were making blue boxes, and according to her I announced that "Steve is a geeeeeeenius!" I sort of remember this, too, and I can picture Laura's response. Unimpressed. Deflated.

Which brings me to Steve Wozniak. Woz. Whenever Woz and Steve met up, they connected like excited children. They'd be so thrilled by their discoveries and breakthroughs, so lifted by the helium of their excitement, that they'd literally jump up and down and all around each other, speaking in sharp, rapid bursts, hysterical yelps, and deep-throated laughs. Their sounds were unnerving to me, worse than fingernails on a blackboard. They'd drive me away from the garage and out of earshot within seconds because the pitch was just so awful.

Woz didn't like sharing Steve with me. Likely they both preferred having me out of the garage when they were working together. But this really wasn't the problem. Nor was it the genius that they rightly shared in all of its explosive joy. No, there was something else about it that jarred my nervous system. If there's ever a musical adaptation of Apple, say an opera, there should be dystopian scenes in the famous garage as ground zero, where sound mangles, torques, warps, and then completely tears the physical world of time and space away from the human dimension. Because this is what it felt like to me. When Steve and Woz were excited like this it was as if they were ripping the fabric of the universe. Now I wonder if this was the precursor to what people would later refer to as Steve's reality distortion field.

Woz was older than Steve and I, and already in college, but he seemed younger in many ways. He had no use for me, a girl, and I must admit I found him alarmingly unattractive and couldn't figure out how to talk to him. He wasn't fun or friendly to me. When one of us found the other with Steve, we'd both be disappointed in some quiet way. We were the two most important people to Steve, and yet we had nothing to say to each other.

Woz and I once shared each other's company on a road trip to see Steve in Portland after he had started at Reed College. We left hours before dawn and when the sun came up near Shasta I commented on how beautiful the clouds were: pinks and yellows and peaches climbing in a fresh blue morning sky. His response? A flat "I've seen better." I remember our stopping at a gas station—this was the same trip—and hurrying back from the bathroom because I had a feeling that Woz was thinking about driving off without me. He did leave me once, at the San Francisco airport. Woz had taken Steve to the airport and I had gone along to see him off. Woz drove away and left me there, claiming later he'd had the impression that I was flying out with Steve. No doubt about it: Woz was ornery then.

Yet for all this, I so admired the monster prankster in these two. They were off-the-charts funny. There was an infectious, pure joy running through them, especially when they would do things that were illegal, but so brilliantly conceived that no one could catch up to them. I remember the time Woz drove to L.A. on Highway 5 months before it had opened to the public. No police. No traffic. No speed limit. No problem. And there was Woz at 150 miles an hour. Then there were the blue boxes, devices that got around having to pay for phone calls. Woz and Steve weren't the first inventors, but they did figure out how to make and improve them. These guys had a gangster brilliance. And there was something exhilarating and enlarging about their teamwork.

A couple of years after Apple had started Woz asked me, through Steve, if I would help him decorate his apartment. It was a surprising request because I knew he had never really liked me. Yet it confirmed to me what everyone knows, that Woz didn't have any malice in his heart. Steve and I went over to Woz's place, where I gave him ideas on color and suggestions on where to place some plants. I felt awkward about it, but he was affable and considerate. I think he had asked me over because he was just becoming interested in women—or maybe *a* woman—and wanted to impress her with his good taste. Maybe, too, he wanted to make amends.

That was the day he showed me his Dial-A-Joke machine. As I remember, it was just a big clunky tape machine connected to the phone to generate nerdy science-guy puns. The jokes were funny only because they were so silly. Silly punny jokes are like the verbal equivalent of slapstick—unexplainably funny. Woz has a gift for this. When he showed me the joke machine, he told me that he sometimes answered the phone and delivered the joke live, pretending he was the recording and then surprising the caller with a live response. That machine was like a prototype for online dating searches; Woz actually used it to attract his first wife, who must have been impressed by his funny, goofy guy puns. So there was real sweetness to him after all.

Steve told me many times, and in oblique ways, that he was terrified he would "lose his humanity in the business world." Sometimes he would couch it in terms of his concern for Woz. "I'm so afraid Woz is going to lose himself in the business world," he'd tell me, widening his eyes dramatically. He never got specific about how or why this might happen and it wasn't the kind of thing I could ask questions about. It was too big for language.

Steve's relationship with time and the future—and just about everything else—was different from that of nearly anyone I ever knew. I gradually became aware that he knew his destiny in big ways and that his intuition had given him very specific information about his life way before he would live it. He knew, for example, that he would be in a relationship with Joan Baez, the folk singer and Dylan's famous former girlfriend. He knew that he would be a multimillionaire. He told me many times that he would die in his early forties; then one day, when we were in our early forties, he changed the prediction to his mid-forties. When he had become a billionaire but hadn't died by his mid-forties, I remember him repeating, "I am living on borrowed time," as if the still-young shaman was angling to carve out a bit more future for himself.

Yet as much as he knew some odd and precise details, Steve was in the dark about others. It was only later, as I was looking at our sleeping daughter in my arms, that I remembered how fearful Steve had been of losing his humanity. That's when my understanding gelled; it wasn't Woz who would lose his humanity, it was Steve. Woz, who had a solid, loving bond with both of his own parents, would be fine. Steve had been talking about himself and he'd known it all along. It was always like him to approach matters of personal concern in riddles. I picture him now as a blind man tapping words out with a white stick—out beyond his feet, out beyond the present—communicating between his false and real selves, wanting to confide in me, to not be alone in the mixture of the terrible fear and irrepressible joy of such a rare destiny.

FIVE

CROSSCURRENTS

My name, Chrisann, comes from the flower, the chrysanthemum. It's the symbol for transformation in many cultures, although in very different ways. In European cultures, the chrysanthemum is seen as the doorway out of this world, and so it is given at funerals. In the ancient Hindu sacred system, the 8th chakra that is above the head is a multiple petal chrysanthemumlike flower. A doorway again—this time between the physical body and the higher realms of self. Japanese and Chinese cultures place a very high value on transcending the ego and in these cultures the chrysanthemum means long life and joy, as it's a symbol for integrating the spirit and soul into the body for true happiness in earthly life. In Japan, the Imperial Order of the Chrysanthemum is the highest Order of Chivalry and the emblem and seal of the emperor himself, wherein this symbol is no less than the full realization of the divine in the human, and the human in the divine. My name, given to me by my mother, was like a blessing in difficult circumstances. It was a bright rose window of a name. And I was going to need it.

I was born in 1954 in Dayton, Ohio, the first born in a new generation of the Brennan clan. I grew up with three siblings: one older half sister, Kathy, and two younger sisters, Jamie and Linda. We were a beautiful little family in Ohio, full of the promise of new beginnings. We lived in a big house at the end of a road that was bordered by a deep, wooded area. Surrounding us were grandparents and great-grandparents, uncles and aunts. You could see a cornfield from our front porch, in the middle of which was a hundred-year-old schoolhouse with its bell still hanging intact. We'd ice skate in the flooded woods in wintertime. In summer we'd make forts and pretend worlds in the trees. On Sundays we'd sit down to big family dinners, and on holidays we'd go to church. Easter was new dresses with matching bonnets. Christmas was ridiculously lush.

When I was seven, my father was promoted and we moved away from Ohio and our extended family to Colorado Springs. My father was transferred two more times after that: to Nebraska and finally California. I was twelve when we moved to Sunnyvale, California. My parents would separate within the year. They would divorce soon after.

My father, James Richard Brennan, had been a handsome and talented athlete in his youth: a crack diver and football star in high school, a competitive boxer in the navy, and a skier until he was sixty-nine. At eighteen he went into the service and never went on to college. But with an affable disposition and the training he received in the navy, he was able to build a successful white-collar career and provide us with a good life.

In his youth my father looked like Marlon Brando, with mystical eyes, a powerful jaw, and a face as open as a big full moon. In older age, he had white hair and laugh lines communicating a sensitive nature that belied a broken nose never reset after a navy boxing match. My father had grown up in a rough neighborhood at a rough time and carried pent-up alarm under the surface of his muscular frame. He was kind, yet extremely defensive, and he set high value on being polite and considerate. That's probably why he was ever mindful to keep his real thoughts and feelings to himself. Though my father could be emotionally distant, he also had a refreshing appreciation of life and a love for his daughters and grandchildren that grew as he aged.

My father was conventional. He had a strong sense of right and

wrong and always played by the rules. As was often the case in the fifties, he left the emotional responsibility for the family to our mother,
while he built his career. As a result, he was wholly unprepared for the
shock as he witnessed his beautiful wife's devolution into mental illness
and the impact of the sixties revolution on his four daughters. When
Steve and my father met, as my father would later recall, Steve presented himself as the arrogant, self-absorbed eternal boy. He told my
father that he planned to grow up to be a bum. Two worlds collided.
The last thing my father needed or wanted was for his daughter to be
smitten with such an immature fellow.

My mother, Virginia Lavern Rickey, was an extremely bright and attractive woman. In the home movies of her early twenties, she appears
as a petite, pretty girl who had a soft feminine look and a somewhat
disconcerting sense of her own sexuality. She had a childish mouth,
like Elizabeth Taylor, an unremarkable nose, and deep gray eyes with a
caught-in-the-headlights look. Years later, when I was in my thirties
and saw my first original Georgia O'Keeffe painting, all I could think
of was my mother's hands.

My mother wasn't a particularly nice woman. She saw herself as
superior to most people. My mother had been a latchkey child in the
thirties while my grandmother had worked full time as a cook for
the VA, supporting her daughter and her then-husband through the
Depression. After the Depression, when her father was no longer
around, my mother adapted to years of long, lonely afternoons. She
read a lot of books and drank small bottles of Coca-Cola from a time,
as she later told us, "when Coke was good!"

My mother lived in fear most of her life. Her father had molested
her when she was very young, and in an unusual move in any era, my
grandmother had thrown him out of the house because of it. When
my mother was nine, her father committed suicide. My grandmother
remarried four times and one of her later husbands also molested my

mother—this time when she was fourteen. She carried damage from those experiences with her for life.

As a teenager in the forties my mother had modeled herself on the hard-bitten femme fatale so popular in the movies of the time. Donning a tough attitude that contrasted with her fragility, she would peer down over her reading glasses, take a big drag on her cigarette, and tell us, "Sincerity and a dime will get you a cup of coffee, kid." Such was the root of her humor.

My mother made sure our homes were clean and beautiful. She took her job as homemaker seriously, in a conventional Midwestern fashion. This expressed itself in an insistence that we play outside every day, watch limited hours of TV, go to bed early, and attend good schools. My mother was a fabulous cook with a repertoire that embraced world cuisines. Much of her creativity expressed itself in the dinners she cooked for us. (She made mixed-seafood scampi so well I'm still searching for a restaurant that comes even halfway close to hers.) I remember my mother sitting at the supper table in the late afternoons in Ohio, Colorado, Nebraska, and California, one leg curled up under her, reading and smoking while the dinner simmered. Cooking while reading, reading while cooking. We didn't have much in the way of literary dinner conversation, but our meals were still filled with authors like Faulkner, D. H. Lawrence, Melville, Stegner, and Capote.

All her life my mother read good literature. She had a huge capacity for abstract thought, and I believe her greatest joy in life came from thinking and talking about expansive ideas. She had the kind of mind for bold, tide-turning thoughts, and would say things like, "Everyone in the world is going to have to deal with the fact of Nazi Germany in themselves." I processed this phrase for years in an attempt to understand what that meant about my own life.

She was definitely brilliant in her own way, and I think she may also have been slightly autistic. She was angry that she'd had so many children and it often seemed that her main goal was to get away from us.

We bored her. In later years, as her mental illness increased, my mother gained a great deal of weight and had a defensive disquietude about her. Her laugh was all-knowing and disdainful, and she would criticize everyone and everything, exhibiting a callous and distinctly ungenerous attitude.

At our house, there were never discussions about what the rest of us thought about things; my mother concentrated on her own thoughts and judgments. It was the time of feminism and she dove into her own search for meaning and identity. As a result there were big holes in my upbringing. I never had a desk for homework or a drafting table, much less an easel and art supplies. On the contrary, in areas where I showed talent and interest, my mother would either ignore or ridicule me. My mother wasn't tuned in to her three younger daughters. She made meals and supervised us while we cleaned the house and mowed the lawn on Saturdays, but after that she clocked out to attend to her own world. She often worked to play all four of us against each other, comparing our talents and IQ scores. In truth, my mother nurtured only my oldest sister's education, providing her with special foods, years of violin lessons, and long conversations about literature. She detested my father by the time we had moved to California, and chose my older sister Kathy as her intellectual partner. The rest of us were left to fend for ourselves. Considering her state, this kind of benign neglect wasn't such a bad thing.

Like a crosscurrent, it was when the first of her four daughters hit adolescence that my mother's mental illness would surface without retreat. After that, one by one, as we all came of age, she fell further into abusive behaviors toward us. My mother had experienced a terrible shattering of her childhood, and I imagine that our burgeoning sexuality with its promise of womanhood triggered a great panic and a sense of loss in her. She had protected us from it until she couldn't anymore. Then her pain moved up through the seams of our homes, starting in Colorado, and began covering everything with dark layers of unspeakable outrage and sadness.

My mother was checked out. I think the newly evolving feminist movement spoke volumes to her and provided an escape route to abandon her family. My mother exchanged her family wholesale for an inspired identity as a feminist intellectual. Aloft and deluded, she went to college, eventually earning a degree with a double major in psychology and literature. She would retreat to her bedroom for hours to write papers at a big white desk that she'd painted and antiqued for herself. She put a bumper sticker on her car that said "Another Student for Peace," choosing it over one that said, "Another Mother for Peace." While she didn't value herself as a mother, she also never challenged herself outside of school by developing a professional life. The line between her mental illness and what seemed like bad character wasn't clear to me. As a teen, I just saw her as fraudulent.

My mother had such a deeply confusing combination of traits for me to understand; I felt bad about myself around her. She hated my creativity, my blooming sexuality, my friends, and my budding philosophies. She talked about adolescence in the most derisive tone, as if I should be embarrassed and even shamed by the fact that I was going through it. Every tender thing that was good about that age brought her ridicule and hatred into sharper focus. All of this took place in the midst of cooking wonderful, well-rounded dinners that she planned for and made every day, giving us a better life than she herself had ever known.

I had experienced the cozy safety and wonder of early childhood in a strong family context, but my teen years were a war zone. In my early twenties, when I was struggling with so much, Cindy, my best friend from the sixth grade, laid it on the line because she had been around our family enough to have seen everything. "I am really sorry to tell you but your mother had it out for you." I wasn't sentimental about a mother's love; obviously I knew even more than she did about how awful my own mother had been. Yet what Cindy was saying with such sincerity confirmed what I knew, and I adored her for her courage to speak up with so much careful kindness. What I didn't know then—and what she did know—was how good a mother could be.

The situation was clear to many. By the time I'd gotten together with Steve my mother's eyes met mine with pure hatred. A friend from this time told me that she saw me as tough and sparkling, fragile and soulfully earnest. Some of my teachers at Homestead knew I had trouble at home but no one really understood mental illness then. I think they chalked it up to mother/daughter issues. After my father moved to another house and my older sister went off to college, my younger sisters and I lived a growing nightmare. Without those two at home there was no mitigating the cruelty and so my mother got worse.

My mother and Steve's first meeting was disturbing. She began by sitting on the floor with us and acting like a teenager, flirting and competing with him over whose literary acumen was more developed, his or hers. It went downhill from there. Steve burrowed into himself and used words sparingly as he moved to hold his position. Soon after arriving, he left the house bristling with anger, and I was left dizzy and disoriented and wondering if I had lost him.

I don't blame my mother. As far back as I can remember my heart has been moved by the way her fragile immaturity and wobbly sense of personal identity combined with her great love of life. Prior to the availability of birth control a lot of women had children before they were ready. Ultimately, I valued the importance she always placed on truth and her exquisite, refined curiosity. I felt she was like an Olympic runner who handed us the dazzling torch of all her work before she was felled from the exhaustion of her cruelty. Yet back then, when she held the power in our home, she was brittle with brutality and self-hatred that she projected outward onto us. There was nothing we could do but escape.

I was in my mid-twenties when my mother was diagnosed with a hodgepodge of mental diseases that included paranoid schizophrenia, clinical depression, and bipolar disorder with episodes of psychosis. I don't think anyone even knew the extent of it, and I wonder if it ever mattered what they'd called it, except that by naming such things it seems easier to have compassion. It would take me years to understand exactly how such terms might be translated into the behaviors we'd endured.

As the full cataclysm of my mother's illness unfolded I worried that I would end up like her and this propelled my interest in all things healthy and alternative. And so it was at twenty-two that I made a plan for handling my own mental illness, should I see signs of it. Number one: I would be responsible for my own health. That became my first priority. Number two: I would not eat meat. Numbers three, four, and five: I would meditate, practice yoga, and work to stay connected to my ideals. I also thought—number six—that developing my own creativity was crucial for my health. I saw that my mother only read and critiqued, but never created anything outside of food, and even then she followed recipes. I understood that people who didn't develop themselves through their creativity would end up redirecting that energy adversely.

These were my mantras—my self-appointed marching orders—and all that would pass for a life plan in my youth. It provided me with a curious, defiant security based on a stunning belief in my own internal resources. With this, I armed myself for destiny, come what may.

Before I left my mother's home to live at my father's, I remember being suspended in a recurring thought: *What if people were just good to each other? What if they only paid attention to what was needed, with deep-hearted common sense and a commitment to kindness for the common wealth?* It was a feeling from a dim radiance centered in my heart but it was without words. And because I didn't have words for it, I developed that "love-in-community project" for years without ever understanding that such an important question was working and working in me. I didn't know how to wrap my arms around my mother's lovelessness, so I avoided her. But I got a second chance later, when I was faced with a similar level of unkindness in Steve, and was forced to navigate through it for our daughter's well-being.

SIX

EDEN

Steve and I found our way into love that spring. We would kiss for hours, at the park and in his car, and we'd try very hard to name exactly what it was that made it so much fun. It was ineffable and we never did figure it out, and soon other things between us needed names, too.

When Steve visited my house he'd come directly to my bedroom so as to avoid my mother. I'd look up to see his sweet glowing face at my window and have to catch my breath. I can still see his eyes from that time—they were the kindest, softest eyes I had ever known. Steve was my sublime haven and I was happy in my skin when we were together.

As spring moved into summer, the four trellised columns on my front porch grew thick with star jasmine and filled the air with a humming fragrance. It was then that Steve and I decided to live together for the summer. This was 1972. I can't recall who suggested it first, but I have a feeling it had to have been coconspiratorial, one idea shimmying its way into the air until we both said, "That's it." Neither of us had any ambivalence about the decision. We were determined and clear-eyed about the whole idea. The seventies gave us some permission and the rest we gave ourselves.

Soon after we'd made our decision I rode my bike to the local junior college where I found an ad on a bulletin board—one room in a cabin in the hills. It sounded perfect, but when I called the landlord he told me that he didn't have space for a couple. I was really disappointed, but figured there was nothing to be done. Later, when I mentioned the missed opportunity to Steve, he surprised me by asking for the guy's number. *Oh, really,* I thought, rifling through my purse for the scrap I had written it on. Long story short—Steve got us an interview, and this alerted me to something remarkable in him. This was a guy who could make things happen. And because of the way he'd asked for the number, I knew he knew it, too.

That weekend we drove in Steve's orange Fiat to what was literally the last house on Stevens Canyon Road in Cupertino. We drove past Stevens Creek dam until the road narrowed into twisting two lanes that carried us deep into the woodsy mountains. We passed a lot of small cabins and a local tavern until finally we got to the last turnoff, a hundred feet before the road dead-ended at a footpath. Turning left, we found ourselves on a flat clearing, deep in a valley between some very high hills. Here stood four little cabins, hunkered down in the delicate sunlight. We drove slowly to the farthest cabin, passing an enormous pig in a muddy pen and lots of free-roaming chickens that clucked as they scattered out of our way. Four wild-eyed goats tiptoed in close on their hooves and eyed us as we got out of the car. It looked like some Appalachian back world of stillness and old things.

Alfonso Tatono greeted us with a mischievous smile, and beckoned us in. His house smelled musty. The first thing I noticed was a big white parachute draped from the ceiling down over the dark wooden walls to increase the lighting in a film project he was working on. We were awed. This was the home of a bona fide hippy. Al showed us around the cabin. The spaces were small and dark and well swept. He had furniture from the forties and fifties, and the accoutrement of the sixties and seventies, including found objects from nature. It was tidy with the kind of care that a man instills on his environment and very far from the ranch-style houses of the stultifying monoculture of the American suburbs we'd just left. I found it exciting and sort of awful all at the same time.

Al was in his mid-twenties and seemed worlds older than we were. He was studying film at San Jose State and working on a film about his Italian immigrant father. When Steve found out that Al had access to the university's film library, he was very interested. As they chatted, I wandered around, wondering what it would be like to live there and sleep in the same bed as Steve. We must have done something right, because Al offered to take the roll-out couch in the living room so that we could have his bedroom for the summer.

It would be two weeks before we'd move to the cabin, two weeks in which I'd lay low and quietly observe the changes in my house. My mother peered at me from behind the scenes during this time, copping an attitude of indifference that seemed to me to betray the depths of her insecurity. I had stayed in her home without being wanted, buried at the bottom of a well of self-doubt, trying to survive her cruelty and cope with her mental illness. She had asked me to leave many times before, and had terrified me by saying she would drop me off at Haight-Ashbury. But now that I was finally going, she was oddly soft and disoriented. There was no wind in her for the hatred. No breath. No force.

I never knew exactly what the parallel scene looked like at Steve's house. Steve didn't talk about it; I don't think that it occurs to teenagers to talk about some things. But I had observed Steve's family and I knew that he was always his own authority. I can see him weathering what I imagine was Paul's disgust about our living together in the quiet way that he dealt with all of Paul's reactions at that time, sad but certain of his choices.

In the end I was confounded that my mother responded with grief, that we pulled it off, and that Paul never exacted any revenge. Unlike my mother, Paul had a way of dissolving his frustrations before they mounted into action. Despite his punctuated outbursts, he was wired for harmlessness in some inexplicable way. Clara fell tight-lipped and distant. She kept her judgments to herself. I could sense her disapproval, but she remained considerate in her behavior.

We invited Steve's parents over for dinner soon after we moved in, but only Clara came. When I recall that dinner now, I remember being surprised by how she allowed herself to be received by us. Clara showed such a sense of grace at being our guest of honor that she made Steve and me happy to have brought her there. We were so proud of making a whole dinner for her, and we flitted about like little birds, serving the food, talking about how we made it, and wanting to know if she liked it. I had somehow expected there to be an undercurrent of dissonance that evening, but there wasn't. Instead, Clara—whom I called Mrs. Jobs—sat still and shy in her delight, while we moved about and showered her with our gladness and our best spaghetti and salad dinner. I saw that she was willing to be charmed by us. And I could understand why Paul had married her.

Our nights at the cabin were an Eden. We would wake up at all hours, so deliriously happy that we were together, incredulous that we didn't have to go home because we *were* home. Sometimes I'd open my eyes in the middle of the night and suddenly remember that we were together. I'd feel and smell him and I would reach for him and then he would wake up, and we would embrace and kiss, laughing and astonished to be so close and so wildly sweet with love. We'd fall back into sleep in each other's arms and then he'd wake me up, to kiss and make love all over again. I remember this time for its joy and the freedom to be and love so purely. Our young dreaming bodies were swept away in a swirl of past, present, and future of all time and all worlds, having everything, knowing nothing.

Within the week, whenever we climbed into bed, Steve began telling me stories of how we were part of an affiliation of poets and visionaries he called the Wheatfield Group. (Steve sometimes spelled it Weatfield.) We were looking out a window together, he said, watching the world with the others. I didn't know what he was talking about, but with all my heart I wanted to see such views. It wasn't a metaphor for me. I knew it was real. I had ached for enchanted narratives all my life and his were not only the first, but some of the most beautiful and urgent I had ever known. I sometimes thought I could see the impression of the shape of a window where the cabin wall stood, that I could feel the silhouettes of the poets mingling in the room with us.

Steve always had a profound sense of self-adoration. His private mythologies made that clear. I cherished them, and wanted to protect his blessed poetic vision and the invisible community into which he gave me entrance. I think that sharing the knowledge of the Wheatfield Group must have been an initiation of some sort, because I later found out that a very small group of people at Steve's funeral put wheat on his casket. He must have carried the Wheatfield Group with him his whole life.

Steve hung a poster of Bob Dylan on the dark, wood-paneled wall over our bed and we covered ourselves in my great-grandmother's down comforter that my family had carried, state by state, all the way from Ohio. That, along with her kerosene lamp, kept us warm and happy in the night. My great-grandmother had used that hourglass-shaped lamp as a matter of necessity. In our electrified world we would use it for its soul quality from a simpler time when technology was more connected to the senses. Every night when we lit the lamp it felt to us that we were the luckiest two people ever. We had such a fortune in each other, and it showed in the soft warm light, the downy comforter, and the window into the poet worlds.

During that summer, Steve and I would stay up late to watch movies with Al and his brother. At a time when there was no such thing as home video, VHS, DVDs, Netflix, or live streaming, the intimate clicking of the reel-to-reel projector was a lush and sensuous pleasure. Mostly we watched the student films that Al found in the film library's archives, many of which contained art from the East. We viewed one gorgeous sacred image after another—mandalas and yantras with intricate symbols worked out thousands of years ago, said to create heightened states of consciousness to balance spirit in matter, and man and woman. These images were extraordinary and perfect in the way that the thick, almost cartoonish art from the sixties was painfully far from achieving. In the late nineties I would come back around to paint this kind of sacred art with an added postmodern, New Age, sci-fi, visionary sensibility.

Often I couldn't keep my eyes open past 9:30 in the evening, so I would go to sleep while Steve stayed up late to write poetry or talk with Al. Steve had his own doorways into these nights. He would lug the typewriter into the living room and I would observe him, in my broken sleep, coming into our room for things he'd forgotten, with the blaring living room light cast over the bed. Delicately self-absorbed, with his hand holding his hair back—partly to see more clearly and partly in an adolescent gesture of self-holding—he'd search for the things he was missing, a pen, more paper, a book.

I would hear his electric typewriter bulleting away in the night until I was completely asleep. He reworked Dylan songs by personalizing them for himself, or for us, or for me. Only now do I understand what he was trying to do. He was a loner and he didn't talk much, and I think he manipulated Dylan's songs to make sense of and reflect his world.

One day he nailed one of these poems—"Mama, Please Stay Out," a reworking of "To Ramona"—to our front door. It was a response to my mother's baffling unkindness toward me and her uneasiness over my having moved out. He'd written it in a silent fury after she had come over to the cabin unannounced to see how I was doing. She guessed I might be pregnant. In fact, I was. I never told her, but she had a lengthy conversation with me about how I had to keep the baby. I was struck by her passionate hypocrisy. She had complained so much about the responsibilities of raising children. And later, after Lisa was born in 1978, she would look at my newborn and ask "Why, oh why did you have this baby?" That was her. But that summer at the cabin, Steve and I had already agreed that I wouldn't have the baby. We were firm in our decision and I had no intention of taking her advice on anything. Still, it upset me.

I can imagine now that for Steve, my mother was a she-monster and that he thought that he could keep her out with his poem, like a talisman. I sort of remember how it went. Part of it was addressed to my mother:

So you think you know us and our pain,
but to know pain means your senses will rise.

Other parts were for me:

I can see that your head
Has been twisted and fed
By worthless foam from the mouth

I wasn't absorbed by Dylan's work at that time. In fact, I was inwardly dismissive of Steve's splice poetry and sort of insulted by his saying that my head had been twisted and fed. I wasn't putting things together as well as he was and he wasn't very discreet about how he saw me. I did not have his Bob Dylan context. What I saw were a lot of Dylan songs with a few changes. I couldn't understand why he, of all people, wasn't more original in his writing. Girls can be so hard on boys.

I had a romantic image of the poet as a pure being who would sooner walk off a cliff than disconnect himself from the truth and law of his being. That's how I perceived Steve—as pure a being as ever there was. But now I see that Dylan's lyrics were brilliant and that Steve was looking for ways to live inside them as if they were mansions, because that's what they were to him. My heart has searched for a way to change that history to a different version, where I take time to read the original lyrics, ask him questions, and deeply commit to understanding his changes.

• • •

Not long after moving in, we discovered that the goats had a nasty practice of bucking us in the back the moment we would get out of the car. These ornery creatures were clever and fast; the whole thing was extremely unpleasant. As soon as we drove off the road and into the valley, the goats would pick up their heads and watch us arrive. Then they'd begin their measured tiptoeing toward the car, holding back ever so slightly so as to not be too obvious. But we knew.

Twenty feet running distance was enough for them to pick us off if we weren't paying attention and sometimes even if we were. After having been bucked one too many times, we got strategic. Steve would run and face the leader of the goats, going for the most aggressive black one, grabbing his long horns to push and wrangle with him while I would get everything from the car and run out of harm's way. Once I got to the top of the porch I would laugh, thrilled by his playful chivalry. Then he'd turn to leap onto the steps as fast as he could to join me, and where we'd laugh and be dismayed together.

The porch was a great lookout, and because of the goats, I didn't go wandering around the property that much. Instead I'd stand there to look around and soak up the sun and fresh air. One day when I was doing this I saw the neighbors on their front porch having some sort of little party. I'm not a nosey person by nature, it's just that the house was only about twenty yards away and I couldn't help but notice. Al had told us in passing that these neighbors did a lot of drugs while they were waiting around for their inheritance. As lifestyles go it didn't interest me much, but they were nice enough. Steve and I never really talked about them, and we didn't talk much to them, either, except to say hi every now and then. But on this occasion, as I was enjoying the fresh air, Steve quietly walked up behind and asked me, "Would you do that?"

I looked back at him and saw that his eyes had narrowed to a slit, as if he were looking through to some distant plane. "Do what?" I asked. He expected me to know what he was thinking.

"Wait for an inheritance," he responded.

"No," I answered, and as I said this, the sense rushed through me that this was not how people should use their time. But so did the sense that I was being surreptitiously tested. And because of this, and because the question was so aimed and dark, I've remembered it. Steve the intuitive knew he was going to be extremely wealthy, he'd told me so. Was it that he wanted to gauge not just my character, but the role I would play in his future? And what about his own role in such a future?

In the middle of the summer Steve and I went to a small theater in San Francisco's North Beach to see *Modern Times*, with Charlie Chaplin. We had very little money and no foreseeable prospects in the future, but he loved classic movies and loved introducing them to me. At the end of the evening I was a bit stressed to realize we had spent most of what we had left on dinner and the movie, but when we discovered a $25 parking ticket on our car, I turned inside out with despair. Steve was calm and didn't seem to really care. The truth was he had that look on his face again—sad, surrendered, and thoughtful. I could tell he was seeing into his future.

We drove to Crissy Field in San Francisco after that, and walked out onto the beach to see the sunset. As we walked, I began talking about money worries for the umpteenth time that day. Steve gave me a long, exasperated look, then reached into his pockets and took all that we had left and threw it into the ocean. Ahh! Who would do that? I was filled with so much frustration and admiration that I started laughing and then crying and then laughing again. How could I not love him? The audacity of the act trumped everything. This was purity. This was the poet, not the one who stayed up late rewriting Dylan's stuff.

Later that week Woz came over to the cabin and gave Steve some money for a blue box he had just sold. Until that moment, I had no idea Steve was making money from those things. I just hadn't connected the dots, likely because they had kept it under my radar. Also up until that time I hadn't really considered that Woz could bring serious goodness into our lives, though I found myself constantly reevaluating my position on him because he was never one thing or the other. As awkward as our relationship was, I could never fully dislike Woz. Maybe because he loved Steve so much. Or maybe because he seemed like a very bright child to me, innocent and still growing.

I gave Woz a lot of space. Small, bright boys sometimes play in a way that is more like a feverish unfolding—breathless, busy, and non-relational. At twenty years old, Woz seemed to still be packed tight and bubbling with things to bring into the world. And here he was grinning and splitting the money with Steve. I was so grateful to him. At the time I thought he was simply being nice to share it. I still hadn't managed to wrap my head around the idea that he and Steve were equal partners in an underground business.

Later that summer, the three of us went to De Anza College to look on their job boards. We found an opening for four people to dress up as Alice in Wonderland characters at a Santa Clara shopping mall. The pay was $250 each for two days work—a lot of money in 1973. We jumped at the chance, and brought along our roommate Al as the fourth.

I looked very much like the original Alice: a large head on a small body, with long ringlets and serious little circles under my eyes. The three guys, who traded off the Mad Hatter and the White Rabbit, would wear these huge head constructions that went down to their knees. That weekend the mall's air conditioner had broken, and the weather was smoldering hot, so they could barely handle being in costume for more than ten minutes at a time. Even after stuffing bags of ice inside the heads, the three of them kept running into the dressing room to trade off heads and drink water. It was painful to watch. Hilarious, too.

Looking back now, it seems so bizarre and fitting: the big heads and the little girl falling down a hole portended the future like nothing else could have. In light of what came later, I think it would be rather nice to be able to package my memories in the form of a fairy tale, something soft and bright and fanciful that I could look at from time to time, and then put safely away.

The truth is, when I shared my world with Steve I made myself into an orphan so that he would feel less lonely. But I was no orphan. Yes, my mother was ill, but I had a big family who loved me and wanted me. I think I imagined I had it all to spare because like many young people—maybe even all people—it's hard to know how much you have and what it all means until it's gone. I let Steve exert the wrong kind of pull on my heart. It took me almost twenty years to understand how much harm I had done to myself by that kind of wrongheaded inspiration, but I can say now that it was a false response that made for huge losses over time.

That fall, before Steve went to college and I returned to high school, I made a painting as a tribute to our summer. The painting, long gone, was of a marionette floating in the middle of starry patches of blues and greens. It was a little French marionette that looked like Steve, with a sad smile inside a big, happy one. It had soft billowy pantaloons with big, lit-up buttons, like chakras running down the front of the body. Big droopy feet poked out from under the pantaloons, and they hung ungrounded in midair. There was only one string to the marionette and it swirled up from his hand and over his head ending in a series of soft, overlapping circles. Steve cherished the picture. Eventually I think we both understood that it was a snapshot of what he would become.

SEVEN

THE HANDBOOK OF BECOMING

Steve left for Reed College in September. Woz and I went to see him in October, leaving before dawn for the nearly twelve-hour drive to Portland. We got there late in the afternoon, locked our luggage in the hatchback, and raced up to find the glorious boy.

Steve's dorm was in an old brick building with gargoyles on the rooftops. These creatures were uniquely grotesque and so realistic that I felt them shifting around, flapping their leathery wings, and peering out from the heights of some medieval authority.

There were about six people in Steve's room when we got there. And in the midst of the flurry of introductions, Steve grabbed my hand and ran, leading me into the privacy of a co-ed bathtub stall where he kissed me like he had never kissed me before.

I didn't see Woz again until it was time to go home.

I stayed with Steve for two days on that first visit. We'd sleep in his narrow student bed and sneak into the bathroom to take baths in a claw-footed tub. I shared Steve's meal plan, with the added guest expense of $1.35 per meal, but when we wanted to be alone we'd eat in his bedroom. We made meals on Steve's Bunsen burner—Campbell's tomato soup with crackers, mostly, which we'd sip out of camping cups and eat with saltines. I'd explore the bookstore when Steve was in class, which is where I found the full set of pictures from a series of cards he had been sending me by a contemporary painter named Muldoon Elder. I remember that I felt moved that Steve and I both loved the same artist's work. I'd also bide my time listening to music (usually Beethoven) in the private world of Steve's headphones. I sang blithely along to the music—until one day Steve came in and started laughing at my tuneless threading notes.

I met Daniel Kottke for the first time on this visit. Like most of Steve's friends from the period, Daniel—with his long blond hair and soft, mustached face—looked like a version of Jesus. But I had a limited picture of what Steve's life was like at Reed because my visits were always brief and we shared little time with others.

When I think back on all this now, I have a much greater appreciation of the intensity of teenage emotions. Steve and I missed each other terribly. It was difficult to live so far apart after being so close in the summer, and we wrote frequently to each other during this time.

Some three years later when Steve was helping me move my things out of my father's garage, he found the large shoebox in which I had stored all of his love letters. I remember him standing there with the S curve of his harlequin body, the soft angle of his long neck gracefully bent as he read. He cast a cold incredulous look at me and said: "Hey, I was romantic!" At the time he said this, our on-again off-again relationship was off, so I felt he was also asking *Why didn't you stay with me?*

Being romantic was so important to Steve; it can hardly be overstated. I've long since lost those letters and all but one of the cards, but I still have some of the books by Kenneth Patchen with Steve's handwritten notes inside the back cover. He would practice his calligraphy in brown or gray inks and disregard the spelling and grammar, which I wouldn't have noticed anyway.

Weatfield club (nighttime branch) invites you to its meetings ~ every night in the weatfield of your mind. bring your lover along too. See you There, OAF.

Sad eyed lady of the low lands, where the sad eyed prophet says that no man comes—my warehouse eyes, my Arabian drums, shall I leave them by your gate or sad eyed lady should i wait? [quoting Bob Dylan]

". . the words on the last page are the same as Miriam Patchen used when talking about her husband and his death. he talked about love that way also, the forces behind things continue, life, love, even hate. it is in this sense that I say that Dylan Thomas and the Wheatfield group are there when we are together."

"All that leaves is always here."

i love you,
Steve

I will love you until the end of time. ~Oaf

I cherished Steve's letters and longed to hear his voice, but phone calls were expensive. (It's amazing to consider that long-distance calls were so costly when gas was only 32 cents a gallon.) Enter the blue box, the now famous electronic device made to circumvent the phone system. Steve and Woz had figured out how to make them and were selling them as an income source. And now I would use one. Steve arranged for Woz to meet me one Saturday on the Homestead campus. We had to use a public telephone because the blue boxes were illegal and could be traced to a home number; the pay phones at Homestead were safe because we used them in the inner quad where they were out of view of the street.

The boxes, approximately three inches square, were made of high quality plastic casing. They were clunky, with push button numbers on top of the box and a wire leading to a small speaker that emitted a series of bleeps, screeches, and tonal undulations that bypassed the need for coins. Setting a call up with a blue box was a two-handed operation as I recall. You had to hold the little speaker to the mouthpiece of the phone while stabilizing the box against your stomach and the shelf below, and then dial 0. Before an operator answered you pressed the numbers in the right order, in response to the sounds that came out of the phone. It was machine on machine. Woz was kind and teacherlike in his explanation and told me that, basically, the blue box talked and responded to the phone system prompts. Later he or Steve wrote the directions on a scrap of paper so I could know the order.

When Steve's phone started ringing, Woz looked up to see the delight on my face. He then stepped out of hearing range, where he waited patiently. I don't recall what Steve and I talked about that day. I do, however, remember looking out to see Woz in my peripheral view, where he stood for over an hour. His arms were folded, and he looked down quietly in his own thoughts for the entire time. I was so very grateful. I was struck by his patience and kind demeanor that day in a way that I had never been before. It was the first time I'd seen him as a whole, mature person, and by that one impression alone I regarded him with new eyes thereafter.

Later Steve and Woz must have decided that it was okay for me to have a blue box because for a while I carried one around in a small paper bag between Steve's visits home. I knew it was FBI illegal, but I never thought about the risk. I didn't believe I was doing any harm, so I had no qualms about it. In fact, it was exciting, heady even, to have in my possession a piece of technology that reduced Ma Bell to a trifle.

Later in the fall, I took a plane to Portland to be with Steve. Our plan was to hitchhike back to the Bay Area together, two days later. The patina of sixties idealism was wearing off and hitchhiking wasn't as safe or easy as it had been, if it ever was. But the romantic in Steve still loved hitchhiking so we made our plans.

My father asked me about the trip. I told him about my flight and that I was going to hitchhike home with Steve. Incredulous, he decreed, "You flat out can't go!" We went round and around arguing for three days until I told him that Steve had arranged for us to catch a ride with a friend who would be driving to the Bay Area. Exhausted, my father seemed to believe my lie. Or maybe he figured he'd let me deal with the consequences of my own dishonesty. He wasn't going to disrespect both of us by asking for proof. I felt awful about it, but I was a determined teenager and though I tried very hard to be considerate of my father's concerns, in situations concerning Steve he was simply no match for my will.

So I flew to Portland and we hung out for two days, and when it was time to return, Steve and I set off a bit too late on Friday afternoon. I think it must have been about 4:30 when we walked to the street next to Reed and got our first ride out to the freeway. Then after a bunch of little rides and dinner, we got stuck for over three hours just outside of Eugene, Oregon.

The ground was frozen and we were cold and I sat on my backpack with my head in my arms, tired and miserably unhappy. I felt terrible about having lied to my father and feared that I had made a big mistake. Steve stayed cheerful and jumped to the road to put his thumb out whenever cars came near. Finally, at about 11:30, a huge semi pulled up and offered what would be our longest ride home. Grateful, and so very relieved, we climbed into the cab with a blast of warmth hitting our faces. The seat was huge, and bouncier than I could have imagined. We sat monstrously high up above the road. I had never been in a semi before and the feeling of being held in the cozy arms of its brute power was marvelous. After about twenty minutes the trucker encouraged me to rest, "Why don't you climb behind the seats and get some sleep, there's a bed back there." *Wow,* I thought. *These things have beds, too?* I wondered if the guy was safe and if the bed was clean, but he insisted in a kind way and because I was so very sleepy, I decided to trust. Steve stayed talking with the driver for about two hours and then he curled up with me for a night of shifting with the curves, happy for the miles we were leaving behind.

Just before dawn the trucker woke us and told us to put ourselves together because he was about to drop us off. The next thing I knew he had pulled over onto a gravelly shoulder next to the road, where the tunnel burrows through about a thousand feet of solid rock above Sausalito. We were near home and the sun was just beginning to peak into dawn.

Sausalito is a magical place with a deep mystery at its center. With jewel-like houses meandering up a steep hillside, it overlooks the San Francisco Bay, Angel Island, Berkeley, and San Francisco itself. Sausalito has a European feel and an interesting history. It's where Anaïs Nin lived in a houseboat and wrote parts of *The Diary,* and where some of the scenes from Orson Welles's classic movie *The Lady from Shanghai* were shot. Sausalito was where many of the beat poets hung out in the fifties. It's also where Otis Redding wrote "Sitting on the Dock of the Bay."

Steve and I dropped out of the truck's dark cab and into the predawn morning. Our breath made big, purple plumes as we braced ourselves in the freezing air. Making sure we had all our stuff at our feet, we waved a fond good-bye to the trucker and watched as he maneuvered the huge beast back out on the road, down the thousand-foot drop right onto the Golden Gate Bridge.

From that location we had the view of the gods, and as we waited for our next ride the sun's rays broke through the buildings that made up the San Francisco skyline. It was the purest light I had ever experienced. And as it rose, it made the Bay Area seem like one luminous room of sea and sky. Steve looked down at me with a smile that was like the beginning of time. He could do that. And we stood there so happy to be alive and close to home, thrilled that we'd gone for the adventure.

We were just kids taking care of our responsibilities in the best way we knew. And being kids, we were living in the moment, too. Although it was, perhaps, too much in the moment for me. I had distinguished myself by winning three awards: for my work in a district-wide painting contest; as a contributor on Mark's film "Hampstead," which won honorable mention in a state competition; and for talent and artistic accomplishment, taking Homestead's highest art award in my graduating class. But I wasn't making plans for college. It wasn't something my parents thought about for me and we never discussed it. To be fair, my father had also won awards in his youth and never thought he could go to college, so that may have been part of it. Still, in the absence of such planning, I hadn't come up with goals to weave into my lust for adventure. I didn't understand that opportunities weren't unlimited, that time was finite. I just filled in the blanks with the notion that there would always be some wonderful next step to take, not actually realizing that you can waste time and opportunity if you don't actually *plan* next steps.

Then came the day in the mix of this mulligan stew (I think it was in early November of that first year or maybe January of the next), that Steve called to tell me he was dropping out of college. It was the first thing he said and it came anguished and without warning. "I just *can't* spend my parent's money like this anymore," he said. I understood; he didn't need to explain. Steve had a keen sense that his education was too great a financial burden on his parents. We had talked about this a few times before he went to Reed, but I thought everything was going to be fine once he was there. My mind raced and I pictured the big boat in the Jobses' driveway; that made me think they could manage the cost. I deeply admired Steve for the way he considered his father's feelings, but I felt that Paul was a small, battling man who complained way too much. These complaints weighed heavily on Steve, who kept his worries and his calculations in a cave to himself. By the time he called me he had made his decision.

He told me that he was going to drop out, and then he paused. "Anyway," he said, "I'm going to start auditing classes."

"Oh," I said, intrigued. "What does 'audit' mean?"

"It means I can take all the classes I want but not pay for them."

I was stunned. "You can do that?" Magical worlds of access unfolded before my eyes.

"Yes, although I won't get any credit."

"Oh," I said again, sort of sad this time.

"But I don't need the credit. I just want the classes." He said this with a sense of steely-eyed realism. And there it was—evidence of the creator's synthesizing mind. Earnest and pared, Steve had figured out how to go to college without using his parents' money.

When I look back on all of this now, I wonder how the adoption lawsuit in Steve's infancy might have factored into not just this decision, but how it had affected his life early on. At a time when adoption was culturally less reflective and variable than it is today, Steve's birth mother, Joanne, seemed uniquely remarkable and courageous to have challenged the placement of her child. And maybe incredibly stupid, too. I imagine her having acted boldly, even in the midst of what must have been nearly unbearable grief over the loss of her son, not to mention his father's departure, the man she must have deeply loved. She was only twenty-three or twenty-four, but her fierceness and sense of authority stand out for me. And so does her lack of reflection and compassion for Steve and his new family's emotional environment.

What I imagine now is that Joanne could have had a back alley abortion but chose to give birth. And in the nine months the child grew in her, she must have thought through what kind of influence she could have on his life when she wouldn't be there. Her blessings would include a Catholic upbringing with its Divine Mother to oversee him all his days; adoptive parents whose higher education would ensure that his environment reflected his birth parents' deep regard for learning; and an adoptive family wealthy enough to afford her child big choices in life. But it all torqued out of shape because the family she'd chosen changed their minds at the last minute and decided they wanted a girl.

The Jobses had not attended college. They weren't Catholic and they weren't wealthy. So after the adoption was finalized, Joanne demanded that her plan for her child be honored. I understand that. But then there are the other painful pieces that float in my mind; Joanne's beauty, her returning to take him away from the Jobses and put him into what she perceived to be a *better* home with *better* people. And the Jobses, first-time parents being told they weren't good enough, fighting like hell to keep the newborn that they'd named Steven Paul. They probably even wondered if they were doing the right thing by fighting. Why not just give the baby up as the mother wanted? All through it I can hear Paul, blustery and pragmatic, saying, "Damn it, lady, you let go of him, he's ours now."

Understandably, the court's impending decision interfered with Clara's ability to feel safe enough to love the infant for his first six months. It was seventeen years after the fact when she told me this and the whole thing still haunted her. The Jobses' home must have tottered with profound uncertainty until they finally won the case. And all of Joanne's bright dreams for her son narrowed to one single requirement: that the Jobs promise that Steve would to go to college. With that agreed, at least it meant that everything was settled.

In light of it all, Clara's later guilt over not wanting to mother such a difficult child when Steve was two makes the picture even more poignant. And because Mona, Steve's sister by his birth mother, later told me that Joanne had never saved any money for *her* college education, it makes me think there was shattering in everyone that had come from both the adoption and lawsuit. It would seem that Steve's existence set off detonations from the very beginning.

Steve had nerve. It was a thin line that ran up through the middle of him. If you plucked it with a less than a careful comment, he would speak harshly about his parentage: "My parents are the ones who raised me, *not* the person who gave birth to me. *She* gave me away. *She* doesn't deserve to be called my *mother*." This refrain seemed to me to acknowledge not just the fact that the Jobses were the ones who did all the work, but Steve's bitter sense of loss and what I imagine were years of Paul Jobs spitting tacks about it and everything else he felt powerless to control.

Back then Steve was so empathic that I think he overidentified with his father and wanted to shore up his insecurities. And so, at the tender age of seventeen, he took things into his own hands. He made the decision to drop out of his degree program and audit courses instead. It was a funny hybrid of his own desire to learn exactly what he pleased without it breaking his parents' bank account, and complying with his birth mother's requirement. I never heard him regret it. Not once. And there were plenty of times he might have, because the next few years were rough.

That his parents allowed for the change is revealing, too. Here was one of the smartest students at a high school known for extremely bright kids, so advanced that he met once a week with a handful of students chosen from a pool of thousands for an elite math class. It seems to me that a child of his intelligence should have been cultivated, but that would not have been the Jobses' context. Once he had made the decision to stop matriculating at Reed, as young as he was, he had in some way become his own man. He wouldn't have given his parents any say in the matter and that, ironically, was consistent with the Jobses' worldview. That would have calmed Paul down and made Steve look good to him.

Steve acted happy about the change and his fledgling confidence grew as he embraced his Grand Experiment. I could feel his slightly overloaded enthusiasm to *fake it until he could make it*. Steve was inventive, for sure, and he was great at finding alternative ways of doing things, like using other people's unused meal tickets and sleeping on couches and on dorm room floors in his sleeping bag. Steve liked being a vagabond in the tradition of Woody Guthrie. He fully enjoyed the experience of being homeless and free with the wind at his back. Steve was an experimental romantic at heart, and may very well have had his eye on the rugged beauty of that former time. I think this was what he meant when he told my father that he wanted to grow up to be "a bum," and to me it suggests a Henry V blueprint of the foolish days of the young prince before he ascends to the throne.

Steve went back and forth between the Bay Area and Oregon a lot over the next year. I'd drive him to an on-ramp entrance of a freeway so he could hitchhike. And driving away from those drop-offs sort of broke my heart because with his shoulders up around his ears and his black hair ruffled and flying in the chill wind he looked like a cold and lonely raven, like a bird on a wire. I remember him smiling and waving good-bye, determined to make the best of it. It still gets to me.

Everything that happened for him at that point was a complete surprise to me. Steve audited Shakespeare, poetry, dance, and calligraphy. I was baffled he didn't take more science and math, because that's what he was good at and what Reed was known for. It's remarkable to me that he followed his instinct to develop himself through the arts. He must have told me twenty times that he loved his dance class. "I'm not very good," he'd say, shaking his head at his willingness to be seen like that, "but I *love* it, I just love it!" He couldn't stop repeating himself. He loved all his audited classes, but . . . *dance*? I tried to imagine him in a leotard, but I couldn't quite see it. Steve had been a competitive swimmer in high school and until he went to India, he had a beautiful swimmer's body with a muscular upper body and arms. But he could also be awkward and clumsy in all things physical. His massages hurt and he was extremely self-conscious, tripping and falling over his own feet more than anyone can possibly imagine. And yet, he also had a sense of sublime grace in many of his movements. I would try to see into how this all might have worked for him in a dance class. I may have snickered a little, too.

At one of the winter breaks, Steve hitchhiked with a friend from Reed to the Bay Area. They stayed at my house, since my father was out of town on a business trip. The two were excited about their clever plan to hitchhike to Mexico on a private airplane flying out of the little airport in Palo Alto, which then was only known as a college town for Stanford. Rainy Portland could be very dreary, and Reed in those days had one of the highest suicide rates of any college in the United States. Bright, sunny, cheap Mexico must have seemed like the best idea anyone had ever thought of. The guys had put an advertisement in the local paper saying they needed a ride, but they got no response, so they decided just to show up at the airport and shake the pilots down for a ride. Steve's body moved like a song and a prayer in the hopes of free air passage.

The three of us spent the next day and a half in Cupertino, and then I dropped them off at the Palo Alto airport in my father's VW bug, fingers crossed that they would be picked up. I knew they had done it when they hadn't called by nightfall. Steve came back a week later, sunburned and happy, bearing a gift to me of a beautiful rainbow-colored Mexican blanket, which I had for years until someone stole it out of the back of my car. (*You know who you are!*)

On the evening they stayed with me before their trip, while Steve and I sat on the couch and talked, I noticed that his friend was wandering around the living room with a look of dumb loss on his face. Steve was completely ignoring his friend, and I felt that the guy was disconnected from us, in a sort of no-man's-land that alarmed me. The change in the two boys' dynamic was subtle, but I found the friend's expression more profoundly disturbing than might easily be explained.

In a flash of indignation I got off the couch to draw his friend back in, and as I got up, I looked back over at Steve to see a hazy, almost drunken look on his face. It was as if he were in an altered state of his own. I couldn't understand it: neither of us used marijuana very often and that night we definitely had not. I was miffed at Steve because I felt he was excluding his friend in some weirdly powerful way. I moved away from Steve and found his friend bedding, food, and water and we talked a bit because I had a strong instinct to care for him. I'm not really the mothering type; as an artist I tend to relish my own experience. But I'm sensitive to people in my environment and on this evening, my attention was reordered in a way that told me that something was way off. I had a feeling that Steve, so crippled that he needed to be the center of my focus, had actually blanked his friend right out of the room.

In retrospect, it seems to me that there was a dark vortex next to Steve for as long as I knew him. But that was the first time I recognized it. After that, I always knew, just below the level of words, when that aspect of Steve would show up. Through the years, I'd see that buttoned-up look of shock and loss overcome people when they went from inclusion to invisibility when they were with him. It always left me pale with the feeling that something was terribly wrong. The words "there it is again" would move silently through me when I saw that lost-from-self look in people.

I never thought of Steve as having serious mood swings because they were so mild back then. But after he became the Steve Jobs the world would know, I would hear about the extremes other people witnessed. I still thought it seemed unlike him until much later, when I better understood my own creativity and so could appreciate his. I know now that it would have been impossible for Steve to keep his extremes hidden after Apple had started because it is through the movement between the highs and the lows that creativity and invention flesh out new spaces. Highs and lows are what it takes to break the mold of previous consciousness and allow world-shattering ideas to be birthed. Not only did Steve have a big hole in him from the adoption, he had an enormous id that fed on nearly everything to fill it up. Looking for the love he missed, he made sure all eyes were on him so he could get what he needed. He'd wipe people out in the process.

But that night in Cupertino, prior to his Mexico trip, I wasn't mature enough to understand that Steve was himself in deep trouble, and that was why he was creating a sense of loss in others. It was over my teenage head and I was just so tired of his haunting social ineptitude that it triggered something self-protective in me and I started to back out of the relationship. I didn't know that I should talk about it with him, much less *how* to talk about it. In this I am sure I was caught by my own limitations as well as by his. I felt like growling and screaming and shouting because he was using his weaknesses to manipulate people who didn't know what was happening. I just didn't have a vocabulary for this and, even if I had, he likely wouldn't have been willing to hear it.

By the spring of '73, I didn't visit Steve at school anymore. Once he had dropped out, there was no place for me to stay and I didn't want to visit him anyway. So our distance, emotional and otherwise, increased. He was distraught.

One day in early spring, Steve called to tell me he had rented a room in a house near Reed. He asked if I would move up to Portland to live with him as soon as I graduated from high school. "No, I'm sorry, but no," I told him. He seemed so sad I hated to refuse, but I didn't have a life up there and I didn't feel good about him at that point. In truth, I felt that all that was unconscious between us was too great to foster happiness. Eventually I came to understand that he had been seeing other girls at this time. He himself bragged and bragged about it years later. He was in college and surrounded by all kinds of beautiful and interesting young women, it made sense. But the real issue—and the one that I didn't understand at the time—is that he asked me to move up there to stop him from having these other relationships. It was his attempt *not* to destroy ours.

I think Steve called with the invitation because he had a beautiful dream for the two of us as a couple. He wanted me to come up Portland and start painting seriously, while he wrote poetry and learned to play the guitar. But this was sort of in the talk bubble above his head where he shelved his imaginary copy of the *Handbook of Becoming Bob Dylan*. It was a great plan but it was far more formulated in his mind than any plan I'd had for myself. I couldn't have made myself into a painter at that time because I didn't know how to focus or work hard. I needed training and experience and more feedback from good teachers. And because I didn't see him as a musician, I didn't have the foundational belief needed to support an idea of marrying our fortunes in such a way.

I was disenchanted.

Steve had come to seem like a floppy marionette that had lost the taut lines connecting to his excellence. I would never lose sight of his beauty or the knowledge that he was extraordinary. I would always believe in him. But he was so spun around and tangled up that I knew of nothing I could have done to help right then. That was when he began his descent into what I think of as one of the darkest periods of honest confusion that I ever saw in Steve. It was embodied in Dylan's paradoxical lines about there being no success like failure and failure being no success at all. I personally never knew how to be so honest while in as much difficulty, as he knew how to be, and so these were some of the times I felt my deepest, most profound awe of him. This was the beginning of when I came to trust failure in Steven Paul Jobs, far more than success.

One day around March of 1973, Steve's mother sort of angled in obliquely to ask if I wanted to live at their house, in Steve's room, until I completed high school. I think she asked in a careful way so as not to shock me. But I was shocked and wondered where the question came from. Why was she offering me a place to live? My mind searched—did she know my mother was mentally ill? It's likely that the whole school knew, but I had no way of talking about it publicly.

Not meaning to be ungrateful to Clara, I mumbled a response, something like "No thank you, no, but thank you." *NO!* I thought to myself as I scanned the implications. The truth was that I had just met Jim, a guy in my art class, and we were spending a lot of time with each other. I could never stay at Steve's parents' house while my affections were blooming with this new boy. It would have been dishonest. But there was more to it. Clara's offer frightened me; I felt like I was an outcast in my own family and I had no idea how to fit into another's. Also it would have felt like a prison. At a time when kids didn't trust the older generation, her offer seemed like a generous bolt from the blue. But I didn't have a close relationship with her and I didn't want her generosity. None of it made sense and it only occurred to me much later that Steve had more than probably asked her to offer this as a way of keeping me in his life. I'm sure she never would have considered it without his first requesting it anyway. It was always very like Steve to ask people to mediate for him.

Spring moved toward summer. I lived at my father's apartment in Cupertino and was free to be and do as I liked when my dad was away on business trips. I would stay out until all hours with Jim and we would walk all over Sunnyvale, Los Altos, and Cupertino, down the long dark

streets and through the blooming cherry and apricot orchards, sometimes until dawn, getting to know each other. This was the bohemian
lifestyle that I have always had a great appetite and natural inclination
for, and I still kept up my grades. Under those deep blue starry nights
we talked quietly and laughed a lot as we walked down quiet streets,
sometimes running over the nights and over the tops of cars in our bare
feet, climbing over fences and out of windows and up onto rooftops,
treetops, hilltops, listening to lonely dogs bark to each other across great
distances. The nighttime had a way of redrawing the daytime territories,
and in this I found my way out of structure and back into full-blown
wonder.

Jim's sensibilities were warm, human, and earthy. Our relationship
wasn't sexual; we were more like happy soulful playmates falling in love,
yet not too seriously. Like me, he liked to live inside alternative worlds.
He was crazy in love with the Tolkien Trilogy and was in the middle of
illustrating the whole thing, beautifully, when we met. Once, when he
was lying on his back on my couch and I was sitting on the floor close up
next to him with our hands and arms playfully entwining between
deep kisses, I felt his breath on my face as he quietly said, "I love you." I
could hardly bear the words before my entire being dropped down to
what felt like hundreds of thousands of miles below all surfaces. The
expression of his love was profound and I confess that later I compared
it to Steve's expressions of love, which at that point seemed more about
insecurity than anything else. Still I was drawn powerfully to Steve
and a love that seemed both broken and big. It *was* big. In this present
age where the tendency is to pathologize everything, it's easy to think
that Steve and I were attracted to each other because we were both, in
essence, motherless kids. But that's not how it was. In fact, it was moth-
erlessness that got in the way of a love that was real. I loved Steve. He
was time and timelessness to me and I measured everything by him. I
would have thrown my lot in with Steve over anyone if I'd known how.
But I didn't know how.

EIGHT

WALKABOUT

Steve moved back to the Bay Area late in the summer of 1973. He was living with a roommate in a house off Skyline Boulevard, a two-lane highway that tears a perfect hilly line between the mountains and the sky. Steve had scored a great place, with a big redwood deck surrounded by old-growth trees. I would visit him at this cabin by hitchhiking up the mountain on 84, taking rides only from pickup trucks so I could sit in the open air and catch the glorious views as the driver ascended the mountain road.

Our relationship was complicated. I couldn't break the connection and I couldn't commit. Steve couldn't either. One night, when he had the cabin to himself, he invited me to spend the night. We slept outside on the deck, on a heated waterbed, which was a kind of perfection in those days, maybe even now, too. Softly entwined outside under huge old evergreens in the deep quiet of night, yet with the protection of the cabin and the comfort of a warm bed . . . it just doesn't get any better. If only we had understood.

In the morning, the air filled with happy birdsong and when we got up, Steve played Cat Stevens's "Morning Has Broken" as we made breakfast and puttered about. Just then a friend of Steve's roommate dropped by. "My God," he exclaimed. "There is so much love in this house!" That may sound like a very seventies thing to say, but the truth is I had never heard anyone say anything even remotely like it. The remark startled me. How could someone else know such a thing when I couldn't see it myself? But when I looked around I realized that the stranger was right: the house was bright and radiant with our love. I was amazed by the power and simplicity of the love between us. Steve had known it all along. I was the one who hadn't realized what we had.

There would be other occasions, other times and places when people would see the love between Steve and me. They'd remark on it, very clearly, and I would be perplexed that others saw what I didn't see. Teens often live in a haphazard state of hit and miss, and they need the insights and the framing that an adult's experience can provide. It took me a while to realize all this, but in the years since there's never been a time when I wasn't mentoring at least one young person. Having come to realize how much I didn't understand when I needed to understand love, I now feel compelled to shorten the years of ridiculous, unnecessary trouble in others.

Steve may have had a long lovely summer at the cabin, but it wasn't carefree for the simple reason that Steve himself wasn't carefree. "I'm already nineteen and I still don't know what I'm supposed to do," he said, fretting about his life's big picture. I was kind of shocked by the statement. Impressed, too. I wondered if men had to be more serious about their futures, because, by comparison, I was just enjoying life and not at all stressed because I didn't know what I was going to do. "But why on earth do you think you could know so much at nineteen?" I asked. At this he became a pantomime of despair. Unable or unwilling to just tell me what the problem was, he threw his arms up into the air in abject frustration. He simply would not use words. And in the silence I wondered what pressures Steve was under. Now I understand that he was both confused and alarmed that his future hadn't yet started. I think he was worried that he might miss it. After all, he thought he was going to die at forty-two, so it stands to reason that he had no time to waste.

After Steve had dropped out of college, and before he went to India, he entered into one long aboriginal-like walkabout. He was an American boy searching for a way to access the huge potential within him. He was, in turns, full of hope and despair, advance and surrender, cheerfulness and devastation. He tried everything. Following his intuition and his common sense, Steve hitchhiked back and forth between Oregon and the Bay Area. He worked. He gathered new ideas. He met new people and stayed with old friends. Sometimes he'd rent a room. He'd find me, too, when he felt the need. His was a case of moving from the sublime to the ridiculous and then back again until one day all the infinitesimally small steps started to piece together. Later in my twenties, when I was floundering, Steve got mad at me. "Look," he said. "If you're having problems, work it through. Chase after everything until you've understood it!" Oh, had he ever earned the right to give that advice.

There were many times in the course of his sojourn when Steve would call out of the blue to tell me he was in town and that he had something to show me. It started with the harmonicas, which he kept in his pockets and backpack. I think he was learning to play them between rides when he was hitchhiking. Then he tried to get me to look into candles, as if they were flickering messages from a higher plane. And then he showed me how to use the *I Ching,* first with coins and then with yarrow sticks, offering his interpretations of the hexagonal combinations that we threw. Steve explained a kind of thinking that was new to me, one that was based on ancient wisdom and the workings of chance. This knowledge had been available to me intuitively, but it took me time to understand that the potential of a moment was readable in the toss of some coins. The *I Ching* actually changed my understanding of time. I used it for years after that.

It was around this period that Steve introduced me to Georgia, a forty-something-year-old woman who lived in San Francisco. Generous and lively, she reminded me of Maude from the movie *Harold and Maude.* Steve was working with her on a color-based therapy system she had developed for clearing past emotional trauma. He was midway through his process when he asked me to work with her, too. I soon found out that she had been a former colleague and girlfriend of Werner Erhard of EST fame. EST was a personal growth regime of weekend seminars that started in the seventies with an overly aggressive template for getting people to take responsibility for their lives. It has since changed a bit, and after renaming itself several times, it's now called The Forum. How Steve first came across Georgia I don't know.

We started with seven pieces of colored paper, red, blue, yellow, brown, purple, green, orange, and one big white sheet, twice the size of the others, which was to be a summary sheet. Then we cut images from magazines and put them on the colored paper of our choice. Mostly Steve and I cut images from back issues of *National Geographic* that we bought used at a resale store in Palo Alto. In the beginning we had no idea what the colors, the sizes, and the images meant. We'd just gather the pictures we were attracted to and glue them to what seemed to us the appropriate color. When that was done, Georgia would interview us, taking notes on our thoughts and explanations for our choices and what they meant to us. Then the boom would fall and she would decode what we had done so that we could see our issues and work to move beyond them.

I remember most of my images and two of Steve's. The best of his was a delicately granulated, color-treated photo of a stone relief depicting an Egyptian god of Intuition. He had placed the image on a piece of orange paper where it just floated with ethereal light. It was breathtaking, and we were, all three, in awe because it was clear that if ever there were a god seeing over Steve, it would be the Egyptian God of Intuition. Steve used one image per colored sheet, evidencing his minimalist aesthetic. We both knew it was superior and he gloated over it. I loved his awareness of his own design excellence, but was a little perplexed by his sense of competition.

My time with Georgia brought new awareness to my thinking. She told me, "I sense you have a huge capacity for love." This comment was like a stunning rebirth after the terrible ways my mother had spoken to me. Georgia valued me and she helped me value myself. But in the end, she became ill and I never completed her program. Later, after I got pregnant with Lisa, I called Georgia in tears and it was then that she told me that Steve had sat with her for hours and hours in grief because I didn't love him enough.

Georgia had some unspecified illness when I knew her, and it was getting worse. One day she told us that Werner Erhard had been stealing her creative energy and that this had been making her ill. I had no idea how to evaluate such a statement. It was so matter-of-fact, yet so outside the borders of accepted reality. But the notion that such a thing might be possible stayed with me. It was terrible, of course, but also exciting because I was ever looking at the way things might be working behind the scenes. All told, Georgia provided me with a much better self-image and offered me my first experience using a color system as a tool for transformation. I would go on to use many others through the years.

Little by little, Steve and I separated. But we were never able to fully let go. We never talked about *breaking up* or *going our separate ways* and we didn't have that conversation where one person says *it's over*. I guess we just didn't know enough to be final about it. Later, Steve would make jokes about our breaking up by telling people, "I knew it was over when she bought a sleeping bag that didn't zip to mine." It was like him to find the defining, humorous spin. But it wasn't quite truthful. Not in my experience.

I remember a different turning point in our relationship, a particularly dramatic moment that played out late one afternoon in August of '73 when Steve was still living on Skyline. My father, my little sister, and I drove Steve home. When we got to the top of the mountain to drop him off, Steve stepped out of the car and held his stomach as if in intense pain. But he looked as if he was stepping out into a desolate no-man's-land. It would have been comical for its extreme drama, but this was real. He couldn't even say good-bye. He spun around on his long spindly legs and staggered from one foot to the other as his stiff body stepped toward his cabin, like a cowboy who had just been shot. I watched, trying to comprehend what was happening. I glanced at my father and sister, who also looked baffled. Had I wounded him? Had there been some misunderstanding? Later I wondered if it was about my being with my family that triggered a sense of profound loneliness and isolation in him.

After that afternoon, we moved increasingly apart. He didn't seek me out as often and our paths didn't cross. I don't really know what he was doing at this time, because I was busy in school and working at a café. But seeing him so rarely allowed me to better grasp the changes he was going through. One day he called to see if I wanted to go for a walk. I hadn't seen him for a while and I didn't know until then that he had moved back into his parents' home. I drove over to Los Altos and walked in to find him sitting on the floor in his bedroom playing a guitar and singing. I can see now that he had staged himself for effect, and he did a good job at it. He was holding a beautiful guitar with a wide tapestry strap; he had a harmonica brace around his neck with a harmonica attached. He looked up at me, a misty depth in his eyes, this time fully channeling himself as the rock star.

I was instantly taken in. He curled his vowels. His phrasing was beautiful. Spit flew as his mouth went back and forth between the words and the harmonica, and I could see that he was mastering the coordination between the energetic intensity of his singing and the grace of the song. Basically he was saying, *Look at me!* I stood there blinking, overwhelmed by how good he was and how far he'd come. Up to that time I simply hadn't believed that he was a musician. Ten different kinds of brokenness in me could have prompted me to make that judgment, or maybe I had been right all along.

Musicians made up a large body of my friends in high school. For those friends, music was a way of life. But it wasn't a way of life for Steve. He knew he was going to be famous, but it's likely he couldn't imagine anything beyond Dylan at that time. That day I was hard pressed not to reconsider all of my assumptions. And I would have, had he kept going with it.

Through the years I have toyed with the idea of an alternate scenario: if, in that moment, I had fallen at his feet in adoration, would it have incited him to become a mystic poet musician instead of a billionaire businessman? His truth and beauty turned me inside out with admiration. But instead of giving over to it, I hung back, uncertain of how to speak and scared to fully acknowledge him and the effect he had on me.

Weeks, if not months, would go by without us having contact, but Steve would always find me. When I worked at the health food café he'd stop by in the off hours. When I worked as a live-in babysitter he would come over in the night and knock at my bedroom window. We'd talk through the screen and sometimes he would stay over. On those nights, after making love, I would fall into a deep sense of peace that would enfold me for days. From this I would walk around trying to fathom how it was that he could make me feel this way. I didn't understand my own experience.

Steve was the person I measured everyone and everything by. If I had entered into a not-so-great relationship with a boy, just seeing Steve would be enough to get me out of it. If he showed me some new thing—Medjool dates, a spiritual book, or that science supply store that used to be in Palo Alto—I'd go back to them repeatedly. He and his eyes brought sanity to my heart and soul. His take on things lit me up. He once said to me, "Do you not sense how deep our history is?" In this he was referring to past lives. "No," I said. "And you do?" I looked up into his face, knowing he'd say yes. He nodded seriously, and scanned the horizon. He knew I didn't get it.

During that floating time Steve traveled to Oregon to go through primal therapy. Between John Lennon's song "Oh My Love," and all that Steve had told me about primal therapy, I had intense expectations.

I looked for the changes when I saw him about four months later, but I noticed nothing. I urged myself to scan more deeply and to be more perceptive, but still, I found absolutely nothing different. I had assumed at the very least that his voice would deepen and that his massages would improve. But his voice was the same and his massages still hurt. Steve had a way of always pushing into the place where skin runs thinnest over the sharpest bone, and an uncanny ability to press on the exact location of a new bruise. This hadn't changed.

Compared to everyone I knew, Steve was the Spock character from *Star Trek* in my life. I had thought—imagined—that primal therapy would make him more human. In the end I discovered that Steve hadn't completed the course. In fact, he'd hardly even started. I sensed something had gone wrong with the therapy or the relationship with the therapist, but when I asked him what had happened, he brushed me aside with "I ran out of money." This didn't ring true. Steve always had money when he needed it. But I knew him well by then, and if he didn't want to tell me something, he simply wasn't going to.

Later, Steve spoke quietly about a trauma that he had dealt with, regarding a memory of his mother, Clara. He was five at the time, and Clara had taken his sister Patty indoors and left Steve outside, alone on the swings. Clara had excluded Steve from her intimate world with Patty and it must have played utter havoc on the psyche of a little boy who felt he'd been abandoned once already by his birth parents. He'd asked his mom about it when he got back to the Bay Area, and I imagine Clara looking into herself to answer as fully as she could because her response was "Patty was an easier child to take care of." Boy, was that the understatement of the century. Clara's words couldn't have been more simple or profound. And they were followed up with an apology: "I didn't mean to leave you out," she had told him. "I didn't know I was hurting you. I am sorry." I'm so very sure she was.

Steve's failure to complete the full primal scream course made a huge impression on me. Here was the magnificent opportunity for transformation and he had just walked away from it. I had fully believed that the miraculous was possible because of how Steve had talked about primal scream therapy. I had so wanted for him to be okay. But when I understood that he had quit, then nothing was sure for me anymore. And for him, I saw a kind of disillusionment set in, maybe even a quiet, slow bitterness at the edge of everything, like ice growing over a pond. It seemed that when the hope of that therapy died, a pragmatism set into Steve's life and soured the tenor of his sweetness. This sort of thing isn't ever totally obvious, and because Steve kept his thoughts and his feelings to himself, I can't point to one big thing that changed, except that he became a little more sarcastic. Steve had exhausted his childhood plan and at that point began to internalize the loss of a dream. He kept himself busy after that—and it wasn't with a guitar.

On one of Steve's hitchhikes home from Oregon, he got picked up by a guy I'll call Thomas. Thomas lived in unincorporated Cupertino, right across from where I was staying at my father's apartment. (I had by this time quit the babysitting job.) I never did meet the man. Steve had his own reasons for keeping people apart, but I remember Thomas because, with all of Steve's hitchhiking, he had never told me about anyone he had taken a ride from, until this guy. Apparently they had made a good connection. Steve even told me that Thomas asked to buy Steve's North Face hiking boots—right off Steve's feet!

Thomas was a scientist in his forties. This was already impressive to me because I saw Steve as a scientist type and I liked that this man was older. But there was something more going on here. I sensed Steve was trying to tell me about it in an oblique way so I found myself listening more deeply. I was confused by the boot story. "What a weird thing for him to ask to buy your boots," I said. "Are you going to sell them?" Steve then threw another line out, hinting: "The guy can get his own." A nonanswer, so I asked, "Then why did he want to buy yours?" Steve gave me a really long look, like I was soooo sloooow. "He wanted contact with me again," he said, slightly embarrassed.

Steve's embarrassment was always charming to me. He had an

unusual quality that I would later see in Mona when I would compliment her writing. It must have been in the DNA. I think there was so much beauty in their extraordinary minds it made them feel uncomfortably cornered when it was acknowledged. Years later, I asked Mona why she behaved that way when she was complimented. She shook her head and with a rush of embarrassment said, "I just don't know what to say."

It was after he met Thomas that Steve started talking about "going through," and how once you're through, "there's no going back." I am sure in their friendship the two men were talking through the nature of truth and enlightenment. I felt that this friendship bolstered Steve, that it helped him with something very important. He would tell me a little obsessively, "No mistake is possible, there is *no* going back, once you've gone through, you're through. You cannot slip back out." I believe he was telling himself this as much as he was telling me. Steve was beating a drum, rhythmically repeating, invoking and hinting, but he would never come right out and say, "I'm going to be enlightened. It's finally happening." All of this is in the tradition of "The Way," Steve would say, "It's like a bush. You can't ever just say what it is. . . . You can only point to it!" This was like Alan Watts's remark about pointing to the truth, something like "You can point to the full moon but you cannot touch it and most people only want to suck your finger." These were the metaphors of the time.

In the extremely refined and sophisticated traditions of the East, you would never say you are enlightened because the tradition abhors it. There are ways of thinking and using language that can turn you away from a true state of awakening. Exclaiming that you're enlightened or going to be enlightened would be one of them. I was always excited about Steve being so remarkable, but the masculine systems of philosophy and spirituality irked me. The systemization of special words and behaviors has always seemed to me to be exclusive and, contrary to all expectation, extremely egoistical. It never touched my heart or engaged my imagination, either. Later I would be apprised that the female aspect was enlightened in a different way. This made sense to me, but no one talked about the differences then, they just said it was all the same when it really wasn't.

It was so like Steve to imply but not actually say anything. I had to read the invisible ink in the air around him to understand what was happening. My take was that Steve was going to go "through," and he would change and never come back. I had some fear of being left out—justifiable, I think, because there was something in Steve that wanted me to feel this fear. A big part of him wanted to get over me and leave me in the dust. But he also was deeply sincere, and that big conversation he had going on in himself since we'd first met was finally starting to accumulate mass and order. He was finally finding the right connections. And as a true fan watching on the sidelines of his life, I was as relieved and happy for him as I was worried for myself.

Months went by and then Steve called to tell me he'd moved into a small cabin in the mountains near downtown Los Gatos. It must have been early spring of '74 when he was earning money working at Atari for a trip to India. I didn't know anything about Atari, just that it was an up-and-coming game company. Later I heard that Steve was put on the night shift because his coworkers were uncomfortable around him. In fact, it's been widely reported that people didn't want to be around Steve because he smelled. That didn't make sense to me; Steve never smelled when I was around him. I had heard that he was moved to the night shift because his coworkers found him so dark and negative. Now that made sense.

Steve invited me to the cabin for dinner. When I got there, I saw that he was living a very simple life on a big property that a divorced couple was sharing for the benefit of their children. The way Steve told me about these people's circumstances was as if he were winking an eye at me and saying: this is what will happen between us. We'll have a child and this is how we'll manage it.

I wondered at such an arrangement.

Steve had the ability to see into the future. I was convinced he could and therefore was hypnotized by his ideas of things to come. I listened too deeply to his take on everything and it never occurred to me not to play into his vision. Or to alter it. Steve planted seeds in my imagination and I just didn't think to say no or to respond with any conditions. I didn't know I could be practical or even magical in my own right, so I just gave in. Was that ever a mistake.

Steve invited me to the Los Gatos cabin only twice. And both times I was talkative in contrast to his stone-cold distance. We were polarizing. Part of me was witnessing it all, while part of me wanted to pull us back together and smooth over our differences. But his mind was made up. He wanted to hold me at a distance. Or more likely, he wanted me to feel unsure of where I stood with him. At the cabin, he had acquired a Japanese meditation pillow, and was reading *Be Here Now*. He gave me a copy on one of those nights and signed it, "With love, Steve" in his brown calligraphy. He turned on some South Indian music that was so outrageously different than anything I had ever heard that I wondered at it even being called music.

On my second visit to the cabin, Steve once again asked me to look into a candle for some mystical insight, but this time he wasn't sweet about it. I felt like I was being tested in a mean way because he bore down on me, repeating, "What do you see? What do you see?" Sadly, I could see no higher level of reality. What I saw instead was that he rather enjoyed that I wasn't *getting it*. I hated his big fat Houdini act.

Until this time Steve had wanted to include me in every adventure but no more. The load of our unconscious on the truth of our love was overwhelming and infuriating to both of us. Steve blamed me, and that indicated a lack of spiritual development on his part. So my feelings about staring into the flame were probably right. It was a cheesy parlor trick: all light and no love, patience, or compassion. Steve's heart had become negative toward me and he used the spiritual techniques as power tools for one-upmanship.

·   ·   ·

Steve had grown up in remarkable nonconformity to the rest of the world, because he was so ahead intellectually and intuitively, but so behind emotionally. As he pursued his destiny with an uncompromising commitment, there wasn't a single misstep he could take that wouldn't eventually come around to serving the greater goal of his emergence. It was going to happen. Ultimately, I'm pretty sure it came down to one remarkable friend, Robert Friedland, to finally usher Steve into his own remarkable life.

I never knew Robert well. He was Steve's friend. They had met at Reed. Nevertheless, I have shared some of the more profound times of my life in Robert's company as a result of his assistance to me. Robert is an extremely bright, ambitious guy, and I would say that in the seventies he was a seeker in the tradition of someone like Ram Dass. He had started out exploring the intellectual traditions of consciousness, then moved to LSD, and from there became a student of Neem Karoli Baba and the mysticism found in the East.

At around nineteen years of age, Robert had gone to prison because he was caught in some kind of drug operation. He went on to spend time in a low-security facility, where he was constantly in trouble with the guards for teaching yoga to the inmates. I know all of this and more because Robert, who was named Sita Ram when I met him, is a master storyteller of his own antics.

When I met Robert he was a smooth youth in his mid-twenties, of average height and build, with long blond hair. Robert was handsome, with a cultivated calmness and a humorist's killer instinct. His large, crystalline eyes would open and close with slow, deliberate blinks and when he told stories, he'd speak in light syllables that created the impression that here was a guy who loved hearing himself talk, and was worth listening to as well. He held his head level with self-awareness, and for all intents and purposes, he looked to me like a Caucasian Krishna.

Robert sat down with me on his farm one day and told me the story of his prison stay. Apparently a deal had been brokered for his release if he would go to college, get straight As, and fulfill extracurricular demands to keep him focused on a new life. It was an appropriate second chance for a really bright kid who had gotten caught up in things over his head. He took the opportunity, which is how he came to be at Reed College. I think he met Steve when he was running for class president (and winning) as a part of his parole obligations.

Robert was older than all of his classmates at Reed. When I knew him, I had the feeling that he had a huge capacity for life. It wasn't just that he was super bright, it was that he had a deep sense of humanity and a meta-level awareness of other people's circumstances. In short, he was someone who could truly meet Steve as he was—the orphan in all his princely constellations—and still have room for more.

I suspect that Robert and Steve connected immediately as kindred souls. And I can imagine how they must have quickened into fast recognition of one another's bold, uncommon intelligence. And even though Steve and Robert were equals as friends, I have always felt that Robert had an aspect of care for Steve that was genuinely fatherlike. It would have been like Robert to step into a role after having seen a need.

Beyond this, I saw that the two would come to identify a shared desire and ability to strategize for elite levels of success, in part through the uses of esoteric knowledge found in the East. And I don't in any way believe that it was by accident or dumb luck that Steve through Apple and Robert through mountaintop mining would both build multibillion dollar businesses within twenty years of meeting.

Back when their facial hair was soft, Robert encouraged Steve to go to India to meet Neem Karoli Baba. India! The golden land on the other side of the world, where Gautama Buddha was born. Where Jesus is said to have walked in the lost years, and where Gandhi developed satyagraha. India! It is one of the few places on earth where both the gods and the goddesses are still visible, complex, and in relationship with each other. It is a place where a huge world-creator type like Steve might well receive something he needed.

After India, Steve would toss aside all therapeutic models and reorganize everything under a spiritual rubric. From my observations, it was in India that the cosmological switch got flipped in Steve. And even though Neem Karoli Baba had died before Steve got there, he was touched by something, because by the time I saw him again, Steve knew his place in the universe.

The morning of the day Steve left for India he came to my house to say good-bye and to give me a $100 bill. He had made a bit of money at Atari and he just wanted to give me this gift. I hadn't seen him in a while and was standing with my new boyfriend at the entrance to the apartment when Steve walked up. Steve touched my forehead to indicate that I was his, which I found outrageous. When I objected to the money, Steve demanded I not play the game of rejecting it. Steve was nothing if not ceremonial in his passages and this money was about him, not me, so I took it and thanked him. The next time I saw him would be four months later after he had returned to the United States and was convalescing at Robert's farm an hour to the south of Portland.

NINE

ALL ONE FARM

Laura Schylur and I decided to celebrate our high school graduation with a three-week road trip. We weren't sure what our graduations meant to us, but we knew that a celebration was in order, so we talked about what we would do and then made the money to do it. I put new tires on my ivory Chevrolet and we took off with a screech, happy to be leaving it all behind before returning to waitress jobs and junior college in the fall.

Everything was planned when, about two weeks before our trip, Steve wrote out of the blue to say he had returned from India and was reacclimating to the United States somewhere in Oregon. I was delighted to hear from him and wrote back saying that Laura and I would soon be traveling through the northwest ourselves. To my surprise, Steve sent another letter inviting us to visit.

Laura and I drove north from San Francisco up the California coast on Highway 1. Our first stop: Eureka, California. It was a long drive made longer by our decision to take the coastal route, where we passed picturesque fishing towns as charming as any Welsh seaport the imagination can conjure. I had read a lot of Dylan Thomas, which is why, I suppose, the notion of the Welsh seaport came to mind. Those outposts of human endeavor colored our drive in every sense of the word, and they turned me inside out with aching wonder about a kind of life I would never know.

The northern California shoreline offers a rugged uncommon beauty. Pristine and wild with riptides that tear at the land, with waves that crash their sloppy magnificence all over craggy cliffs and sharp jutting rocks. We stopped to swim when we found a bank of sandy access to the water's edge with a safe place to pull off the road and park. I had been taking cold showers all that spring which enabled me to walk straight into the ocean without anything but pure lust for its bracing coldness. This was a new kind of freedom, like sprouting wings or, something just as fantastic, swimming bare skinned into the northern Pacific as if it were temperate.

In Eureka we stayed with both of our older sisters, who lived there with their boyfriends and attended Humboldt State. We visited for four days, taking hikes in the damp wilderness, walking around the cute college town, and spending good time with family before setting off for Oregon, All One Farm, and Steve. If we stopped overnight in a camping ground on the way, I don't remember now; I just remember that from Humboldt we turned inland, and that it was a relief to trade the winding road of the coastal highway for the ease and speed of the open freeway. I also remember that it was a small thrill to cross the state line into Oregon.

Getting close to our destination by midafternoon, but not sure of the directions, Laura and I took turns calling the farm from gas station pay phones. A woman named Abha always answered—Abha with the lovely ethereal voice—and she would hand the phone over to her husband, Robert, who would direct us from our newest lost location. It didn't matter that we called six times, Robert was patient and kind each time he spoke to us. Eventually, we found our way.

We could hear the gravel kick out from under our fat tires as we drove down the long drive to All One Farm. We followed some tire tracks under a hood of deepest greens, until suddenly everything opened into broad daylight and we saw a bright expanse of burnished silver rolling hills, dotted with dark pockets of lacy trees, and a sky of confident blue overhead.

Laura was driving when we reached the farm. She sat with her left leg tucked under her, leaning forward to peer carefully ahead on the long, cool, driveway. Her feminine conscientiousness always made me wonder what it felt like to be her. With her big sometimes care-laden blue eyes and her high sweet voice, she didn't look as if she could get angry. And she couldn't. Not convincingly, anyway. (She would eventually become a kindergarten teacher.) Laura was a large-boned, well-proportioned young woman with a little girl's sweetness in her beautiful face. She could have been the immortal inspiration to a German clockmaker of an earlier time. Maybe her great-great-grandmother had been such a muse. Laura was bright-faced, intricately watchful, towering, a little unsure of herself because she ran so tall, too big to hide. But that's where the laughter came in, like waves of delicate chimes at the top of every hour. No choice but to crest and fall into laughing at it all. Laura and I loved to laugh. And we laughed a lot.

We parked where we were told—just north of a big tree—and got out to stretch. We looked at each other from over the top of the car with raised eyebrows. Laura was teasing me, wiggling her brows up and down. She knew my stomach was filled with butterflies to see Steve again. It felt good to shut the motor off and repressurize to the weightless expanse of the great outdoors. The air was fragrant with fresh smells of nature and bright with the sun overhead. I still remember the smells. Looking around at our home for the next week, we saw an old, weathered barn, a large vegetable garden, and a big cow that we'd later find out had come along with the purchase of the farm. The main house was to the south.

It was Robert Friedland who greeted us. He went over everything about being on the farm and sort of humorously laid down the law: we were to get up at dawn to meditate under the big tree with everyone else, and we were to help with the work. Robert, who was then called Sita Ram, was nicer than I expected, but I was on my best behavior because I'd only met him a few times (and briefly), when he came with Steve to the café where I worked, and at Reed. I assured Robert that Steve had told me about the requirements and that we would be very happy to contribute in every way we could, *and* to meditate, too.

Robert then pointed to the barn down the hill and told us there would be a small room to the right in the back of the barn's main hall where we could stay. From my dyslexic blur I straightened up and got myself to suss out right from left, and we then proceeded, lugging our backpacks and sleeping bags.

We found Steve resting in his blue sleeping bag in the center of the main room of the cavernous barn. He looked terrible. Worse than I had ever seen him. "Hi," he groaned out. "I'm sick with parasites." He was so ill and he was also reserved. I sensed that he was ambivalent about my being there, and it made me a little mad because he had invited me. I wanted him to be happy to see me, but he didn't show it if he was. Nonetheless, he was kind enough, and encouraged us to run around and meet everyone.

Laura and I were both shy but we made our way up to the kitchen to meet Abha. In the early evening of that first day we helped lay colorful blankets on the grass in preparation for the dinner. We also brought out huge bowls of salad, which everyone ate with chopsticks, sitting on the blankets picnic fashion. I was curious to find that there were three or four different salads served at every meal, and a strong emphasis on zwieback breads and almond butter over peanut butter. The whole farm was vegan, with a focus on nonmucus forming foods. The Mucusless Diet! Its helps the emotional, physical, intellectual, and spiritual bodies integrate, and this place was serious about it. About eighteen people sat down for dinner that night—some who lived and worked there and some, like us, who were there for a short stay. Steve was too sick to join the group for the meal, so I felt freer to meet people on my own terms. The conversation moved like popcorn and I enjoyed the fond familiarity and the cajoling about the day's work. I was delighted to be sitting with these people, each of whom was under thirty.

That first night, after the dishes had been done, Laura and I returned to the barn and laid out our sleeping bags. I was deeply aware
that Steve was sleeping less than twenty feet away from me. Laura and I
whispered about the day so as not to disturb him. Then she fell asleep
and the barn came to life with miniscule and unfamiliar sounds: little
animals, creaking timbers, and the quiet shuffles of people coming in
at all hours. I heard them moving about as they got ready for bed, and
imagined them lighting tiny candles, and meditating, in the transparent windswept building. I lay awake for a long time feeling the massive
structure as if it were an extension of my own body.

The next day Laura and I worked in the kitchen canning dill pickles with Abha and two other women. We were like extras grafted onto a
movie scene. The circa 1940s kitchen was clean and orderly, with eggshell-
colored enamel painted many times over. Abha had scores of shining
glass jars on shelves high up around the walls: grains, pasta, beans, lentils,
seaweeds, dried fruits, and vegetables. The variation and abundance was
beautiful to look at, a gorgeous sense of order in multiplicity of the
gifts from the earth.

I had canned before, but never pickled. Abha boiled the jars and
lids and we listened, comically carefully, to her instructions before moving into action. We stood in the middle of the production line and
filled our hands with the herbs and spices, packing half a Meyer lemon,
a couple of garlic cloves, a small hot red pepper, turmeric, and fresh dill
into each cucumber-filled Mason jar. We moved quickly so as to not drag
the system, cleaning up spills whenever there was a moment. After the
spices, another woman poured in vinegar and boiling hot water over this
cluster of good things, then placed the liner caps on the jars until they
cooled. Every finished jar caught the light and became its own jeweled
world of deep, forest greens. I looked into each one for its compositional
beauty as if they were drawings of the same still life. At the end of the
first day we had lined up about twenty jars of pickles. They were magnificent. The next day we checked them and screwed their lids on tight.
It was completely delightful to complete the job, and I was awed to real-

ize that our work in this one week would extend into the community's future. I imagined Abha reaching for the jars throughout the year to come and I remember thinking it a real pity that I wouldn't taste any part of it. I didn't know then that I would return within the year.

At about twenty-eight, Abha was five years older that Robert. She was six months pregnant with their child when I first met her, and she had a magical daughter of three from a previous marriage, whom Robert would later adopt. Tall and radiant with a healthy pregnancy, Abha seemed both powerful and very sweet at the same time. Her face was covered in bronze freckles and her hair was a deep bronze with coppery pink highlights. Abha's gold-flecked eyes were more than piercing: they appeared to look straight through people. And when she laughed her face broke into a thousand lit-up facets.

Abha was as solid as she was aloof, in the way you would expect of someone who cared for so many people while simultaneously being so cosmic. She managed the kitchen well and was a remarkably gifted cook. I learned about new food combinations from her, like cottage cheese with dulse seaweed or fresh dill and soy sauce and farmer cheese or brewer's yeast tofu stroganoff. I would watch Abha's face when she cooked and tasted the food, her mouth mulling over flavors, her facial muscles tuned in to decide what more, if anything, was needed. Watching her face when she was tasting gave me pathways into my own new recipe ideas.

Years later, after Lisa's birth and after Steve became well-known, I felt I had to hide my identity when meeting new people because they had far too many projections—both negative and positive—and far too many questions. I'd just keep my mouth shut and become more and more quiet as Steve became more and more famous. However, over time, keeping a low profile turned into a problem. My history was filled with Steve and hiding it diminished my presence in a room of people. In effect, it silenced me.

All of this came to a head years later when I began taking classes to learn how to visualize information for corporations. As part of the process we were given huge sheets of paper—four by eight feet—on which to use our histories to illustrate the paths our lives had taken. I think I did about six of them in different group settings. It was only as a result of being forced to reveal myself at these classes that I first became conscious of how truly uncomfortable I was about being seen—and unseen. I certainly didn't want to put my life and everything on display in a professional environment. I couldn't handle it and had decided my colleagues couldn't either.

Now I regret that I wasn't more outrageous and inventive. I could have drawn a big black gangly vortex and strung the disasters one by one, around and around, tunneling inward into the center where a tiny exhausted figure holding a baby looked up from the bottom of a great hole. But I didn't. And after taking a number of these classes and being extremely conscious of all I sanitized (and embarrassed by what looked like a milquetoast life), I eventually realized that I could use food to refer to my past and develop my timeline in a public way. It would be through food and cooking that I could talk about all the people who had introduced me to new ideas. It would be through food that I could talk about my life and illustrate my timelines and my passions. This was the subject that would braid itself into an easy narrative. And in this version of my history, Abha would be the first of my influences, once I had left my mother's home. I thought I was brilliant when I finally figured it out, because the subject of food is always a way to be visible, personable, and enthusiastic while staying private. Finally, I could smile inside myself for having found a happy little middle ground in which to stand and be a part of the world without raising eyebrows.

After that first day of being in the kitchen, Abha apparently told Robert that Laura and I were great workers and so we were welcomed into the community. We hadn't understood that this was such a big deal at the farm, but when we had learned that we'd passed with flying colors, we soaked up the unexpected happiness of this approval.

The farm must have been a bold experiment for Robert, who owned it with his uncle, Marcel. If I remember correctly, it was Robert's job in the partnership to get the farm into good shape so he and his uncle could turn it around and sell it for a profit. As there were innumerable projects that needed hands, Robert had ongoing ads in classifieds all the way up to Portland in the never-ending search for people who would work in exchange for fresh garden food and a place to live in the country. This business structure—extra farmhands working in exchange for food and a room—was an old farming model with an added new twist: hippies and meditation.

Two types of people seemed to respond to Robert's ads: those I thought of as spiritually oriented and those that I thought of as normal— young people who had moved to the farm to work, eat well, and live in nature, but who were not so spiritually motivated. The combination was a true yin and yang: the mystical and the mundane, and the comic spin between the two.

The nonspiritual people thought the spiritual people were hilarious. Informed, for the most part, by a materialistic and matter-of-fact view of life, they laughed at what they thought was the comedy of an overly spiritual perspective. When, for example, the spiritual people at All One called each other saints—"Oh, you're a saint," someone would say. Or "Would you be a saint and do this or that for me?"—the nonspiritual ones would roll their eyes. But it was all in good fun, and it seems to me now that no one believed they had the single scoop on truth, which was why this group of people was so important to me. We coexisted in a kind of common wealth, bonding over the bounty of the place, the daily work, the healthy meals, and the naturally forming relationships. It all held together in some basic and very agreeable way.

There was so much to do and so many rich conversations at all levels that I felt endlessly happy at All One Farm. The sense of space and time, the hands-on work, and the variety of people so filled the hours that by the end of the first day I was baffled to think that only one day had passed. Truly, it seemed as if an entire month had gone by since dawn. Laura felt the same. The next night, as I pulled into my sleeping bag, I checked myself for the sense of expanded time and I saw that it had happened once again. And the day after that . . . and the day after that. In the end I decided that time must behave differently on a farm. It was a little insight I tucked away for future reference.

I didn't see Steve very much those first few days. I was busy, having fun meeting people and working. Of course he wasn't feeling well and he was grumpy; even so, I wondered if he still liked me. Teenage girls are always wondering if someone does or doesn't like them. It's a total waste of time, but there you have it.

On day two, Abha gave me a huge bowl of the densest green parsley salad I have ever seen to bring across the field and up the plank into the barn to Steve, who was so miserably sick it was alarming. She made these salads just for him, to kill off the parasites in his liver, and calm the itchy bumps from the bedbugs he'd brought back with him from India. I arrived with these "lunches" a couple of times and Steve would stir himself slowly, then lean heavily onto one elbow to reach for the bowl. I sat next to him while he ate, happy to have an excuse to see him. I really wondered if this was going to do the job, especially since eating this much parsley seemed like a lot of work. But he committed himself to it with resignation and eventually some interest.

The care that Robert and Abha bestowed on Steve was clear and dear. It was as if he were a son or a beloved younger brother. I would watch them look at him with humor and tenderness. They called him "Steven." In fact everyone was called by their longer names at All One Farm, which felt rather grown-up and loving to me. It seemed like more of a person's whole self was present when people used the full name that their parents had given them. *I* even felt more intact when I heard another's name fully pronounced. I'm sure that was the point.

During the week of our stay I met Greg Calhoun—Gregor—who was funny and smart and terribly cute. He had also gone to Reed with Robert and Steve, and had moved to the farm to live after he graduated. Greg's father had died when he was young and his stepfather was an

Episcopalian minister. Greg was one of the spiritual ones—a tight-muscled, petite man with a trimmed blond beard and mustache. He had a sweet temperament and twinkling steel gray eyes with huge blond lashes that swept the landscapes as he thought. He played the piano and a number of other instruments, including the bagpipes.

On the farm Greg had remodeled an existing chicken coop into a home for himself. I found it to be the nicest dwelling on the property, though it had no plumbing.

On one afternoon, Greg walked me around All One to show me the different projects that were being worked on, or were soon to come up. He showed me the apple orchard from which Apple derives its name. It was a good twenty-minute amble from the main house and it was the oldest orchard I have ever seen. The trees had a crazed growth pattern with branches going every which way, covered with layers of lichen in all colors, like peeling paint. The orchard had not been pruned in what seemed like a hundred years and it had a scarecrow quality. Greg called them "old soldiers."

Soon after this, all the young men on the farm would be at work to revitalize them. I have the pretty image that their working in that orchard was for Steve a St. Francis-like rebirth. After he had gone to India and then been so ill, it must have been wonderful to return to life there, with all his friends working together like a brotherhood in the bright, limitless air. Orchards are a kind of church in any case. You walk under limbs that meet in graceful flying arches, filling up with blossoms and birds and rain in the spring and then grateful heavy fruit in the fall.

I looked for ways to talk with Steve through his sickness and our distance. He had done a lot of work to separate from me, but I wanted to know who we were now and what my place with him was. On a few nights, I tiptoed out to where he lay in the barn and slipped into his sleeping bag next to his feverish, skinny, scabby body. We curled up together for hours, and there were a few moments of real tenderness and love, but we both knew it wasn't a good idea. I'm not sure why I was reaching out; neither of us could have opened up to each other at that point. I think I was just trying to feel the perimeter of the changes in him and in us. Holding out for what might be possible, I was trying to connect beyond the strangeness, too. I missed him, and I imagine that he was trying to see if he could sleep next to me without being attached in the old way. After all his longing, which was truly overwhelming to me in the first two years of our knowing each other, our new distance unbalanced my sense of everything. As exhilarating as it is, change grieves me. And I've never quite understood separations or endings.

Since that first day on the farm, I'd had to cope within myself with Steve's growing distance. That earlier deep, young love had changed. With just a few exceptions Steve didn't extend himself to me and I hardly saw him. I voiced a complaint on one of the days when he was up walking around, concave and fragile. As we happened to be standing near each other without anyone else nearby I said, "You seem to not even like me!" It was the verbal equivalent of stamping my foot on the ground in hurt and frustration, but I was sinking rapidly from the effect of his apparent indifference, and I felt I had to say something or go under. In response to my little bomb of outrage he said that one of his friends at the farm had just told him, after meeting me: "Steve, I knew you had taste." *Oh,* I thought, *he said this about me to compliment Steve.* It felt like a lifeline, a connection, and an acknowledgment of my value but with a curious twist. It was as if he'd reached into his pocket to find something to offer, gracious and immediately given, to ease my pain and confusion. Yet in the alchemy of gift giving I think it surprised both of us because it was so brilliantly crafted for good-bye. I found a confidence in that statement that set me free. After that, I felt I didn't need to pull on Steve for affections he didn't want to give. I was unburdened, happier, set up on an even keel with wind in my sails.

The very fact that Steve had invited me to All One was a gift of sharing something he cared about with me, and for me. I do know this: Steve had a generous spirit when it came to bright things. Over the next fifteen years he would invite me to a number of events at Apple and it would always be a puzzle, because once I actually did all the work to show up he would invariably ignore me. Likely he was acting on moments of inspiration because he liked my mind and wanted to share with me, but in the end he could never remember or carry it out with sustained friendliness. I always had a hard time holding up under it, too.

One day in the late afternoon, toward the end of Laura's and my stay, I walked into the kitchen to discover that a new wave of visitors had arrived. Among them was a woman with her four-year-old daughter. The two stood center stage on the kitchen floor with about ten people surrounding them, including me. The little girl was wearing a long dress and sandals. Her mother was dressed in long hippie skirt with a pretty blouse and flip-flops. She was a confident tree of goodness, standing tall and firm next to her little one. Everyone was talking, as women do, pouring praise and greetings onto them. Someone said the child was born in the month of May and was a Taurus. *Oh,* I thought dreamily, *a little Taurus!* I was very taken by the child because she had such a powerful soul-light around her. Without thinking, and in a complete wonder, I floated a new thought: *I want a little girl like this one, a little Taurus!* I knew the woman was a single parent, but in this one moment even that looked good to me. So fast and full did the wish fly through me, so at-one was I with my dream that I didn't fully understand that I was engaged in an act of creation.

Years later other women—at least three that I know of—would look at my child and would also decide to have one like her. All had been taken by Lisa as I had been by that child at All One Farm and all went on to have daughters of their own. Incredibly, each one sought me out after the fact, to proudly tell me, as if from a hushed secret society, "I now have a daughter and she is like Lisa." Tipping their heads forward, they would smile, clear-eyed and glowing with pride as if to say what couldn't be said, "My daughter is also like *her*."

I wept when Laura and I left the farm at the end of the week. It felt like home to me in a way that nothing ever had. It wasn't just about Steve because he was way too ouchy to be around without others to dilute the hurt with laughter and kindness. It was the farm and the life at All One itself that I loved. There was some rare, incomparable nutrient that had saturated my being in that place, a quality that, as Rumi says, "your whole life yearns for." Getting up at dawn to meditate, the rich gold feeling deep in the bone of focused work with others, and yet so much more on the side of the ineffable. Maybe it was Neem Karoli Baba's influence, because it sure seemed like someone with that kind of love over-lit the place. Steve used to frame things as being greater than the sum of their parts, and this described All One. I wanted to stay forever and ever. Nothing in me could hide the depth and purity of the sorrow I felt about leaving. I had a commitment to drive on with Laura but I stood outside the car door and cried. Next lifetime, though, I'm staying.

All One Farm was a wisdom society when we were all still so young and foolish. It was a spiritual community working to turn a profit. A sanctuary. It was the time and place where Apple got its name and where I first had the yearning for my chirpy, happy, soulful daughter.

TEN

THE PRACTICAL AND THE POETIC

I have always had the odd talent of being able to find the very best books, films, and clothing; to walk into a store and locate the one item I want without having to shop, sort, or compare. It's the perfect sense of the true find. That's what happened in the spring of '75 when I came upon a restaurant in downtown Los Altos, called Pan's. I was charmed by this little place, by the way the front door was set back from the street in a little alcove. And so I went in.

A man in his mid-thirties with a shaved head stood behind the counter preparing food. His body was slightly stocky, and he had a large chest and grounded feet, as if he had a bit of the hobbit in his bloodline. His eyes had a diamond hardness: not harsh, but crystal clear and intentional. The air around him was so palpably quiet and focused it seemed as if I had entered another world. The place was empty besides the two of us, and at first the thick silence in the room felt suffocating. But that soon gave way to something peaceful. Eventually he asked me what I wanted, then turned his back to complete some other task before starting on my order.

I fidgeted as I waited. On the counter next to the register I saw a brochure about a Zen Buddhist community in Los Altos; it attracted my attention in a fierce way. "You ought to check it out," the man said. He then returned his full attention to the work. I took the brochure and sat down to read it, glancing at the man as he prepared my lunch. He moved at a glacial pace, shaking tiny droplets of water from the lettuce one leaf at a time, then stepping back to place them onto the bread he had just cut. Finally he set the sandwich in front of me with such care that I got the awkward feeling of being served by someone of great spiritual development. It was in that sandwich piled high with a mountain of sprouts that the world of Zen first entered me. The man's name was Steve Bodhian and he was an ordained monk.

I saw Steve Bodhian in his robes the following Wednesday at Haiku Zendo of Los Altos, the place on the brochure. Haiku Zendo was located in a two-car garage that had been converted into a tricked-out Japanese meditation center. When I first peeked into it I saw beautiful wheat-colored tatami mats covering the floor, and a balconylike tier of seating around the walls—also covered with tatami mats. The front wall had a central island stage built out into the room for the teacher, with two recessive platforms behind him where advanced students would sit. Regal-looking scrolls with Japanese calligraphy hung on the wall behind the teacher's seat and ceremonial accoutrements were arranged up front: an incense cup; pillows on which two different sizes of bowl-like bells had been placed; mallets; and a long stick. The place wasn't that big—it only seated about seventeen people—but it was so ordered and beautiful that the room's emptiness felt spacious.

I had called during the week and was told to come on Wednesday at 5:30 p.m. so that I could learn how to "sit" and conduct myself when the group arrived an hour later. A thin man in his thirties was already there. We removed our shoes, and then he took two round meditation pillows called zafus, and two soft mats called zabutons, from a wooden bin outside. He handed me a pillow and a mat, then put his pillow and mat under his arm. I followed suit, and then we began.

Upon entering the room I was instructed to bow as soon as I stepped in. Then we quietly crossed over to a wooden platform where I was shown three different ways to sit. One was with my legs folded under me on each side of the pillow. He said this was the way Japanese women in a dress would sit. The other positions were half lotus or full lotus, whereupon my guide pointed out the stability I could obtain by triangulating my bottom on the pillow and my knees on the mat. He told me, "Do whatever you can manage for a time." I was playful with his instruction, making little jokes to make a personal connection with him. "Is falling off the pillow like falling off the wagon?" I asked. But he was all business, and so I settled down and focused. He then showed me how to cup my hands into a symmetrical shape called a hand mudra, and to place this cupping against my lower belly, just below the navel. When the time came, I was to face the wall in complete silence with my chin slightly tucked and the top of my head angled upward so that the back of my spine was straight. I was also to keep my eyelids partly open and unfocused. This way of meditating with open eyes is particular to Zen. Moreover, the exactness of form the body holds is said to be enlightenment itself. In Zen, you don't strive for enlightenment; logic has it that you are already enlightened, so there is no journey and nothing to attain. It is powerful, elegant, and deceptively simple.

In time I would discover that all the people at the Zendo were bright and a little peculiar, that they were quiet and paid attention and laughed kindly at odd things. They seemed to all be poets and/or scientists, or married to poets and/or scientists. Most had some affiliation with Stanford University. I would learn that Japanese Buddhism had, in part, been developed for the Japanese intellectual class as a practice for emptying the mind of *intellectual sediments*. Eventually this all fit together in my understanding, but on that first day it was as if I had stumbled into the middle of an old-growth forest of tree people.

That evening I sat up in half lotus through a nearly unbearable forty minutes of meditation, until a delicate bell finally rang out. As the tone sounded, signaling the end of the period, everyone bowed. Still maintaining a careful inward focus, people scooted around on their bottoms, continuing to look downward, but this time facing the group and the teacher. Stillness returned to the room at this point, and I felt a deep resonant space open up, each person being a booming well of silence. The room was filled with a profound sense of acceptance. The quiet of the collective power was impressive while the teacher found his words. The teacher was slow to speak—and I was in such agony—that I stole a glance around to make sure everything was as it should be. *Oh God! Were we really all just going to keep sitting like this?*

Finally the teacher spoke and with his first words came the most delicate, careful speech. I had never heard such profound and gentle confidence. I remember him saying, "We go to truth with nothing and we return with nothing." This was the practice of Zazen and it moved straight into me. I could not take my eyes off the teacher, nor did I want to, though I guessed it was probably impolite. The teacher's robes were layered and beautiful with long, looping table runner–like sleeves. Mostly he was covered in gracious folds of black material with ivory and white underlayers peeking through at the neck and wrists. His posture was tranquil and very present. Every expression was evident on his face, moving from seriousness to humor with infinite nuance. It was the first time I had listened so deeply to anyone from Japan, and between the truth in his kind face and the soft accented words of his amber voice, I became aware of an extraordinary weave of refinement.

With the powerful teacher and the mature students, my young restlessness calmed and I came to be at one in a room of sitting Buddhas. Over the hour, as the teacher spoke, incense streamed up in a single blue line, only to flutter and disperse a foot above the burn, and tip its fine white ash back into the cup from whence it came. As the sun set, the sky turned dark and a delicate candlelight lit the interior space. Afloat on the teacher's words and thoughts, a feeling of *just we few* came into me, but this time with a generosity that seemed to include the whole world. It was like happening upon a perfect bright shell, complex and whole, lying on a shore—a gift from a tourmaline sea. *What have I found?* I wondered to myself. Over the next three years, I would sit and listen to many lectures like this first one.

Suddenly the teacher stopped speaking and a cloud cover went over his eyes as he left us to look inward. Two people came in with jingling trays of white cups, two pots of green tea, and small cookies. One by one every person in the room was served—cup, tea, napkin, and cookie—both servers going down the rows, bowing to each person, going down on their knees, and then up again to step forward to the next.

After the sitting, the lecture, the tea, and the retrieval of the cups, a tiny bell rang and everyone bowed together. It was over. People moved onto their knees to push their pillows back into shape, and then stood up. Holding zafu and zabuton under one arm, they individually bowed with one hand to the place they had just been sitting, paying homage to the space that had held them. Then everyone moved to walk out silently with one final bow at the door before stepping into the cool night. Outside, people talked and laughed in hushed tones as they put their shoes on, their slacks bulging at the knees.

I was trying to work out the teacher's name with one of the lay monks, a guy named Trout who had kindly introduced himself. But his demeanor changed when I referred to his teacher, incorrectly, as "Chino." The teacher's first name was Kobun and his last name was Chino. Kobun Chino Sensei—"sensei" meaning "teacher." Later he would become Kobun Chino Roshi—"roshi" meaning "master." All the syllables of the teacher's name were so completely unfamiliar to me that I didn't know where any of the sounds began or ended. I was just doing my best with the whole thing, but my guesses were wrong and I had apparently offended the monk who now seemed incensed. "How would you like it if I called you 'Brennan'?" the monk exclaimed. *My, but you're easily offended!* I thought. Later I would find Trout's requirement for exactitude the key to many important things.

Soon afterward, I learned that Kobun, who was then in his forties, had come to the United States to became the Abbot of Tassajara at the request of Suzuki Roshi, and had left Japan without his teacher's blessing. In a culture of such ceremonial order, refinement, and conformity,

Kobun had taken a huge risk in coming to America. Only later—much later—would his teacher praise him in full, telling him he had done well.

That night at the Zendo made my head swim. As I was gathering up my very first impressions and getting ready to leave, I looked over, and to my utter amazement, there was Steve, just eight feet away. I hadn't seen or heard from him in months, not since Robert's farm. He was standing apart from the group, waiting in the half-light. The teacher had his back turned to him, having Steve wait while he greeted people who approached as a part of the evening's ritual. A student's waiting for his teacher's attention is as old as time itself. Steve had that third eye focus, but he looked so thin and vulnerable—he seemed to be barely hanging on. My heart gripped with pity, but I was also simply happy to see him, so walked over to say hello. Once he'd caught sight of me, however, I saw the shadow of a thought cross his face: *Oh no, not you.*

"When did you return from the farm?" I asked. "Are you living at your parents' house?" Steve gave me vague, one-word answers and peered down into me as if I were at the bottom of a very deep gorge. He had become a stranger and it shook me to my core. I said good-bye and left as quickly as I could.

At the next Wednesday night meditation, I ignored Steve to avoid making either of us uncomfortable again, but at the end of the evening he approached me and asked if I would like to come over to his parents' for lunch the following week. I accepted.

I was glad to see Clara again, and in the short time we talked I felt that there was something lighter and more gracious about her. She led me to the backyard where Steve was sitting on a little grassy mound watching the sky. He had a pleasant, bewildered look on his face and a buzz of energy around him like someone had just clapped him between two massive cymbals.

Backyards in the California suburbs are often bordered at the property lines by six-foot-high redwood fences. Typically, they're comprised of small bean-shaped lawns with bean-shaped patios and bean-shaped pools. They had always seemed miniscule to me after having lived with the huge swaths of green found in the Midwest; but extraordinary, too, like beautiful garden rooms furnished with exotic flowers and sunshine. And I'd always liked the way they seemed to create a private plot of sky— very special and sort of stingy at the same time.

The Jobses' backyard had been a barren moonscape for as long as I'd known them. Far from a private little paradise, theirs had been an empty box with an obligatory crabgrass lawn and water stains that looped up the dark fencing like an intricate army of wood-eating lice. But that day I found a transformation from Kansas to Oz. A verdant garden, about sixty feet across and thirty feet deep, covered the back third of the property. A cornucopia of crazed activity, the garden had stakes and twine and circular metal forms holding plants in a cacophonous sem-blance of order. It was as if the space had waited all these years for this outrageous justice.

In India it is said that there is no way that a child can return the favor of a life of care that parents have bestowed. I read this in the book by Ram Dass that Steve had given me, *Be Here Now*. Gratitude to your parents didn't exactly find favor in sixties or seventies America, but Steve broke rank on that one. It seemed that the first order of business for him when he returned from India was to thank his parents for all they had done for him. This beautiful garden represented his gratitude. It was one of Steve's great signatures in the world to merge the practical and the poetic. After that, for as long as I knew them, the Jobses always planted a garden in the spring and it seemed they were happier people for it.

Steve looked over to me from a little raised hill on the right. With a small sigh he got up and as I stood in the doorway holding the screen door open with my body, somehow expecting a greeting or at least a smile, he edged past me to the kitchen. His acknowledgment was so casual—even disappointed—that I wondered if I'd come on the wrong day. Why such indifference? He went to the stove and began to sauté brown rice. At a loss, I walked over to see what he was doing. I had never seen rice cooked like this—perfect, fat grains of translucent short brown rice toasting in tiny bubbles of sesame oil. I was riveted. Even the long-handled saucepan that held it was beautiful. This approach to cooking rice was so completely new to me that it set off a small revolution inside me. I cannot overstate the effect it had. I stood beside him, babbling with excitement, narrating the beauty I saw because I couldn't stop myself. He remained silent. His manner was off-putting, seemingly as harsh as it was indifferent. I feared my presence must be barely tolerable to him, and all of this while the cooking itself was so transcendent.

I stepped back to the far end of the small kitchen. Steve then poured water over the sauté and placed a lid on the pan. Everything felt awkward. Not only would he not talk to me, but his attitude canceled my words midair with something like an interference pattern. Then, as he put some steamed string beans from the garden into a bowl, adding salt, I finally realized with relief that he *had* prepared for my coming. "Sit down!" he commanded, whereupon he threw the beans across the table at me and barked, "Eat!"

There is a tradition in the East about killing the ego in tough ways. Hindus, Tibetan Buddhists, even Sufi mystics, believe that anything is justified in order to save a person from his own ignorant ego. As the stories go, if a guru tells you to jump off a cliff, you run to the closest one and toss yourself over it headlong because it means your next life will be more awakened. In our own time the celebrated yoga teacher Iyengar has literally punched his students when he felt they were showing off with their yoga. This treatment would get you sued in the United States, but in the East you would consider yourself lucky to have such a teacher.

Steve was apparently trying on the role of teacher, with me as his student. It was a bit over the top to be practicing on me like this, especially since I had no context. The teacher/student relationship is usually agreed on by both—but I had never made such an agreement with him. It seemed I was to be the object of his charade throughout the entire lunch, and I felt a piercing hurt because he wasn't talking to *me*. I wanted to walk out, but I gritted my teeth and stayed. Later, I discovered that everyone newly engaged in an Eastern spiritual practice tries on the behaviors of their spiritual teacher. It's embarrassing, but everyone goes through it in some way or other depending upon the teacher they are imitating. By the looks of it all, Steve was imitating the sixty-year-old Indian guru, Neem Karoli Baba, because he was scrunching up his face to create the deep lines and big nose of the older man. How can you not want to emulate a master once you actually understand the wisdom he or she represents?

Sitting at the table, I pulled the plate of beans toward me. I had never liked string beans and was expecting disappointment on top of disappointment while I fulfilled my role as guest. Then I would go home and cry. That was my plan. But that first bite was so unexpectedly delicious that my focus turned to delight and I started babbling at him again. In all my life I had never eaten such amazingly good string beans; in fact I hadn't eaten anything as good in any category of food as those beans on that day. And, like the perfect setting of a precious stone into fine metal, it clicked: Steve had something worthy going on.

Steve's unkindness, in combination with this beautiful cooking, the quality and taste of the food, and our being together in one room, was a jarring juxtaposition of extreme lights and darks. It was as if the whole scene had been filmed with time-lapse photography. I looked for light and right, and ignored the rest. It was a poor strategy, but it was the one I had used to survive my mother and it had given me a bright outlook on life. After lunch, as I was leaving, Steve invited me back the following Saturday. I accepted and braced myself for what might be next. I definitely wanted more beans, though he never served them again. So Steve!

Paul was lighter when I returned the following Saturday. Lighter than I had ever seen him, though it was light with a bit of a vengeance mixed in. When I stepped into the Jobses' backyard in the late morning, everything was in bustling motion—choreographed. Steve as the all-knowing director had a great calm and a decided sense of satisfaction as he pointed and told his parents what to do. Paul came tooling past me driving a wheelbarrow three-quarters filled with weeds half-wilted by the sun. He had a big smile on his face and grumbled something at me as he passed. He was, as ever, Paul Jobs, but now he was as transparent as a bright happy child. This time the fragility in him sparkled with wild-eyed joy. Gardens have a way of infecting people with confounding levels of excitement and replenishment. Paul's happiness was proof of this for me.

Over the next couple of months, as Steve and I spent time together, things got a little easier between us. Though we weren't terribly reflective about how we communicated, I deeply respected the changes he was going through. He must have liked having me around because he invited me over . . . semi-regularly. Steve had converted the toolshed in the backyard of his parent's house into a bedroom. It was a little thin hut of a structure, but it was perfect for adjusting to the United States after India. He slept in his sleeping bag on a foam mat on the bare, wooden floor. It was clean and orderly, and held minimal possessions— a few spiritual books, a candle, and his meditation pillow. The simplicity was just so beautiful and honest that my old admiration of him was resurfacing.

One night Steve invited me over at about 11:00 p.m. after I had been out with friends. When I arrived he told me to take off my clothes. Holding out a bottle of Dr. Bronner's All One Peppermint Soap he said something like, "We need to wash you off." Steve loved Dr. Bronner's All One soap. For him it was the perfect commercial achievement: its broad usefulness; its ecological foundation; its philosophically monistic aesthetic. He was holding the garden hose as he told me what to do.

"I'll spray you with the water. Then you'll scrub yourself down with this," he said, gesturing toward the minty soap. "Then I'll hose you off again."

This wasn't the first time that one of us thought that the other had gone completely bonkers. It was a cold night, the water would be freezing, and I was in his parents' yard, not more than fifteen feet from the back door to their house. Three strikes, he was out.

"No way!" I said with in a hushed yell. "Your parents could come out and find me naked!"

But he was so intent on my following his instructions that he got angry. His words became a fast blur—demanding, but sort of pleading, too. "Just do it!" he said, glowering. "My parents aren't going to come into the backyard at this hour! Come on Chris—"

"I won't," I hissed back. "You've got to be kidding, it's freezing out here. *And* you don't know that your parents won't come out!"

I was so alarmed, the harshness of the request felt hateful. I can imagine now that he thought I needed to "wake up" like an ascetic doing penance through flesh-denying ablutions. For all I knew he had just given himself the treatment before I got there, but again, he gave me no context and I wasn't one to follow orders any more than he was one to explain.

In general, I resisted Steve's many Pygmalion impulses out of principle. When I think on it now, it seems like all the times I had to say no to Steve connected inside me like a system of inner caves. He may have been completely convinced that he should be my guru, my teacher, my leader—a theme that would present itself for many years to come—but it was never the truth for me. I think I felt sorry for both of us that night.

And yet, how could I not be absolutely taken by him when he was so driven by purpose? Steve, the bewildered lunatic shaman, the extraordinary darling, was more extraordinary than ever that summer and I found myself, as always, moved to protect his shattered and shattering beauty. We didn't have a sexual relationship at that time. A ball of light had been let loose in Steve in India and I think he was holding himself separate for what that would yield. I don't even think he knew what was happening to him. I appreciated this and respected him for it because it was real.

I didn't know what he meant to me. He didn't know what I meant to him. We didn't know what we meant to each other. I was just trying to get along because he was important to me in some inexplicable mountain range of a way. My feeling is that he was in an amorphous state, not exactly one thing or another but blinking in and out, neither and both. That he trusted what was happening to him when he was so unstable seems phenomenal to me now. And although I'm sure I don't know the whole story, it might be fair to say that during this period Steve was stabilizing himself after the blowout from India. That he was preparing himself for the man he would become.

In the science about the transformation of insects there is a term called *imaginal disks* that refers to a group of cells in the body that get activated for metamorphosis. I think people have imaginal disks, too. Not everyone realizes such full potential, but Steve did. And this was the time that it began its unfolding to deliver a new kind of code for the massive changes through which he would develop. He was coming into a master level of consciousness.

But it was a tricky thing because I think he was off register, too. In all his exquisite effort to achieve some kind of higher, purer state, I felt and saw that Steve also started to reject the feminine aspect as inferior to the glorious masculine. Oh, yes, that ancient theme. Once he had returned, I felt increasingly uneasy about his view of me, and women in general. He had plenty of views on the subject of women, and he wasn't afraid to voice them. He would level sharp critiques full of dramatic repetitions, like "a bad woman is like a snake in the grass" (that comment came out of *Be Here Now*) and "if women were good, they wouldn't experience labor pain." I wish I could remember more. What I do remember is that these comments would be followed by an all-knowing laugh or a buttoned-up silence, also all-knowing. When it came to the female, Steve didn't question his right to critique or assign value. If Steve had one God-given talent it was an authoritative voice. But his ideas about women were bizarrely fundamentalist.

Steve was in some kind of profound spiritual transformation, but he was also coming of age in a man's world and adopting the negative myths men have forged about women throughout time. One was melded to the other. I remember that when I was growing up people used to honk their horns whenever they saw a newly married couple. Just Married would be written all over the wedding car in shaving cream or washable paint, and tin cans would be tied to the rear bumper. When my father heard these honks, he would look up and say, "Ah, another good man bites the dust." At the time, this seemed extremely funny to me and I would laugh at his joke, but the deeper reality of this view meant that I would have no place to stand as a female and no future as a woman in a relationship with a man that wasn't problematic. Steve left me with that same sense of having "no place."

When President Kennedy's space program and the feminist movement came into my girlhood awareness, I decided I wanted to be an astronaut. I never thought of wanting to be the wife of a man who walked on the moon because it was always clear to me that I wanted and could have adventures of my own. Now I think the space program couldn't have existed without the women's movement. That they erupted at the same time indicated that they were a part of the collective dialogue between the masculine and the feminine. Sorting out the whole concept of what it meant to be a man and a woman was very much a part of the confusion of my time. But at least the dreams of little girls became bigger and bolder then, and this put pressure on all of us to form a future in which those dreams might be realized.

Steve brought new spiritual ideas home from India and craved experiences based on them. That's probably why, not so long after the Dr. Bronner's incident, it all broke open between us when he asked if I would make tantric love with him in his garden shed. The question came flying out of him like a cry. In an instant, I felt paralyzed, as my head raced. Cautious but calculating fast, I wondered, *Did Steve want to use tantra because it justified sex when he was so committed to being some kind of ascetic?* Did he even know how to practice tantra?

I'm generally open to taking risks (perhaps too open), but with this request I felt a deep sense of self-preservation—in part because of how Steve was asking me, and in part because of the way he had been treating me. The one thing I knew about real tantra is that you're not supposed to mess with it unless you are an initiate, prepared over time with purifications, and overseen by a master. I didn't think Steve had been prepared. I sure knew that I hadn't. Did Steve think he was smart enough to figure it out for both of us? Did he even think?

Tantra is the qualified use of spirit in matter. It takes training and purity to manage the energy of spiritual movement called the kundalini in the body. I knew that the kundalini could be released in one person or between two people, in divine union. However, without the right approach, the kundalini fire can rip through the etheric body so fast that it will cause incalculable harm for life. As far as I was concerned, raising the kundalini was the biggest mistake you could make if you did it wrong, and the most important thing you could ever do right. Who knows why I knew so much, but I did because this was the kind of thing I pay attention to. I was worried about what powers could be let loose through us, or just as bad, that nothing would be different and that I would be party to Steve's self-deception. But I didn't say any of this to Steve. I just didn't know how. The only word I had was an emphatic "No."

I think a lot of people have to fulfill something spiritual in themselves before they go into their true professions. Branch Rickey, my great-uncle, went to divinity school before going into baseball and changing race relations in U.S. sports. Steve went to India because, with all due respect to Bob Dylan, he needed something bigger than the singer-songwriter to inspire him to do what he would go on to do.

They say that we don't choose the gods but that they choose us when we are ready, and I felt that something like this happened to Steve in India. Some big archetypal god had chosen Steve. He seemed so different after he returned that I felt he had been marked. He knew something deep inside. He seemed more comfortable in his skin. Despite, or perhaps because of his extreme vulnerability and instability, I could see that something in Steve had been lit and confirmed. He was in the awkward middle stage (he was living in the backyard shed at the time), before he had fully integrated the transformation. But it was coming.

In India, the divine masculine principle is represented by a trinity of gods. There is Brahma, the creator; Shiva, the destroyer; and Vishnu, the preserver—all of whom are creator gods but in different ways. I now think it was Shiva, the Destroyer, who chose Steve because his fingerprints were all over the boy. Shiva, the trickster. Shiva the austere one. Shiva the arrogant creator who destroys all that comes before in order to bring forth the new. Steve went on to change everything he ever touched and the world has never been the same.

ELEVEN

THE GUARDIAN AT THE GATE

Since Steve and I could not come together in a meaningful way, we went on with our lives. Steve worked in earnest with Kobun and Woz, and others, too. I went to junior college to work with the best art teacher I have ever had the privilege of studying with.

Gordon Holler was a phenomenon. His talks on the evolution of art were brilliant and he was so cuttingly honest, so awake, that he was actually scary. I remember one lecture in the middle of a semester when the lights went off and a classmate leaned over and whispered, "Buckle up!" It was good advice. And I took it. Gordon Holler was a model for young artists, not just because his work had been bought and hung by the major art museums in New York, but because he and his work were so beautiful, intelligent, and frightening. He taught that Jackson Pollack's action paintings were about the age of nuclear war, that they themselves contained the energy of the bomb. He taught us to recognize that more often than not the spills on the floor—like skid marks on the road—had more energy than our paintings. He encouraged people to make art, not from what we knew, but from the moment of direct perception. And for better and for worse, he convinced me to stay true to myself as an artist. I have never stopped working, in large part, because of his influence.

In studio drawing classes, where most art teachers try to get their students to simply draw well, Holler talked about the energetic power of visual information itself. He worked like a demon to get us to make images from a nonnarrative level of awareness. We used all sizes and weights of charcoal, along with smudgy rags, sponges, brushes, and sticks we found on the ground, which we dipped in ink solutions, from total black to soft subtle grays. The idea here, he said, was to use materials that would stop the student from getting too precise. Holler liked energy and he liked the energy of mistakes. "If you're going to make a mistake," he would say, "make the biggest mistake possible because then at least you'll learn from it." Yet in all of his hollering we were expected to create exquisite images. Because even though he bombarded us with a wholly new kind of instruction, good image making was ever the goal.

Beyond the class hours of studio work were several weekends of around-the-clock conceptual art events. People made all kinds of projects for these weekends. I especially remember a guy who let someone give him a haircut on stage, during which he talked continually about what it was like for him to be willing to trust someone with his image in the world, and why that was important to him. We may have been at a small junior college in Los Altos Hills, but we were connected to an important art movement, and to a teacher who was the real thing.

Gordon Holler had weekend-long conceptual art events of his own work, too. He set up rooms where naked, half-lit young men floated in luminous tanks of water or were mummified in plastic wrap. The men were wired with stethoscopes on their beating hearts and their rhythmic, heavy breathing amplified throughout the performance space. People milled around looking at everything as Holler photographed the models: he'd later make the photos into large-format silkscreens. His homoerotic images were brutal and off-the-charts disturbing, and yet they were so sublimely beautiful. You wanted to look and look away at the same time. And this made sense since he always talked about simultaneity.

Gordon Holler was star fire, lighting everyone up. The students who gathered around him were full of whatever it is that makes people remarkable. I got As from him, which he rarely gave out. One day he told the class not to worry about their grades, that he gave only about five As a year and that the people who got them didn't care. This was true. I didn't care.

In the mix of all this Greg Calhoun came down from All One Farm and I let myself fall in love with him. He was sexy and smart and cute. We had fun, and as our affections grew, we decided to live together. I moved up to his renovated chicken coop and became a part of the life at All One Farm for about six months.

Greg drew little glyphlike pictures, the first drawings of abbreviated form and light and sound that I had ever seen. They had a brightness that I could feel and sounds I could hear. After so much time rendering complex form in art classes, I marveled at the power of his little line drawings. I still have them. Years later, still inspired, I developed a kind of alphabet to visualize information generated in corporate meetings. I even started a business around it. Like so many things from All One Farm, Greg's drawings were a nod to the future because this type of graphic facilitation wasn't widely used until the mid-nineties.

Inevitably, or so it seemed at the time, Greg and I decided to go to India. Almost everyone we knew was either in India, yearning for India, making money for India, or just back and recovering from India. Traveling to the subcontinent was the most exciting possibility anyone could think of. And Greg and I were next in line. So we moved back to the Bay Area because it was the best place to make money for the trip. We were just about to sign a rental agreement for a place to live when Steve stepped in to tell us that he didn't have a good feeling about the place or the people we were about to commit to. Moreover, he had found us a better place to live, with *better people*. I imagined him in his hippie van, driving around to housing boards, checking out places on our behalf. It was very like Steve to be vigilant and generous in this way. As it turns out, Steve had been right. Once we moved in, we really liked our house, as well as our roommates. When we threw parties, Steve was always invited.

During the time we worked and saved, Steve warned Greg not to take me to India with him because, as he said, I would interfere with Greg's spiritual experience and development. I guess he didn't place any value on my own spiritual development. Steve said, "All the women who go to India just get fat!" Steve could mete out convictions like a blacksmith hammers an anvil. While his thoughts usually had at least some flying sparks of truth, he rarely had it completely right. At the time he offered this unasked-for advice, Greg and I just looked at each other and rolled our eyes.

It took us six months, but we made enough money and left for India. Steve drove us to the airport and handed us a last bit of advice on the way: "Be sure to drink the water as soon as you arrive so that you get sick right away and get it over with. That way you'll be free to drink the water everywhere you go and not have to worry about getting sick again." We didn't ask the obvious questions about parasites. We just thought it was a brilliant piece of advice and said so.

Greg and I landed in Hong Kong after an exhausting twenty-three hours of traveling, which included two hours spent in Anchorage due to engine trouble. We had one night in Hong Kong in which to grab some sleep, stretch our legs, and walk around in the city seaport before we boarded our next flight. I had chosen Frank Herbert's *Dune* as my airplane reading and continued with it on the plane to New Delhi. Talk about *imaginal disks*. Flying over the parched deserts of India while reading about a boy who discovers he's an avatar on a sand-covered planet was nothing less than surreal. I finished the book exactly upon landing in New Delhi, our home base for the next year.

We'd been warned about the beggars at the airport, men and women who held tiny drugged babies with arms and legs cut off to elicit horror and money from newly arriving tourists. We'd also been warned that the cabbies and rickshaw drivers would take newbies all over the city to plump up their meters before arriving at their hotels, sometimes hours later. Luckily, friends had told us what to expect to pay, so Greg moved into action and negotiated our bill in advance of getting into the car. He was damned well going to make sure that we weren't going to get ripped off and I was glad for it.

We drove over potholes in a tin can car that zigzagged through the traffic-filled streets. Dazzled by the sun and the heat and the noise, I was glad to arrive at the dingy little hotel that Steve had recommended. Greg checked us in while the porter took our luggage and led me up to our dark and meager room. As I laid down my things to reach in my wallet for a tip, the young Indian man shut the door and grabbed me, exclaiming with the kind of dramatic gesture found in a Bollywood extravaganza, "It is because of your eyes that I am in love with you!"

Alvin Toffler's book *Future Shock* had warned me that something like that could happen, but nothing could have prepared me for that or the hot spicy food or the twenty-four-hour nonstop noise or the relentless heat. We were barely able to eat or sleep those first days. Still, we had each other and a room. And we were okay.

Two days after we arrived, Sita Ram—aka Robert Friedland— brought us to Vrindavan. Luckily, his current time in India overlapped with ours. Robert was wonderfully convivial on the two-hour bus ride, sharing stories and answering questions before it even occurred to us to ask them. Robert said, "Westerners have been traveling to India en masse for over ten years. The Indians have seen it all, so don't worry about making mistakes."

The brightly ornamented bus to Vrindavan was loud and lurched in a top-heavy, big bus way. It had an altar on the dash with lit incense. Heck, the whole bus was like a mobile altar to the gods, with its glittery ribbons and framed pictures of deities like Ganesh displayed upfront. (There's always a Ganesh, because he's the remover of obstacles both spiritual and material.) Some of the buses even play devotional songs on loud scratchy speakers—whether you like it or not. Blessedly, not this one. We could, at least, hear each other talk.

Robert sat on the seat behind us and leaned forward. "The thing is," he said, "you only need about two hundred and fifty words to speak Hindi." And to prove it, he translated some chatter he heard in the bus. But he stopped translating when the Indians spoke about me, a female traveling with two men. "It is really too terrible to repeat," he said. I wanted him to tell me what they were saying, but he tactfully moved the conversation on to a young woman he knew, an American around my age who was studying Indian singing with her guru. "She was on one note for an entire a year," he exclaimed. "After she mastered it, the guru gave her three more notes." He continued. "She is so beautiful, she could be a model in the United States, but she gave it all up, all the men and all the glamour, to study music with this guru." He also talked about her diet, which was sattvic, meaning of pure high vibration, and said that if she traveled and ate onions it would take her two weeks to recover her notes again. I was amazed that an American woman would have been given access to this level of sacred Hindu musical instruction. I wondered, too, how she made her way to that decision or if Robert wasn't fibbing just a little. Mainly I sensed he was working to engage my spiritual imagination.

The commentary continued. "The Indians eat too many sweets," he told us. "It's because they're so bored. Look, there's a sweetshop every three doors." He was right, too. Small hole-in-the-wall sweetshops dotted every town we passed. Robert's comments and insights had a flat realism that made me listen more deeply. I would often find myself asking, *What did I just hear?* On this day he was as much talking to himself as to us, and his eyes turned deep gray with study and recognition, as if he were someone's uncle talking about the character flaw of a family member. It was like he was wearing big Paul Bunyan boots while wading all throughout India, collecting a stunning minutiae of detail.

We checked into a hotel as soon as we arrived in Vrindavan. Shortly after, Robert shuttled us off to the Yamuna River for a holy bath. The Yamuna River is one of the holiest rivers in India, and as we walked, Robert filled us in with stories of Krishna's childhood. Vrindavan is where Krishna is said to have grown up four thousand years ago. You can tell by all the shrines in the village—as plentiful as ATMs in any

American city—that Krishna is considered a god in a human form. Devout Hindus have two distinct views on history of the god incarnate. Some feel Krishna was his most perfected self when he was a baby, with all the innocence and pure love that implies. Others believe it was when he was a young man, newly in love with his divine female complement, Radha. That the question of whether a god's perfection is to be found as a baby or a young lover is tossed around as a part of a cultural dialogue in India just floors me. This definitely engages my spiritual imagination.

We took a circuitous route to the river, trailing through sandy white backstreets that were more like tiny alleys. The Indian people walked very slowly, which made sense in that heat. Robert, however, had a Mad Hatter quality about him, and he walked quickly, with no time to waste, his ivory-colored clothing flowing. His arm encircled Greg, who was shorter, as he ushered us around on speeding legs, offering us advice: what to avoid, where to find proper clothing and the best sweets. I was only half tracking it because I don't pay enough attention to this kind of detail and also because I was in so much culture shock. The two walked ahead most of the time, leaving me to take in the surroundings as I trailed behind them. I was amazed by the many free-roaming peacocks all over the town—on the ground at our feet, in the trees, and running to get out of the way of the rickshaws—and by the gracefulness of the women's colorful floating saris. Indian women seemed to have elegant wear for the most mundane activities. I was too tired to talk, but Greg and Robert were chatting away and laughing nonstop. I had two contrary impulses: go back to the hotel room to hide, or keep up with them because I didn't want to miss a thing.

When we neared the river, Robert told me I was going to have to bathe by myself because there was no way a woman and two men could be seen bathing together at the river, "especially Westerners." I felt sort of left out and terrified to be by myself, but he gave me instructions about how to bathe in a sacred river, and they moved on. The boys walked around a dune, their voices trailing off, until the only sound I heard was the deafening roar of the river. By myself and not at all comfortable, I looked around and up at the huge, blue sky overhead. I took off way too many clothes—I would later realize this with great alarm—and walked into the river.

Following directions has never been my strong suit, and I couldn't remember what Robert told me to do, so I made up my own ritual and then dunked myself in an act of self-baptism, feeling too self-conscious to fully give myself over to the experience. When I stood, the water was up to my ribs. I scanned inside myself for any differences, and then looked around. My surroundings were so stark I could have been on the moon.

The Yamuna is broad, maybe a hundred feet across, with a light gray sandy bank. I felt the pull of gravity down in the river's trough and the force of the water sweeping around my body. It was all just sand, sky, and this wide, thick water. No clutter of voices. I breathed a big sigh, my whole body having finally slowed down to its natural rhythms after days of travel, heat, and terrible sleep patterns. At last I felt at one in my body with my environment.

Standing in this peace for a while I noticed something floating about ten feet away, in the fast moving center of the river. I strained to make it out. With a jolt of recognition, I understood that it was part of a human shoulder attached to a bit of torso. A disconnected hand bobbed after it. Horrified beyond words, I was suddenly terrified that I couldn't see my feet in the opaque water. Straining to drag myself free of the river, I made it to the shore, naked and panicked and small, like Eve thrown out of the garden.

I dressed as fast as I could, tugging and pulling the clothing over my body, the whole process slowed down by the wetness. The realities of the sacred and the physical were oddly juxtaposed in this one bizarre moment. There was nothing to do but wait for Greg and Robert to return. My skin felt the kind of refreshed well-being that comes after cold water and dry clothes under a beautiful warm sky. Calming, I saw the river was smooth and unending and remembered not just Robert's words, "the Indians have seen it all," but the words of others who had told me that "Mother India allows for everything." On that day, I dearly hoped that included me.

Later I learned that there must have been a funeral ghat upstream where they dumped the body before it had fully burned because the relatives didn't have the money to buy enough wood to completely cremate their family member. At the time, though, only three days in the country, all I knew was that body parts were floating past. *Get out now!* was all I could think of.

After bathing, Robert showed us how to smoke bong, which is Indian marijuana that has been ground to a thick paste. Hemp grows in many parts of India, and it was stunning to see hillsides covered with these spiky green hands on undernourished plants. It's not high quality stuff, and I wondered if the process of grinding it into a paste, which is done between two rocks, somehow extracts the narcotic properties to improve the smoke. It was sticky and wet and amazing that it even caught fire. After we got stoned I was in trouble because marijuana makes me vulnerable to fear, of which there was no end on my third day in India. I fell silent and that night became very sick with a temperature of 106 that lasted for a week. Greg became equally sick just as I got well. After that, we did have some kind of silvery immunity as we traveled through India. Steve had been right. We never got sick again.

When Steve had returned from India, he told me he had gone on retreat with a teacher who sang to his students early every morning. He described it in such beautiful detail that I was beside myself with longing to see this for myself. Completely coincidentally Greg and I ended up at one of this teacher's retreats—then five or so more after that. But on the morning I first heard S. N. Goenka sing, my memory floated back to Steve's story. The deep resonance of his voice sounded through the meditation hall and I knew it had to be the same guy. It was his songs that swept through us every morning, that cleared us up and strengthened our resolve for ten days of deep vipassana meditation.

Much later, after my return from India, Daniel Kottke, who had traveled with Steve, told me that it was only he, Daniel, who had meditated with this teacher. Steve hadn't gone; he had only heard about it from Daniel. I was shocked. Why would Steve lie?

The taking of another's story as your own is a type of thievery, charming or otherwise, that claims attention under a surface awareness. As an adult I've learned to give young people plenty of latitude to experiment with lying because imagination and what we call reality are just a continuum. And because the sixth sense is the most developed and inclusive of all the others, sometimes what we call a lie is actually a sixth sense that cannot be seen or proven—yet.

It may be that, for Steve, deception was a radical form of creating. He once told Howard, a mutual friend from high school, that Bob Dylan had sent his Lear jet to take him to a concert. Steve was seventeen years old at the time of this lie so he was just barely young enough to get by with it, but definitely old enough to be playing beyond the edges of acceptable behavior. "What a liar!" I told Howie. I was incredulous and twenty-one. I'd had no idea Steve was telling people stuff like this back then. However, over the years, I began to think more along the lines of, *what an extraordinary lie.* At the very least, Steve had the courage to tell a massive one. And later, when he owned his own Lear jet, how could I not appreciate the nonlocal kinds of space and time in which the magician was playing. It was both a lie and a creation.

I believe Steve held multiple purposes in a single act of deception. Creativity, as I've said, was one. But it seems to me that he also lied to study people's responses in order to gather intelligence. Sometimes I think he lied simply to make himself look more interesting because he thought he was too oafish and regular and didn't think he was enough as he was. And I think he lied to tweak people's insecurity, and in so doing, take charge of the environment. After he became well-known, Steve was able to manage perceptions to separate people and to discourage communication about things that he wanted to hide. It's all so fascinating, of course, because the man who went on to be a part of creating technologies that connected people all around the world was himself so effective at keeping those nearby disconnected from each other. I mean this on both a business and a personal level. I'm pretty sure Steve was consciously strategic about the paradox. He was an acomplished trickster who operated outside other people's awareness. In the end I found it disturbing not because he lied, but because he used a masterful awareness of other people's blind spots to create and manage perception for personal advantage.

In May or June, Greg and I moved to Dalhousie in the state of Uttar Pradesh, India, to get out of the heat. Dalhousie was an English hill station during the time of the English occupation and was used by the British to escape the scorching summer months. From our front yard there was a view of a seven-thousand-foot drop to the plains to where an indistinct arc of the horizon met the seemingly endless sky. The great Indian poet Rabindranath Tagore had lived on the very top of the mountain we were perched on, where there was the most extraordinary view of the Himalayan peaks. Nothing I have ever known has come close to the magnificence of this view.

After helping me to get settled in Dalhousie, Greg bused through Pakistan and Afghanistan to Tehran, Iran, to teach English and make money so that we could stay in India longer. I was way too dyslexic to teach English; likely any Iranian would have had a better grasp of English grammar than I did, so I stayed on the hill.

About twenty Westerners from all over the United States and Europe had moved to the mountain to get out of the heat that season, and a month after most of us had arrived, Larry Brilliant came with his wife, Girija. From 1973 to 1976, Brilliant had worked with the World Health Organization (WHO) to eradicate smallpox from India. While he was doing this, Girija was writing her Ph.D. dissertation on women's studies. We were all excited to meet them, then one day word spread that everyone on the hill had been invited to their house for dinner.

The only thing I remember about that evening's festivities was

Girija's talking about her research. She said that the highest suicide rate in India was among young Hindu wives in new marriages. Seriousness sets the memory like nothing else, and I remember studying her closely because the fact of this was so horrendous. Girija was very present and had a plucky graciousness that was impressive. Her colors were pretty and light: a gossamer shirt and a wide-patterned skirt that brushed the floor as she stood, walked, cooked, and talked. It swished in a way that reminded me of a waltz in a Disney cartoon. This was a happy woman and I wondered at her marriage—it seemed like a good one.

As Girija spoke, hers were the words of a careful reporter who had seen behind the scenes and into what I now consider to be a crime against humanity. She was careful and articulate as she spoke; the whites of her eyes widened to convey the full impact of what she knew beyond her words. She shared all this with us as a group but I wanted to know more. She told me that when young women are married in India, they move into their husband's huge family homes. The young Indian wife has no status and no power. She is the least valued, least cared for, and least understood in the new family. If the family is cruel, which they often could be, she is in trouble; the mothers-in-law may take over raising her children and her sisters-in-law might put stones in her food so that she will break her teeth or worse. If the emotional environment is intolerable, the young wives will often see suicide as the only way out. But Girija went on to explain, "If she survives the ordeal, this woman might well grow old enough to take over the raising of her own daughters-in-laws' children." I remember thinking, *What a terrible cycle*. It may be that the goddesses are on equal footing with the gods in India and Hinduism, but the real women were suffering terribly. You can tell a lot about a culture's values by how they treat particular segments of their populations. In this case, it was how they treated the young women who carried and gave birth to the babies and the future of the whole nation.

After Greg returned from Iran, there was a day when, unexpectedly, two friends we had met in New Delhi told us that the 16th Karmapa was in town at the ritzy Ashoka Hotel, and that we could have private darshan with him. The Karmapa lineage is Tibetan and pre-dates the lineage of the Dalai Lama by two centuries. Catching the spirit like a cowgirl and a cowboy, Greg and I freshened up and took a rickshaw to the Ashoka where we met our friends in the lobby. We would be seen immediately. It was such a straight passage through, it felt like a free fall into the sky.

Before entering the inner sanctuary where the Karmapa sat, high-level monks worked with the four of us in an anterior room to show us how to conduct ourselves in the presence of a Karmapa. We were instructed to stand upright while holding our hands together in prayer over the tops of our heads. Next we were to bring our hands down to the level of our third eye, and then to our hearts. After that we were to stick our tongues out pointing downward toward our chins and force our eyeballs up into the top of our heads and bow. Each bow, and there were to be three of them, was a full body prostration on the floor before the station of this man. I was utterly embarrassed, but jumped in ready to do whatever it took to be in his presence.

We were led into the room and His Holiness sat watching us perform the dizzying routine until at last we lined up like Four Musketeers catching our breath for what would be next. From a Western perspective the following won't necessarily make sense, but I will say it anyway. It is true that we were all four standing together, but it was also true that each of us was having a private audience with His Holiness. Brilliant and glittery-eyed cartwheels of light turned in his eyes, as he looked into our eyes, individually and simultaneously. From this I knew I was in the presence of a fully awakened, multidimensional human being. I felt vastly expanded and lit up under his gaze. I would later look at his picture hanging in a Palo Alto spiritual bookstore and feel the same thing.

The Karmapa asked questions through a translator and seemed to be laughing at us in the most marvelous way the whole time. Part of the deal of receiving a blessing from him was that he would give us each a Tibetan name. In the East, teachers and gurus often give you a god name. I had been given other names, Paravati and Sharda, by two different teachers, and this would be my third. I had not intended to collect sacred names for myself, it is just what happened. The Karmapa was about to receive his lunch so we were told to come back the next day for the naming. When we returned at the appointed hour we went through the round of bows and, once again, felt the exhilaration that we were all being seen individually, as if he had four heads and eight eyes. He had the monks reach into a hat and pull out slips of paper one at a time. Each name was typewritten in Tibetan script and read aloud, then handed to the translator, who explained the meanings in English and then handed it to each of us. I do not remember my Tibetan name but I do remember its translation: "The Guardian of the Gate." The Karmapa encouraged us to ask questions, and after a short Q and A, we were sent on our way out into the super-crowded, sun-blasted, noisy streets of downtown New Delhi.

I had gone to India because I wanted to be touched and changed by something as huge as the force that had touched and changed Steve. Seeing the Karmapa lit a fire in me that can hardly be overstated. The name that he gave me was a very powerful riddle that would take more than thirty years for me to understand.

Steve would later criticize me by saying that my trip to India was more of a vacation than a pilgrimage. But he missed it entirely. And only now after so much time has passed, and I have the depth of insight that a lot of work and a long life have afforded me, I am completely certain that India could never be a "vacation" for anyone who was there for over three weeks—it is too profound a place. That Steve couldn't or wouldn't see this, that he couldn't allow me to have my own sacred experience without his distorting interpretations, is something that took me way too long to understand.

Before I left to go on my trip to India, the Zen teacher, Kobun, had told me, "If you feel like coming home, first wait two weeks and then if you still feel like coming home, *come home!*" I had been in India for a year when I finally knew I was done. I also knew that my relationship with Greg was over. Our approach to living was so different that we were a constant aggravation to one another. It did not seem like a life partnership would be possible, and so I returned to the United States by myself.

TWELVE

PURE FUNCTION

The afternoon I flew into Oakland airport from Hong Kong, I had to take public transportation across the bay because my family was confused by the dateline and thought I was arriving the next day. The doors were locked when I got to the house in Saratoga and no one would be around for hours. With little else to do, I sat outside and waited. It felt odd to be back in the grand materialism of California. Our neighborhood, with its empty streets and perfect lawns, seemed sterile after India. It was a mind-blowing contrast.

By evening, however, my family had returned and I had the most wonderful time regaling my younger sisters and my father and his wife with stories of the year's amazements. I had been a stranger in a strange land far too long and it was so good to be home. Home, where people knew me and I knew them. The next day I called Steve, who, at this point, was simply my friend. We met for dinner later that evening and ended up at his parents' house, where he was living at the time. Paul and Clara were watching TV when we walked in. We said hello and went into Steve's bedroom, where we sat on the floor and had a glass of port. I told Steve about my trip, and I remember that we talked about Deuteronomy that night, because I had read some contemporary essays about it on the flight home that had lit new concepts in my mind. I'd found

Deuteronomy a mysterious and ugly word before reading about it, but afterward I was thrilled by the way it tumbled out of my mouth. I think this represented a new me to Steve.

I had intended to go home that night, but Steve made a bed on the floor for us and we made love. It was two o'clock in the morning when Clara knocked on his door. "Is everything alright?" she asked. I was paralyzed with fear thinking that she would walk in and find me there, but the voice that emerged from Steve repatterned the very air with its blend of soft confident power. "I have been on a long, long journey," he told her. He was looking at me but angling his voice toward the door. "Okay," Clara said. She didn't need to know more and so returned to bed. This call-and-response between mother and son was truth and it was beauty, and he had protected our space with it. This was a new Steve for me.

Steve was haunted his whole life by the nature of his relationship with his parents but more than that, it was the nature of the life he had grown up in. I think he wondered if he was even in the right life. He made a lot of jokes about there being *a big mistake,* and something about *a case of mistaken identity.* It was one of his shticks. It was so charming to see him fall into this act because he was just so honest and funny about the loss. At bottom though, I think it showed that he worried constantly that something had been damaged or irrevocably lost due to the bungling at the time of the adoption, or perhaps because of the adoption itself.

QUESTION: What does a person do about something that was
   lost in the past?
ANSWER: Worry about how that loss might translate into losses
   in the future.

It's my feeling that these issues were coming to a head for Steve just as I had returned from India. I felt he looked to those around him to weigh in on his questions in a deeply sincere way. *Had something been lost?* Turning to others to give value to something in myself is not what I'm inclined to do, at least not in the same way. I've never felt that kind of trust. Yet, it's a tender and honest trait that I've observed not just in Steve, but in our daughter, Lisa, and in Steve's sister, Mona. Perhaps it's an innate quality carried in their ancient Syrian DNA, connected to the importance of group consensus; it's a characteristic that is completely open and vulnerable and looks to the group to ask, "Can you see, am I worthy?" Sometimes this quality strikes me as too dependent upon the opinions of others, while at other times it appears to me as the most remarkable wisdom. Steve usually radiated the sense of his being more precious and important than anyone in the world. But at that time he was looking outward for evaluation and his concerns touched my heart.

Though I don't remember any distinct conversations (except a bit of one with Robert Friedland), I do recall the sense of mounting consensus that seemed to lay down the necessary level of confidence in order for Steve to move into his destiny. I think that, prince that he was, Steve was looking to others to somehow move beyond his parents and reclaim his throne. It's hard to say, but I do remember opening the Jobses' screen door on a beautiful spring day and being struck with the feeling that not only were they okay for Steve, but maybe even perfect. In my mind, Paul, who was so practical and clear about the business of his days, and Clara, who was something of a giantess of good intention, were the right parents for Steve, or at least right enough. Perhaps they were what providence had arranged for. As I looked at their neutral sensibilities—the adamant no-frills quality of their lives, the blue-collar work ethic—I saw that all combined to provide the right endowment for what Steve needed for the man he would become.

I now believe that Kobun was behind everything. Eastern masters can remove a student's karmic negativities so that he or she can progress with greater ease. It's called the grace of the guru in India, and though I don't know what this kind of knowledge is called in the Japanese tradition of enlightenment, I know it exists there, too. Kobun had many capacities as a spiritual teacher. He was skilled at unifying perceptions between groups of people, and at opening doors to allow for greater access. But was it the place of a spiritual teacher to remove a person's karmic obstacles in order to engage in a business enterprise? Could it have been that Kobun was so inspired by Steve's genius that he stepped out of his spiritual integrity to give the lad a leg up? Was Kobun a spiritual materialist? Maybe he was flipping switches behind his curtain without really understanding the implications. Members of the Zen community said many times that Kobun never abused his power. That made me uneasy, because people often repeat things when the opposite is true. Kobun was extraordinary and he was also beloved. But he was decidedly tricky.

The great value of developing through difficulty, whether you think in terms of karma or psychology, is that it humanizes people. Being human is about the challenge of surmounting obstacles. Too much grace and we don't really understand what things mean, and we can lose our way. Too much hardship and we never find our way. It's a fine line to walk: while we want to succeed, the road that gets us there must be just bumpy enough to allow an appreciation for the effort made. That, in turn, allows compassion to flower and bear fruit. Was Kobun wise enough to have found the right balance for Steve?

Compassion might not be valued highly enough today. Our elaborate systems of business and politics consider humanity to be less important than the bottom line. Long ago in 1976, Kobun gave Steve something—many things—that were good. But I also felt there was a kind of nudge-nudge wink-wink complicity between them. It seems to me that Kobun lifted Steve up, and in so doing, helped Steve avoid some bumps he would have done well to encounter. And maybe it is in this way that Steve lost some human breadth along the way.

Steve and I fell in love again. And one day that spring he bowed his head and told me that he knew we would fall in love months before I had returned from my trip. It was a profound admission, said with life-altering honesty. We were older now, diving deeper and redefining. This was our next step and it indicated larger responsibilities, which we both yearned for. Steve was open and in love with me, and sometimes at the end of his day when I walked into his office, I could feel and see the bright true colors of love come over him when he saw me. Steve's reception of me was profound and that drew me closer. Our kisses were deeper and our lovemaking was of a different order. We were growing up and the stakes were higher. Steve and I had both changed.

I was around to see how all of Steve's changes were affecting his parents, too. They were so proud of him, but they were also hurt that Kobun had such influence in their son's life. Though I don't think there were flare-ups or that anyone said anything directly, at least when I was around, I knew they were sad and angered because I watched their expressions. Steve had taken the greatest care to thank his parents with the garden, and many other considerations—yet they seemed awkwardly displaced in their own home once the Zen master had taken over the inner sanctuary level of Steve's education. In Eastern cultures, this transition—that of such a teacher choosing Steve as his student—would have been cause for the greatest possible pride and joy. Though poignant, it would have been the mark of all success and distinction. But Paul and Clara didn't have this frame of reference, and I saw Steve walking very carefully around their pain. They thought they were being replaced—and in a sense they were.

One night when I was waiting for Steve to come home from work, I sat down to watch TV with Paul and Clara. TV was an important part of the Jobs household. They worked hard and had a wholesome tiredness that hung on mind and body, and this is how they relaxed and closed their days. Clara would sit on the La-Z-Boy chair, feet up, and slowly move the ball of her right foot back and forth for hours, as if keeping time for her family.

The Jobses' living room was something of a terminal for me, a way station between events. But I have come to appreciate that it was also the stage on which many important changes would be flagged. On this night, as I waited in what could be considered the most social time I'd ever had with Paul and Clara, the lights were low and the TV was blasting. It was dark outside and the blue screen took over the room with its aggressive noise. When Steve walked in, Clara turned off the TV, leaving the room painfully lit by a lamp's single bulb, but blessedly quiet.

Steve was carrying the first prototype of computer casing to show his parents. I watched as they oooh-ed and ahhh-ed over it, the whites of their eyes shining in the dim light. Steve stood at the end of the couch, tall and impressive, turning the hard plastic shell between his hands. That evening it seemed like Paul and Clara were the children, and Steve the proud parent. He was happy with the design and told us that the Italian company Apple had originally hired had come up with a literal head shape for the TV screen. A head for a computer screen! Steve shut his eyes and shuddered.

It was on this one hallmark of an evening that I realized how unaware I was of everything he was doing during his workday. If I had not known Steve personally, I never would have paid attention to a rising star in the world of computers. If the Apple products had been ugly, I would have been even later to the show. I confess I don't know Apple's history except where it intersected with my own. Steve thought I lacked curiosity, but it wasn't that. There was a level of hype around Apple and Steve that I could never key into. I found Steve interesting and beautiful for his refinement and intuition and poetic sensibilities, but I found his business personality caustic and unappealing. Still, the plastic case he was holding was concrete, and that night I began to pay more attention.

One of the most unusual changes I'd noticed in Steve was his new way of watching TV. It had been a passive thing before, but now he sat up very close to the screen and studied. All the muscles in his supersensitive face twitched along with the drama, while his eyes followed every minute action. He watched as if he was reading, as if he was processing an enormous amount of information. Completely engaged, he strained to collect and calculate, peering into the TV as if he was trying to see

around doorways and through walls. To this day, I have never seen anyone watch TV as he did. Not by a long shot. At the time I felt that he
used the phenomenon of the TV to accelerate his learning about the
world of power and sexual relationships. I also noticed that he turned
the TV and the radio off if there was messaging in the program that he
didn't want to receive. It was a kind of spiritual discernment and disci-
pline for him. Most people vegetate, taking everything in when they
watch a show, but for Steve, TV had been turned into a tool for creative
self-imagining and insight into building power.

Another day that spring I noticed a piece of paper with my name
on it lying on the Jobses' dining room table. I was running through the
house to the backyard when I saw it. Swinging to a stop, I picked it up,
and found that Steve had had my astrological chart drawn up. There
was one for him, too. Steve walked up as I was looking at it.

"Whoa," I said. "Did you have this done?" I was surprised and also
curious that he'd taken the initiative because he'd once told me that
astrology wasn't a worthy symbol-system for self-analysis.

"Yes . . . there's a computer program that does astrological charts
and I had them done for us."

"Why?" was the only thing I could think to ask. As I examined the
colorful diagrammatic splays I noticed that all of Steve's planets were on
the top of the horizon and that all of mine, except one, were below. I had
one planet in the upper hemisphere in the 7th house.

"Wow, all your planets are above and most of mine are below."

"What do you think it means?" he asked.

"I don't know at all," I said. "Do you?"

He just looked at me. In the past when Steve asked me what I thought
something meant, he was kind. But this time his lack of response had a
different quality. Despite what I had considered our renewed closeness, I
was beginning to notice a deep unfriendliness etching into our relationship. And I was dodging it more often than I liked to admit.

With regard to the astrological charts, I soon found out that the top
hemisphere meant a life out in the world while the bottom indicated a

predominately introspective life. I was disappointed to hear this because I'm naturally so extroverted and was looking forward to a big life. This must have been obvious to the astrologer explaining it to me, because he took pains to point out that both ways of life can be fulfilling.

Perhaps Kobun was influencing Steve's attitude toward me at the time. During my first meeting with the sensei—this was long before I went to India—he spoke to me about my clothing. He said, "Clothing is not just for you. It's for other people who look at you, too." He said it should be modest and simple and not offend people. Not *more* modest and simple, but modest and simple. It wasn't a bad first teaching because clothing speaks to the intersection of the inner and outer realities—where personality and spirituality express as one and individual meets community. But I was modest in my dress and wondered why he was telling me this. It seemed so superficial. Moreover, I felt that Kobun was slightly shaming me with this information, that he was telling me that I wasn't enough as I was. In total it alerted me that something was missing. I remember thinking, *This isn't what we should be talking about.* More to the point, *This guy doesn't see me. He doesn't know who I am.* I felt angry and invisible. I didn't know how respond to him.

Later, when I was more savvy, I wondered about the socioeconomic dynamic around Kobun. Japanese culture has a system in place to support spiritual teachers of Kobun's stature. American culture does not. Japanese culture is highly structured, American culture is not. When Kobun came to the United States, he was surrounded by an elite group of educated, wealthy, and in some cases, famous people. It made sense: these were the people who would be naturally attracted to Zen coming into America. They were the forward thinkers, the early adopters. With these backers, Kobun had every hope and expectation that he would become the best Zen master he could possibly be. I didn't have the markings of elite society: no wealth, no fabulous education, but I am smart and I've always been something of an early adopter.

I wonder now if Kobun didn't see who I was or if he had simply decided that I wouldn't be useful to him. I was the youngest female in a community of accomplished people five to twenty-five years my senior. I had little life experience and no promise of fame, so perhaps Kobun decided that I was not important. It wasn't that he was unkind, but if he was looking to externals as an indicator of my capacity, I can imagine that I didn't look like much. These are my guesses, but I still wonder why he was not awake to the seeds *inside* all the people who came to him? What kind of master was he? Why didn't he recognize *me*?

Kobun was a worthy teacher. I returned again and again to listen to his talks, to practice zazen, and to call on his advice. The Los Altos Zendo had a huge door with a wide opening. I felt welcome. Indeed, people had told me, "You get what is going on here." I am sure I was at the right place at the right time. But I would never receive any kind of real teachings from this teacher. Eventually I'd understood this because of how he treated me compared to Steve.

When I had returned from India, Kobun told me, "You weren't human before you left but now you are. What happened over there?" There were many times that he asked me, "What happened in India?" Repeating and repeating, "You weren't human before." He would laugh and sort of tease me when he said this, but he seemed genuinely curious. I didn't know how I was supposed to answer such an ignorant question. I tried to respond politely, while inwardly I thought his frank views were cruel.

Years later, a spiritual teacher told me that Kobun had not worked with me because, as she said, "He simply did not recognize you as an American female destined for enlightenment in this lifetime. He'd never seen it in your form before." At the time, however, I didn't know enough to move on from Kobun because I didn't know how to ask the right questions. People who know how to articulate good questions amaze me. It denotes layers of experience that I didn't have back then. Jim Black—Trout—was such a person. A lay monk at the Zendo (he was the person who got me straight about Kobun's name on my first evening there), he looked like my idea of Little John in Robin Hood's band of Merry Men. He worked with children, had a jovial round belly, and a face that was sane, kind, and intelligent.

Trout had a knack for getting the details straight. One day he asked me, "Who of the two of you, Steve or you, Chrisann, found the Zendo first?" I told him the truth; that we had found it completely independent of each other, at about the same time. He then told me when he had asked Steve the same question, that Steve told him that he had found it and brought me there. The lie was typical of Steve. (I just didn't know it yet.) And questioning was typical of Trout. That he would even think to ask me the question after Steve had given his answer alerted me that he was giving us equal consideration. Moreover, that he didn't necessarily buy into Steve's authority. Amazing.

One day Kobun talked to me about Steve, telling me that he, Kobun, had always wanted a student who was strong. He emphasized the word "strong," at the back of his throat. With his lips curled outward and his chest puffed high as he held his arms away from his side, Kobun looked like he was crowing. He told me, "No man who ever went to Tassajara could possibly be strong." But now he would have a leader! Kobun was keenly aware of having a special student in Steve. "I have never had a student master the information in so short a time. Three months!" he exclaimed, his eyes wide, his mouth dramatically elongated. "It is the shortest time possible for anyone to understand." His happiness was thick and evident.

I have always liked it when men confide in me from their worlds, and I was truly happy for Kobun. However, on this day and in this conversation, I had a feeling that something wasn't right. Kobun was gloating. Why was he comparing Steve to the zazen practioners from Tassajara? At some level, even though I knew I had been ignored and passed over by Kobun, I wasn't jealous because I loved Steve and his daring-to-fully-be qualities as much as Kobun did. But as Kobun and I walked through his house that day, stopping and starting as he exclaimed this and that about Steve, I wondered what might be under his communication. Why was he sharing this level of their relationship with me? He never had before.

An addendum to this conversation came a few months later. Kobun told me that when Steve was painfully ambivalent about going forward with Apple, he said: *Just do it*. Kobun spoke with bright urgency, making sure I understood his pivotal position of importance. "I said this to him!" he repeated. And here it was, Kobun was coming to me and he wanted me to understand that he was the one who'd given the boy wings. And here, in this conversation, I picked up on the ever so slight change in the teacher's power and position. Steve had already flown the coop, and Kobun was expressing the loss of his importance, and to me of all people. More to the point, he may have been lamenting Steve's lack of acknowledgment. I would see this play out badly over time.

After I returned from India I realized that Steve was entering the world stage through two bastions of male power from two hemispheres. Through Apple, it was the value system of American big business: big money, big stakes, big players, and big know-how. Through Kobun, it was twenty-five hundred years of Buddhism translated by way of Japan, home to one of the most refined cultures our world has ever known.

Steve's trajectory was being fueled by some combination of highly refined plutonium and a royal jelly nutrient-rich superfood that made for the highest-grade energy possible. Of course, he was young and could easily put in ten- to sixteen-hour days, six to seven days a week. And at least once a week in the evenings he was also being supercharged and focused by a Zen master's more metaphysical practices for building power. East fueled West and West fueled East. Steve was some new kind of shaman, walking between the worlds. He must have seemed like a boy wonder to them all as he wove into himself the business of the day, the esoteric teachings of the night.

I heard people say that Steve was just lucky in the beginning. But I didn't think it was luck, even back then. Not only because Steve had told me it was going to happen, but because I saw how some of it unfolded. I believe that in the beginning it was Robert Friedland who, in a very intentional way, tied the spiritual-esoteric dimension to business. And I think that together he and Steve wanted to see how far they could go. And I am certain that they collaborated and compared notes about this. Both of them used food and cleansing diets in combination with spiritual practices to open up and build consciousness. Fasting and meditation is the time-honored approach that creates the intense practical alchemy required for massive change. I did enough fasting to know that it created heightened awareness and new insight. But while Indian lore contains cautionary tales about not adapting spiritual insight and practices for worldly gain, this kind of power building for ambition is not that common in the West. Steve and Robert may have been alert to the dangers, but in the face of such exciting opportunity, perhaps they simply didn't care. Maybe the point was to be an outrageous worldly success by any means possible.

Beyond those times with Robert, Steve's work was greatly furthered with a similar kind of collaboration with Kobun. Except that Kobun's spiritual development was mind-bogglingly more advanced. It had to have been a very rare thing in the history of the world, for a full-on, bona fide spiritual master to help a young entrepreneur succeed with a world-changing technology. What I saw was that through Kobun's vast capacity and Steve's warriorlike ability to develop his business acumen, Steve was becoming unstoppable—streamlined, less personal, and highly charged. Pure function.

So what were the ingredients that made for Steve's "luck?" I think it was a confluence of aesthetics: the broad-based usefulness and the capacity of the microchip, combined with Steve's deep need to be acknowledged. Then there was his super-food diet, a Zen master in his back pocket, and his willingness to be shot through the cultural equivalent of a cannon onto the world stage. This East/West combination seemed to have offered Steve the most delicious sense of purpose. And in the beginning at least, the honest blend of his genius and humility seemed to deepen and flower. I witnessed Steve gear up for power, moving through one level after another, literally looking over his own shoulder to see the remarkable stages of his becoming—the once hapless marionette turning into a prime player.

THIRTEEN

LIFE ON TWO LEVELS

While I wasn't prepared for the culture shock I experienced upon my arrival in India, I knew to expect it. What I never saw coming was the culture shock I felt on returning to the United States. I needed big spaces, fresh air, and nature. Lots of nature. So, within two months of coming back from India, I left my father's home and moved to a place called Duveneck Ranch in Los Altos Hills. Once a single-family farm, Duveneck had developed into a hostel and an environmental education center, a place for children from all over the Bay Area to come and learn about nature, farm life, and ecology. It's still going strong, but now, after Josephine and Frank Duveneck have died, it's called Hidden Villa Ranch. Living at the ranch after India would give me the best environment to ease back into American life. And it would give Steve and me a place to spend the nights together.

The ranch sits between about eight hills on a relatively wide valley floor that fans out to Moody Road, a bending two-lane highway that will take you into town or, if followed long enough, to the Pacific Ocean. Duveneck had farm animals, gardens, hiking trails, olive trees, and a big clinking bamboo garden. And it had barn-type buildings for every kind of farm need, crouched in corners all over the property, delightful in total. Back then, in any given year, the Duveneck had a cow or two, lots of chickens, about four sheep, and two to three pigs. The numbers would increase with newborns in spring, and would decrease again in the fall.

I lived at Duveneck for four months, moving into one of the rear cabins in exchange for thirteen hours of work each week. I did odd jobs at first, but it was Trout who suggested I teach. In addition to being a lay monk at the Zendo, Trout was the head of the children's nature program at Duveneck Ranch. He saw me playing with newborn lambs one day and had the children stop and hang with me because, I think, he wanted them to pick up on how much affection I felt for the sweet floppy creatures. Soon after that, he invited me to be a part of the teaching staff for the city kids who came to visit. I am a born teacher but Trout wouldn't have known that. It was the philosophy at the farm to teach children, not through filling them with lots of information, but by allowing a natural passion for nature and animals in the children themselves. Feelings first, names and facts later, and only after children had connected to their awe and were asking questions from a place of intrinsic curiosity.

It was a gift to me to be given a job that was inclusive, playful, and interesting. I'm sure Trout knew this. The two most remarkable groups of kids to come through the program were a group of wealthy children from a school for the gifted in Hillsborough, and a disadvantaged group from East Palo Alto. So it was the wealthiest and most highly served children and the poorest and most underserved children who touched me the most. The kids from East Palo Alto had so much joy moving through them—so much life—that I can still feel their explosive wonder. And the kids from the gifted school were just so off all charts in terms of being self-possessed and intelligent, that I tagged that memory and would later send my own child there.

I had spent some time at the ranch before I'd left for India—Steve, too—because five times a year the Los Altos Zen Center made it into a Zendo for their meditation retreats. At these times the sangha members transformed the hostel into a monastery by removing the furniture in the dusty old community center and covering the floors with tatami mats. We cleaned windows, swept porches, and placed pictures and statues of Bodhidharma and Gautama Buddha around the walls and on altars. Outside we hung huge bells and slabs of wood with big mallets for the 3:55 a.m. wake up, and the other calls to meditation that the strict monastic schedule required.

In 1974 and 1975, after Steve had returned from India but before I went, we both sat for many retreats. My impression of those times was of Steve setting himself apart from almost everyone. He seemed frail and alone, without root but gathering strength under the pressures of solitude. Steve chose whom he wanted to befriend, but otherwise seemed to glare at people. There was a kind of dark buzz around him that came up to the edges of his body and ate at him. To me he was both magnificent and tragic.

Steve seemed slightly amused by my presence at those retreats in 1975; but it was a bemusement mixed with slight hostility. (It was how I imagined the early Christian and Buddhist monks felt about women.) He stood apart from me, and if he considered me at all, it was from a wary distance. For my part, I was a little magnetized, but also afraid to look at him. I tried not to pay any attention, but unless I was disciplined, I ended up tracking his locations. And I always knew where his meditation pillow was. If Steve and I caught each other's eyes, we mirrored each other with feelings that I did not want to feel. I would shudder at the cold darkness in him. I wanted to reach beyond, but didn't dare. He sort of called the shots because he was so harsh. Other times he was friendly like the old friend he was.

But in the spring of 1977, Steve and I were close again and though I could remember what he was like before, this was a new time and we were falling in love all over again. Steve would come to find me at the farm after work, wearing Birkenstocks, jeans, and pressed white shirts wrinkled in all the right places. With his soft-mustached face and his dark sparkling eyes, he would arrive with the bright air of his well-spent hours. I loved seeing him at the end of the day. When he came early enough we went out for dinner, and three or four nights a week we'd spend the night together in my threadbare little cabin, which I otherwise shared with some spiders. When Steve came in late he'd throw his clothes on the bunk that was against the other wall, then get into bed with me, all laughing and gorgeous. I would see him in the moonlight that cut through the old cabin windows, and it was in this brief breezeway between the earth bed and the towers of the skies that my India and his mounting trajectory at Apple swirled together and then scrambled.

Steve and I had opposite qualities running through us then. His days were defining, accelerating, and focused. He was working in an office carrying out a big plan with older businessmen. My days were spent outside in the fresh air with animals and children, doing odd jobs and living a be-here-now life. It was the promise of everything anyone could hope for between a young man and a young woman. I believed that I'd always loved Steve, that there had never been a time when he wasn't important to me. And though he had been harsh off and on since he was twenty, I knew the same was true for him. Through the lens of the double negative, he'd also never not loved me.

At Duveneck I had the room to integrate back into Western life. India had given me a way to more naturally know the feminine in myself. In that ancient matriarchal society I could literally make the physical motion of covering my head with my sari and look down, a gesture that would communicate the right of the female to go inward. Walking around with a little tent of color over my head gave me such a luscious feeling of quiet protection in the chaos of the marketplace. But in the United States, I felt undefended in my femininity. I knew of no equivalent action I could take to be in the world, while also being covered. It was a relief that at Duveneck, I could camouflage myself within the subtlety of nature.

Steve wrestled in his sleep. And I think it was in his ascent to power that he worked out many things from his dream states. One of the most dramatic expressions of this happened on a night when we were together at Duveneck and he sat bolt upright from a dead sleep and shouted: "A man must lead." With his right arm outstretched, Steve repeated this even louder, in a noble, Shakespearian tone, "A MAN MUST LEAD!" God, he was cute. I didn't know if he was talking to me or if he was on the steppes of Mongolia roaring at the world, but I knew for sure that the message had Kobun's signature on it. Inevitably after these outbursts, he would fall back onto his pillow, completely asleep, and I would be left awake and wondering.

I would bet that, when one value system takes over another, or we're wrestling with big changes in ourselves, the evolution manifests itself first in our dreams. Steve and I were not only working out the power dynamics between us, but he was processing the power that was being newly vested in him from the other aspects of his life as well. That's what I believe I witnessed when Steve got really sick with a fever and Clara asked if I would take care of him through the night. We were in Patty's bedroom for some reason, and I sat in a chair beside the bed where he lay, watching him toss and turn, breathlessly fighting, shouting out and mumbling. I had never seen anything like it: an archon in a blur of sound and movement, wild with anxiety and fever. It would seem that Steve was processing a huge amount of information, that vast territories of time and space were being argued over, chosen, and cut up. He wanted me there with him, but whenever I touched his forehead or searched for his hand to offer comfort he'd scream, "Get away!" and the sharp crack of his voice would rip through me.

Then there were the nights when I wrestled in my own stunning dreams. In one recurring nightmare I was being suffocated underneath hundreds of masks. In the way of dreams, these masks were also prison locks. And not just normal prison locks, but prison locks of such technical sophistication that I knew, even within the dream state, that they could not have been of my own making. One night in the middle of one of these dreams, I woke up and pulled myself out from under the layers of the locks to get myself down to the bathroom. But when I stepped outside the cabin door, I saw a ghost for the first in my life. At least it certainly seemed like a ghost and not fifteen feet away. It was

My parents, Virginia and James Brennan, on their wedding day, full of the hope of new beginnings.

Photograph courtesy of the author.

A monk at the Tibetan Buddhist monastery I stayed at in Benares, India, in 1975. That day I was lucky to be served a special Tibetan sticky rice. *Photograph courtesy of the author.*

Proud father, with three-day-old Lisa.
Photograph courtesy of Robert Friedland.

A two-year-old Lisa with me outside my dad's house in Saratoga.

Photograph courtesy of the author.

Daniel Kottke (holding Lisa) and I sitting outside a café in Palo Alto, flanked by friends Steve Follmer (left) and Walter Greenleaf. *Photograph courtesy of Steve Follmer.*

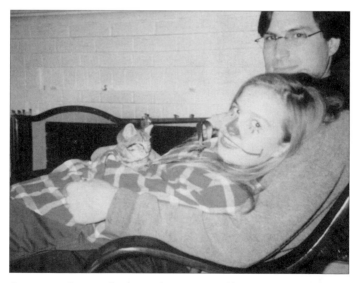

Steve made sure he was there on Halloween 1986 when Lisa was dressed as Raggedy Ann.

Photograph courtesy of the author.

Lisa with Steve and Mona in 1987.

Photograph courtesy of the author.

Two-year-old Lisa with me and my sisters Jamie (left) and Linda (standing) laughing at a joke our older sister, Kathy, made off-camera.

Photograph courtesy of the author.

Ten-year-old Lisa is concentrating hard on my instructions about how to draw a foot. *Photograph by Michael Barry.*

Tina Redse's cousin, filmmaker Fin Taylor, Steve, Tina, and Mona, exhausted but happy after the 1988 NeXT launch in San Francisco, watching coverage of the launch on TV.

Photograph courtesy of the author.

My boyfriend, Ilan Chabay, with Lisa in 1989.

Photograph courtesy of the author.

Steve in repose after a long skate with Lisa in Palo Alto, around 1989.

Photograph courtesy of the author.

With coworkers Richard Johnson (left) and Bob Martinengo at
Apple's offices. We were proud to ship the computers boxed behind
us, the most Apple ever had produced in five days. A far cry from the
3-million-plus devices they sell in that same amount of time today!

Photograph courtesy of Richard Johnson.

Lisa flanked by my father and his wife, Glenda Faye, at Lisa's Harvard
graduation.   *Photograph courtesy of the author.*

Lisa and me in a Waterloo tube station photo booth, in London, 2000. *Photograph courtesy of the author.*

glowing and it had the silhouette of Kobun in his robes. I told Steve about it when he came to visit me later that week, but he must have been in league with the ghost because he jumped up with a big circus smile and asked, "Well, did you shake his hand?"

At Duveneck, I went about thinking about next steps for my life on both a practical and metaphysical level. I worked hard at my meditations every morning because I had the sense that there was a ledge I needed to climb up and onto. Josephine Duveneck inspired me in this. A Quaker and a very practical woman, she was also metaphysical. Her farm—the very land—was alive with these two qualities. Later she would write a book about it, called *Life on Two Levels*. This impressed me as a wonderful way to be. Indeed it was. And the longer I was at Duveneck—the more I worked and developed newfound capacities to see beyond the mundane—the more I, too, began to live life on two levels.

One day I was sitting on a log in the cool damp valley area behind the hostel cabins, under some big spreading bay trees. A buck approached and stood in dappled sunlight. It was about eighteen feet away and we stared straight into each other's eyes for at least ten minutes. While we stared, I would shut my eyes for breaks and when I did, images appeared in my mind's eye, rendered in a style of art I had never seen before. They were not unlike Peter Max's artwork from the sixties, except these were fresher and bolder, with an aesthetic brevity of startling honesty. The images were of hills and dales and flowers and sky, with flowing water and various plants, all in primary colors. These simplified images were clear, soft yet boldly shaped. I felt without question this was cross-species communication, and from the deer's huge unblinking eyes I knew that he knew he was sending me these pictures. I still find it almost unbearably touching that the buck trusted me enough to show me its world. It was as if he were saying; "These things I know and love and I share them with you."

I attempted to tell Steve about the buck and the pictures that week and he told me, "Humans are not meant to mate with animals." He said this calmly as if he were giving me some sage advice. I just blinked. This was the type of comment that my mentally ill mother could have made, insinuating bestiality and missing the point of the story by a million miles. The way Steve's mind perceived me at times like this caused me to retreat into my own silent world, overwhelmed. I literally couldn't get myself to respond. It represented an enormous betrayal, and a warning that I couldn't trust him to understand me.

Steve lived in a symbolic world of his own and always had. He had a rich and meaningful inner life and it was by his example that I learned to pay attention to my own inner symbolic life. Yet in this most essential connection between us he was unable or unwilling to allow me my gifts. It was around this time that Steve asked for my opinion on the first draft of possible Apple logos. He rarely asked for my contributions in regard to his work, but he wanted my reactions now. It seemed to me he went out of his way to pull me aside. He showed me a page full of adeptly rendered ideas on a single sheet of semitransparent paper, and asked, "Which one do you like?" The word "Apple" was sketched out in all kinds of fonts and combined with about ten to fifteen different images of apples. As I recall, the apples all had bites out of them. I scanned the images and calculated what the symbol meant. Bite out of the apple? Eve going for knowledge, Eve carrying the blame for the fall of mankind, Steve making a business out of knowledge management? At that time, I very much appreciated, close to awe, that the logo, a singular image, could tell such a huge story. I told Steve that I liked the one with the horizontal rainbow stripes. (I loved that it looked like a piece of jewelry.) He said that a number of people had responded to that one, too. Then I added, "And by the way, what you really want is an image that's so strong and appealing that there is immediate recognition of your company without the word 'Apple' written under it. Image speaks louder and with more immediacy and power to people. And that apple is beautiful!"

"That shows how little you know!" he spat.

Steve had been protective of me before, but now he was jealous and acting as nasty as a mean old snake. Except I didn't understand this then. His meanness had a way of making me blank and confused in self-doubt. Steve sometimes asked me where all my confidence was going, with as much blame as confusion. He wasn't reflective enough to make the link between how he was treating me and how I was losing myself. I believed in him. I let myself be influenced by him. And I let my defenses down because I loved him. But this was a mistake. Ironically, when I made myself vulnerable to Steve I fell prey to his vulnerabilities and projections. Steve felt so bad about himself that he wanted to win at everything with everyone. Including me. And yet—irony upon irony—it was Steve's belief in his own specialness than made him look so disapprovingly at me.

I shrunk, I did not understand his new rules. I thought that if I could just *be* better, it would all work out. Mostly we were getting along well but when these spikes hit, I froze or argued and worried. I was not putting it all together. Part of the time Steve was kind, other times he was competing with me, while at other times he presumed I should be all-giving and have no needs of my own. Steve was driving insecurity in me by his changing moods as I sat back and tried to guess who I was supposed to be. It was emotionally primitive territory and it was starting to resemble those behavioral rat studies that had so intrigued him five years earlier, where inconsistent feedback drove the rats crazy.

If Steve had just been mean, I would have left. If he had been more self-reflective and considerate and tried to make things work, I would have grown to love and to trust him more profoundly. But he was kind and he was mean and he was attentive and he was aloof. Sometimes he did not return my calls and other times he called constantly. And those mixed messages played havoc with my instincts. I was losing sight of what was meaningful to me and I was losing sight of my value.

There is no creation myth in Buddhism. No Adam and no Eve. No Vishnu floating in a sea of bliss. No God. No big bang. It is without beginning and without end. This is the band of awareness Buddhism focuses on. And since it is all so endless, Buddhism places a huge importance on wisdom and compassion. Hungry Ghosts are lost souls who wander in unquenchable hunger without end. The offerings to the Hungry Ghosts are said to penetrate deep into the darkest places so that those suffering get some relief and understanding, so that their conditions and all conditions might be transcended. This kind of transcendent possibility for the happiness of all beings appeals to me no end and reminds me of the happy comforting knowledge I felt in my childhood about all being well, even though I must say, I do love a great creation myth.

Later that spring the full moon came in May and with it the time of the Buddha's birthday meditation retreat. The hostel got changed into its Zendo self again and I signed up for the week. I would sit in lotus position for hours with intermittent walking meditation, focusing on my breath, like everyone else. When my mind wandered in that environment it was always rich, escaping into everything from the perplexing details of Truffaut's film *Day for Night,* to what *the sound of one hand clapping* really was about, to a fragment of song lyric that came into my head, to the way light flitted through the trees nearby. Then I would suddenly remember to get my attention back to my breath and posture.

I signed up to make the noon offerings to the Hungry Ghosts that week. But one day I forgot about the offering and held lunch up for ten minutes. I just wasn't paying attention. When I finally got into the kitchen the cook handed me the offering plate and pushed me out the door into the main meditation room, telling me not to write until I'd found work. It was a joke, and I had to immediately cut the impulse to laugh out loud in the completely quiet room. I regained composure as quickly as I could and carried the little tray of foods to the central table where I bowed quietly and made the offering. I lit the stick of incense in the center of all that rarified focus, using the candle and then waving the flame out in the air so as not to use my breath. I placed the stick into the beautiful handmade cup filled with the fine heavy silt from trillions of other incense ashes. After this I carefully bowed and, as consciously as possible, laid the offering on the altar and then bowed once more and took a step backward and away. Kobun gave me a chastening look that seared every cell in my body. I wouldn't miss the call again.

Kobun told Steve that I had a very refined sense of transmission. "Transmission" being the word that indicates the way a student receives teachings from the master. Steve was respectful when he told me this, but his respect was blinking in and out at this point and I didn't feel I could rely on it. I wondered if it would make a difference in how he would treat me in the future. It was soon after this that Kobun told me, "You must do a better job of understanding Steve's work." I thought I probably could and should do better, but I resisted. I recognized that some part of me was immature and that Steve was entering an important stage of responsibility for which I needed to step up, but it wasn't as black-and-white as that. How could I be responsive to Steve when I felt so diminished? Besides this, I also sensed that Steve was finding support in Kobun for the double standards he was applying. I would have needed a stellar committee of advisers to manage how I was being treated by both Steve and Kobun and to know how to take care of myself. I didn't have this stellar committee of advisers; I didn't even have a mother.

After that spring retreat, I met and fell a little in love with the son of one of the older sangha members. Chris had joined a sitting period during one of the sesshins; we had introduced ourselves at the break. Tall and blond with light freckles on his face and arms, Chris had a streak of light across an unburdened brow. He and I liked each other immediately. In time, I learned that when I was with Chris I wasn't cliff hanging. I didn't feel the constant challenge to my self-worth. I wasn't ungrounded or disaffected. I was confident and happy. I was myself.

Chris had a generous spirit. He didn't need to fold me into the corners of his self-importance. Steve, of course, hated my spending time with him. It drove him crazy, but he dealt with it in an honest way. Later, however, Steve wasn't so honest, and he tried to use my friendship with Chris to off-load responsibility for his own child.

The dark clouds had been gathering between Steve and me. The signs were everywhere, and yet the love and our youth kept us focused on the next bright thing as we moved toward what we hoped would be a good relationship with each other. We always felt it was just over the horizon. Within two months we would move into a house so we could live together again.

FOURTEEN

SNAKES AND LADDERS

Steve often said that he had a strong sense of having had a past life as a World War II pilot. He'd tell me how, when driving, he felt a strong impulse to pull the steering wheel back as if for takeoff. It was a curious thing for him to say, but he did have that sense of unadorned glamour from the forties. He loved the big band sound of Tommy Dorsey, Benny Goodman, and Count Basie. At the first Apple party he even danced like he was from the forties. So I could see the fit: Steve as a young man with all that American ingenuity from a less encumbered time, with that simple sense of right and wrong. But that's not how I pictured him in 1977. Apple was taking off and Steve wasn't in an airplane, he was in a rocket ship blasting out beyond the atmosphere of what anyone imagined possible. And he was changing.

It was around this time that Steve, Daniel, and I moved into a rental in Cupertino. It was a four-bedroom ranch style house on Presidio Drive, close to Apple's first offices. Steve told me that he didn't want to get a house with just the two of us because it felt insufficient to him. Steve wanted his buddy Daniel to live with him because he believed it would break up the intensity of what wasn't working between us. Our relationship was running hot and cold. We were completely crazy about each other and utterly bored in turns. I had suggested to Steve that we separate, but he told me that he just couldn't bring himself to say good-bye. I was glad to hear this but I was also, by this time, deferring to his ideas way too often.

Steve also didn't want us to share a room at the Presidio house. He said he didn't want us to play assumed roles and that he wanted to choose when we would be together. I was hurt by this, but reasoned that he had a point, that we both needed a sense of space and choice. And so I went along with it. But I wasn't asking myself what I wanted. Nor did I know how to negotiate for myself with who and what Steve was becoming. I wasn't a person who played hardball. I looked for consensus and I ex-pected fairness. Despite all evidence, I didn't get a read on the situation partly because I assumed way too much about his being honest.

Steve selected the bedroom in the front of the house. It was like him to want to position himself as the captain of the ship—in front. He was always vying for that superior position. I chose the master bed-room and settled in, knowing I had the best room. Daniel, who was sort of charmingly odd, slept in the living room on the floor next to his piano. But after a month Steve literally picked me up and moved every-thing I owned and took over the master bedroom. He'd finally realized that I had the better deal: a larger room with an en suite bath and the privacy of the backyard. Steve had paid the security deposit for the rental so was, in fact, entitled to the room he wanted. But he was so graceless that I felt humiliated and outraged.

Even after swapping rooms in this way, Steve and I still shared nights of lovemaking so profound that, astonishingly, some fifteen years later, he called me out of the blue to thank me for them. He was married at the time of his call and all I could think of was, *Whoa . . . men . . . are . . . really . . . different.* Imagine if I had called him to say such a thing.

We remembered different things. Mainly I recalled how awful he was becoming and how I was starting to flounder. But he was right: our lovemaking had been sublime. At the time of Steve's phone call, I found that as I listened I was as awed by the memory as by his strange need to risk an expression of such intimacy. After I hung up I stood still and thought, *Maybe Steve thinks that love has its own laws and imperatives. But why call now?*

His timing had always been so particular.

In the Buddhist scriptures, it's laid out that our environment influences one full third of who we are and what we become. (The other two thirds are divided between karma/DNA and personal choice.) I witnessed this firsthand when I went to Tassajara Zen Mountain Center for a two-week stint as a guest-student in the summer of 1977, before I moved in with Steve. I didn't have a car, so Steve and Daniel drove me down the coast a little past Carmel, California, and then east, inland from the ocean, through the hills to Tassajara. After the four-hour drive, they stayed to hike, to sit in the hot sulfur baths, and enjoy a great vegetarian meal before returning that night to Los Altos.

That day at Tassajara I saw how powerful an influence environment can be. Steve became another person there. His former profound kindness resurfaced. Softness came back into his face. His gestures were more refined and lighter. The contrast was huge because as Apple grew, Steve was becoming quick and tough. Until that moment, I had forgotten so much had changed.

Kobun believed that Steve was another St. Francis. He said so many times—it was part of the way he romanticized Steve, to imbue him with the image of the gentle monk by whose hands a church would be built. Seeing Steve at the monastery that day, I was caught by the contrast and could understand why Kobun held his ideal of him. And though it was so ephemeral, I knew this was the more integrated and mature Steve—the truer one.

It was around this time when, back home in the Bay Area, Steve had started a disturbing habit. Whenever he walked past a bush or a flowering tree, he'd rip the leaves and petals off, tear them into tiny bits, and throw them to the ground as he talked. It was as if it helped him think. I'll wager that absolutely everyone who walked outdoors with

Steve after 1977 was witness to his mad leaf-tearing practice. He always did it. It drove me crazy and I would often plead with him to stop. It seemed so insensitive and most definitely not the kind of thing St. Francis would do. But that day, watching Steve at Tassajara, I finally understood that he was more true and kind in the rarified environment around Kobun and the monastery. This gave me pause and I heard some higher part of myself say, *You must remember how different he is here.*

I stayed at Tassajara for two weeks and then returned to my father's house in Saratoga. Steve breezed by the day after I had come home to take me to a pool party for Apple employees. Since Apple was small, the party was small. I think it was the first time I met many of the spouses and significant others of the Apple employees. I remember one woman in particular, the wife of one of Apple's top executives. Everything about her was picture-perfect: her clothing, her haircut, her healthy youth, and her bell-like laughter. I was completely entranced by her sense of ease.

She talked about how she used to be concerned about the integrity of her husband's business dealings—specifically, about where the money was coming from—but now she just didn't care anymore. She was about six years older than me and here she was saying quite plainly that she no longer bothered about how the money all came and went. I have no idea who this woman was or if she has since changed her mind on the subject. All I do know is at that pool party, languid and self-assured in front of about seven people, she was detached and bemused as she accounted for a change in herself. She was actually admitting that she had dropped her ethical vigilance. Was it because she and her husband were becoming so wealthy that they no longer needed the value system that most people lived by? Or was it something else? I felt that a similar change of values was taking place in Steve, and wondered at the coincidence of hearing the warning implicit in the woman's comments that day. Was there something happening at Apple to cause the change?

·　　·　　·

Living with Steve in Cupertino was not as I had expected it to be. We shared nice dinners and some beautiful evenings, but we could barely sustain a sense of emotional intimacy, much less build on it. It was like a game of Snakes and Ladders, with Steve as the game master. The ups were hopeful and the downs were extreme. I didn't know how to hold my own with him because he didn't play fair. He just played to win— and win at any cost. I knew that a solid relationship couldn't be built on any one person winning, but I couldn't understand why things kept slip-sliding away and breaking into pieces.

When we first moved into that house, I was by myself during the days when Steve and Daniel went off to Apple. I was deeply frustrated by my lack of creative focus. I had made the commitment to myself to be an artist but I had no idea how to do it. There was so much pain between me and my work that I didn't know where to begin or how to direct myself. So when my friend Ellen offered to help me get a waitressing job at a restaurant in Palo Alto, I jumped at the chance. I wanted to be around others, to make money, and to wash Steve and Daniel out of my hair on a regular basis. I needed my own independent life and perspective away from that house. I wanted to be around other people so I could remember who I was and what interested me. I also thought that it would help Steve and me to get on a better footing or, if we couldn't, for me to find my own feet to walk out of the relationship if that's what I needed to do.

Unfortunately I had to turn down that job because I didn't have a car and so couldn't get to Palo Alto. So I ended up working at Apple in Cupertino, driving in the mornings with Steve and Daniel and walking home in the evenings if we didn't have plans together after work. Eventually I started to take art classes at De Anza, which was conveniently located between Apple and our home. At Apple I worked in the shipping department where, if I remember correctly, I soldered disconnected chips onto boards and also screwed those same boards into Apple II cases for final assembly. The work wasn't interesting, but the banter and laughter with my cohorts, Richard Johnson and Bob Martinengo, kept me amused.

At that time Apple had about one thousand square feet to its name, divided into three rooms total: one for shipping, one as a kind of tech lab for R & D, and one larger office for all the executives and secretaries. One day I remember a bunch of us standing around Steve's desk when John Draper, aka Captain Crunch, called. (Draper is well known for his contribution to the blue box technology.) Steve put Draper on the speakerphone so that everyone could hear without Draper's knowing we were all listening. Draper was full of anxiety, pleading with Steve to do something for him. I don't remember what now, but I do know that people were quietly laughing at him. This is nothing in the annals of Steve Jobs stories, but I remember it because Steve's lack of fair play seemed shameless to me. I didn't care who he was making fun of. I just didn't like it.

On the nights when Steve and I didn't have something to do together— and there were more and more of these—he would often come home late and wake me up to talk and make love. On the nights he just wanted to talk, I knew he had been with Kobun. I would wake up to find Steve gently ecstatic, speaking to me in symbolic language with the Zen master's distinct speech pattern. A number of times he spoke to me about how he had been given "five brilliant flowers." His demeanor would gleam when he said this, and I would listen to find out what the symbol meant to him. My best guess after months of these reveries was that the flowers were five different people whose enlightenment Steve would be involved in. These blooms apparently included me. In the beginning he talked about "one brilliant flower" and he would touch my nose when he said it, as if to say, "That's you!" but then it rose to three and then five. I'd wondered who the others were.

Steve was assuming the role of my spiritual master once again and I felt uneasy about it. What if I didn't want to be one of his brilliant flowers. Beyond this, the general lack of transparency when it came to Steve and Kobun didn't feel right, especially when it involved me. A few years earlier Steve had tried to get me to primal scream "Mommy,

Daddy, Mommy, Daddy" when we had taken LSD because he thought he was fit to oversee that kind of opening up in me just from having read a book. The fact that he had never gone through primal therapy himself didn't seem to concern him. It was that Pygmalion thing again. Now he and Kobun thought Steve should oversee my enlightenment?

Also during this time Steve bragged about being lazy. He was working like a maniac but he'd throw his head back with his eyes unfocused and croon, "I am just the laziest man in the world." After about the tenth refrain I quietly translated this to mean that he was only active in response to inspiration, and so in this way, action was effortless, thus, he was lazy. It smacked of the coded language between him and Kobun. Further, it felt self-aggrandizing. I was left out of the late-night conversations between master and student, but I got these trailers when I was half asleep. Some of it was beautiful and I was glad Steve wanted to share it with me, but some of it felt really skewed. Steve had a way of being spiritually advanced while also being emotionally underdeveloped, and I started to wonder why Kobun didn't understand this. Why indeed.

I was wary because I didn't think enlightened people bragged, and I sensed that these two were too infatuated with themselves. The touch on the nose was patronizing. Steve, who was my boyfriend, not my guru, had some confusion about me surrendering to his ego instead of to my own higher purpose and presence. In the end, I think he may have been jealous of me for having my own power and insight. He seemed to want either to own everything or diminish its value.

One evening, Steve and I had a party at the Presidio house. I don't remember much about the party or who was there—likely, Bill Fernadez, Woz, and Daniel, and their girlfriends. What I do remember is that the next morning there was a confusing moment when Steve, looking around and squinting, asked what we should do with "it." I didn't understand the question until I realized that he was asking if there was a service we could call in to take care of the dirty dishes. Doing the dishes ourselves was simply no longer an option for Steve. He had entered into an elite world where others took care of the lower-level functions so that he could operate with more efficiency, on his presumably higher plane. I not too happily cleaned them up by myself. This put me into the wrong kind of position with him, because in no world should I ever have been in a service role to Steve in this way. I just didn't understand how to take care of myself in the face of his enlarged sense of self-importance.

A few weeks after the party Steve started telling me that I had too many wrinkles on my forehead. I'm of Irish and French descent and have thin skin from the Irish side. In my early twenties, I had a wrinkle-free face, but when I raised my eyebrows, I had a bazillion tiny lines, like pages of a book. Steve would point this out and then, like a stage mother, literally reach over and smooth my forehead whenever I furrowed my brow. This was a new Steve. I have never liked this sort of thing in mothers, much less in boyfriends.

I am not the kind of woman who places high stakes in her appearance. That's not a natural outcome of who I am. But I was puzzled. Steve had always really liked the way I looked before, but now my very face was not okay? I fell to tears, rejected and burdened by it all.

I now understand that Steve was learning how to gain power by insinuating negative self-images onto others. He was starting to define me more by what I wasn't, than by what I was. This was a whole new category of unkindness and it confused me. It was mean and I felt rejected, but I just didn't have a comeback.

I needed a more mature level of insight, so I went to Kobun's house one afternoon to talk to him about it. He was there with two of his more advanced students, men who had always been impressive to me. Not only because they were older and had flown across the country to be with Kobun, but because each had such a deep, clear kindness in his face. On that day, though, I was surprised and somewhat uncomfortable that Kobun had scheduled my time when others were present. He had never done this before. At first Kobun sat with me in the well-lit dining area of his house as I told him in a whisper what was happening. I was so afraid that he would conclude, "Yes, you are not beautiful enough for Steve's growing fame and now you know."

Instead, he sighed. "So, Steve has said this to you?" he asked. "Yes," I told him. "He has." And as we talked, I started to calm down in the presence of Kobun's vast sense of allowance.

About twenty minutes later Kobun signaled the two men into the room with us. I was so embarrassed I wanted to bolt. I couldn't believe he had done this. But I didn't bolt and the men sat with me as Kobun told them what had happened. At once they understood. At once they were gracious. These men were kind and honorable. They told me I was lovely and they were sincere about it. About forty minutes later I left Kobun's house fragile and shaken, but feeling more solid because what we talked through made sense. Months later one of the men sent me a short story by Sherwood Anderson about the beauty in women. It transcended everything Steve had said to me.

As Apple grew, so did Steve's sense of self-entitlement; in parallel they both seemed to take on lives of their own. And his behaviors didn't improve with success, they changed from adolescent and dopey to just plain vicious. For example, in the pre-Apple days whenever we'd go out for dinner (which wasn't that often), Steve would often be sarcastic toward the restaurant staff. The host would say, "Two?" and Steve would reply, "No, fifteen!" driving for the implicit "DUH!" But after Apple started we ate out a lot more and Steve's behavior toward service people changed into a different kind of disempowerment.

Steve would order the same meal night after night, yet he'd complain bitterly each evening about the little side sauces that were served with it, cutting the air with disdain for the waitstaff who would serve up such greasy-salty-tasteless-mock-fine cuisine. He seemed to assume that everyone at the restaurant should know better than to serve up such wallpaper paste—not only to him, but at all. Steve would run down the waitstaff like a demon, detailing the finer points of good service, which included the notion that "they should be seen only when he needed them." Steve was uncontrollably critical. His reactions had a Tourette's quality—as if he couldn't stop himself.

Of course, it must have been sort of wild to have your genius recognized at the age of twenty-two, to be thrust into such a role of authority. Steve had always been a brilliant misfit, but at this time—to be generous—he wasn't managing his growing power very well. In fact, he was positively despotic. Excellence had always been a gorgeous thing in Steve, but now he was using it like a weapon. He'd look for excellence and when he didn't find it, he'd behave badly and take it out on people. It was as if the values of aesthetics were replacing decency and ethics in the mad pursuit to be the best of the best.

Steve may simply have lacked maturity, like a lot of techie types for whom a breadth of emotional awareness just isn't the point. It could have been the result of the creative process and the effect of designing with such Bauhaus minimalism that made him so severe. After all, what we create, in turn creates us. Or maybe Steve had lost a sense of grace and spaciousness in his desire to pare everything down to the flat and the essential. (Wasn't that the point in Zen and in computer design—to pare everything down to the essential?) Maybe it was that brilliant myopic quality found in the sciences, so supreme in its capacity to focus on the almighty goal that it somehow disconnects people from having perspective. Or then again it could have been Steve's extraordinary competitiveness, the desire to win at all costs that clicked into his sensibilities and took over every other consideration.

I also felt that there might have been some sort of mean by-product to Steve's rocketing ascent, a kind of fallout from the acceleration—the Faust particle. Thus seduced by the mind and the possibility of total technical excellence, Steve was unable to keep his soul wired into the whole of his life. (Although ironically, his "religion of excellence" would inspire a cultlike following.) It's my current working theory, and goodness knows I've had plenty, that it was by creating a world-changing technology that every excellent and broken thing on earth rose up through

Steve as a part of everything he created and became. So it was in this way that the mutable young man came to express some of the best and worst of our time.

As Steve's first girlfriend I increasingly experienced what it felt like to have him turn against me. And so was at this time that I began to perceive that awesome and awful could be but a hair's breadth apart. And where Steve's fullness met mine with staggering beauty (there was a reason he called fifteen years later to acknowledge the importance of the nights we'd shared), he was also becoming so creatively unstable, so out of integrity with himself that everything could slip out of alignment in an instant. That's when my heart would freeze over. That's when I'd be left speechless and gasping. Though I would try to adapt to the change, it all soon outweighed his value to me.

FIFTEEN

THE WORLD OF MEN

At age twenty-three I was just beginning to enter the world of grown men. The way I perceived men, and my relationships with them, was influenced as much by the changing values of the time as it was by personal experience. My father, who kept himself emotionally hidden, was a man of his time. He had little sadistic and masochistic streaks that would show up when he didn't know how to handle things, but mainly, he was wired for goodness and duty. He was always a solid income earner for his family, and he defined himself by being able to make good money and hold his liquor. He followed a traditional white-collar path, working hard from the bottom up to build his career, earning the position of vice president in marketing at a number of big companies. He bought increasingly nicer homes for us in every state we moved to, with spacious lawns and two-car garages. But he never developed a life that reflected his own profound way of being, as this was something few of his era expected of their lives.

When I was a little girl I saw my father as shiny and smooth like Roy Rogers, "the King of the Cowboys." He was sparkly and intensely interesting to me, no matter if he was shaving or hosing down the driveway. I liked to watch him work. On Saturday mornings he would come into the TV room and laugh so hard at our cartoons that tears would stream down his face, which made them hundreds of times funnier to us. And at the dinner table he would use knives to introduce our little minds to the concept of infinity. He would model thought experiments by demonstrating how you could use a knife to cut something in half, then in half again, and again and again and again to show us that there was never an end to all the halves and that this was infinity. Then he'd watch our faces to see the marvelous notion land and sink in.

When we lived in Colorado I saved up and bought a $40 reflector telescope from the back of a cereal box. Life changed at our house when it arrived. My father would spend one evening a week focusing and refocusing the telescope to get a look at the night skies. Everyone got lots of turns looking through the telescope, and our whole neighborhood of parents and children would join us on our back patio for hours of viewing. Brilliant Jupiter and her four large moons thrilled me. Mars was a ruddy red. And then there were the perfect crystalline patterns from the meteorites that bit into the surface of the moon thousands of years ago and had exploded outward for what must have been literally thousands of miles—the visual equivalent of a symphony.

My father had a sense of grace and when he came into a room I could swear I saw the lights turn a blue hue, which fed my spirit and made me feel safe. Yet I also knew that there was something not so straightforward about him. When he talked about infinity it seemed like the knife's endless cutting didn't always expand his vision as much as drive it into sad, truncated corners. Children may think their fathers hold up the sky, but I discovered early on that there was a sense of intellectual chaos in the one I got. It seems to me that we all tried to help him with the lifting, but eventually the effort made us, a house of five females, disappointed and angry.

My father raised four daughters and cherished all of us, but I think I irritated him more than the rest of my sisters put together. Instead of supporting my creativity, he was often embarrassed by it. He dismissed my art supplies as "cancers," ignored my work, and yelled at me in front of my friends when he found us in a darkened room taking turns wrapping each other up in paper and twine to experience "breaking out." It was a seventies thing. To us it was harmless and full of hilarity. But to my father it was messy and utterly incomprehensible. It made him mad. Another time, my dad arrived home from a business trip. It was early (he had taken a red-eye) and he came in to find Steve and me sleeping together on the floor. He didn't say a thing but later I heard him telling his friends, "If anyone had told me two years ago that I would find one of my daughters sleeping with a boy in the middle of the living room floor, I would have thrown him through the window." As a teen I rendered my dear dad outraged and mute, in turns.

My father wanted a daughter who was compliant and who dressed in matching sweater sets. But I was out in a wilderness, experimenting with what interested me because I was never happier than when I was on the outer edge of new experience. I couldn't comply, and having my dad not meet me in my teenage world meant that I never had the advantage of being able to confide in a man for whom my best interest was in his best interest. Sadly, all this resulted in the kind of miscommunication that created betrayals between us. And when I was twenty-two, and my father saw that Steve was disrespectful toward him and dangerously unconscious of me, we weren't able to talk it through.

It stuns me now to imagine the world in which my mother lived. When my family was still living in Nebraska, she inappropriately confided to us that she would be able to legally divorce our dad once we got to California. As late as 1968, it was illegal for a woman to divorce her husband in Nebraska. We girls knew by that time that she didn't like him very much. I think her sense of powerlessness to free herself from the marriage may have triggered the onset of her inevitable mental illness. My father, for his part, repeated to us a number of times while I was in my late teens, "I should never have let your mother go to college. It gave her ideas." This confounds me for its cluelessness by a man with four daughters in the time of burgeoning feminism. My father would later catch up and understand in spades, but the seventies were a time of slow awakening for the stalwarts who kept to their secret alliances inside male-dominated companies. Also, he had a point: by 1970 some in the feminist movement had lost the threads of its greater purposes and had so radicalized out of total frustration that they were basically directing women to throw the babies out with the bathwater.

I didn't really have enough experience to understand the Women's Movement or why someone would say, "A woman without a man is like a fish without a bicycle." It was a hilarious statement that begged to be understood. I also didn't know what to make of it when I overheard Kobun finishing a phone call in which he bemoaned the qualities of American women. I stood at the edge of the door waiting as Kobun, kneeling on the floor at the far end of his office, laughed and said something like, "Oh, they are not like these *American women. . . .*" implying the superiority of some other group of women who were more deferential to men. Perhaps he had intended to signal me since he knew I was standing within earshot.

I witnessed many such things long before I had enough experience to understand their implications, much less respond to them. But one thing was certain: during the seventies the antagonism between the sexes was crazy-pronounced and weighed in no one's interest—not the men, not the women, and definitely not the children. I might have been more of a casualty of the times were it not for my eventually meeting a couple of spiritual teachers who helped me resolve the polarizing perspectives I'd grown up with. Now I like to think that the real truth behind the discordant seventies is that it was all a work in progress. Or better yet, like the discombobulated strains of an orchestra warming up before a performance. Perhaps the period of my coming-of-age was just the messy beginnings of the good coming into form.

I'm a careful optimist. Later, my heart would be exalted to hear the Dalai Lama proclaim to a group of Nobel laureates at the Vancouver Peace Summit that "the Western woman will save the world." Though I personally don't think it will necessarily just be the Western women to save us—there are some mighty fine examples of girls and women coming forward from the East and the Middle East and Africa—I nevertheless know that sometimes we have to work a long while before a worthy vision is anchored into the world. But that it will come and that it will be worth all the work, I have no doubt.

Having lived in a largely female household for most of my life, moving in with Steve and Daniel was a big change for me. I liked sharing the Presidio house with them. At least in the beginning. I enjoyed the way they'd analyze things to get at the gold nugget of truth, and then erupt into helpless laughter for how crazy the world was. Steve and Daniel radiated a refined sweetness in their friendship, and their conversations centered around technology and enlightenment and food. I remember one comment that Steve made regarding the best use of personal energy: "To totally express yourself is to refine. To refrain from self-expression is to build power from within." Wow.

Daniel added a cheerful presence to the house. Like a child, he took infinite delight not only in what interested him, but in the meta level of *how* it interested him. And as Steve became more preoccupied at work, I shared hours at the house with Daniel and we got to know each other better. He taught himself to play the piano. I cooked and baked bread, and made myself clothes from cheap Indian tapestries I'd found at Cost Plus stores. The seventies experienced a resurgence in attention to homemaking skills. After the ludicrously mechanized, industrial ideals of the fifties, the sixties and seventies ushered in earthier, healthier practices. This was the counterculture that I embraced. Steve couldn't have cared less about this aspect of my creativity; he tuned in with a different kind of attention. But Daniel often expressed a wonderful appreciation of my sewing, baking, and cooking. He seemed to like everything I did and expressed amazement that I could accomplish things without recipes and patterns, telling me I had a "native genius." I didn't know exactly what that meant, but it sounded great to me. I don't think it ever occurred to Daniel that I actually had no idea how to follow a recipe or a pattern.

My mind was so impatient when it came to rules that I was continually working everything out anew.

While I was never attracted to Daniel, I could be charmed by him. Steve acknowledged my creativity in an entirely different way, always more interested in studying my approach to things. Daniel simply made me feel seen in ways Steve never really cared about. But this was only part of the picture. I would soon find out that Steve and Daniel's relationship was based on the most idiotic level of entitlement I had ever seen close-up. I found them chock-full of so many negative female images and projections it might have been cute for being such a caricature, if only I had been endowed with an outrageous sense of humor. In truth, Steve and Daniel played off the very best and very worst qualities in one another. I was often amazed by their lightness while simultaneously being stunned at their insensitivity. Maybe the opposite was true for them of me. I never thought to ask. I just watched them bond as if they were absurdist insiders in the life's-a-great-big-joke club. As time passed I began to understand that all the joking was the main, if not the only, avenue of exchange between them. And it became very predictable.

Eventually I would figure out that Steve was a role model and maybe even a father figure to Daniel Kottke, not unlike Robert Friedland was to Steve. And though all three of them were equal as friends, I think a sense of hierarchy was inevitable because Robert (and then Steve) had a thirst for power, whereas Daniel was ambivalent about it, more inclined to align with those he perceived to have power than to hold the reins of it himself. It was for this reason that I thought of Daniel as the acolyte in that brotherhood.

After about a month of all of us living together, Steve began to exclaim that "men are just so much more interesting than women." And then Daniel followed suit and repeated the same line and sentiment. It was a dismissive statement, but if it was meant to destabilize and disable me, it didn't. Instead I just quietly wondered why Steve would take pride in such thinking. Was this some kind of wonky stage of male maturation? Later it dawned on me that brotherhoods, in their less developed states, are about building consensus, celebrating sameness, and jousting to sharpen wits. It's an arrangement that offsets existential and personal insecurity. And it glorifies manhood to ensure what men, or at least some men, see as security in the world. Steve was looking for sameness soon after Apple started; he seemed to have lost sight of the fact that my value to him was because I was not the same.

This *sameness* would gather momentum. In the years that followed the second coming of Steve at Apple, I began to notice that the world had been infiltrated by an army of Steve look-alikes: black turtlenecks, buzz cuts, John Lennon glasses, and blue jeans. Steve's European casual look was being adopted by men in every American city. It was cultivated simplicity and it was cool. I now believe Steve had an almost unfathomable desire to see himself reflected back. And so it happened. "The Steves" were everywhere. For me, though, it was jarring. This bony, shaved-head look of his seemed to me to have had its origin in Paul Jobs. From my perspective, Steve strove relentlessly for approval from men, Paul being the first. Replicating Paul's militaristic look was part of that.

What I really wanted and needed at that time was to have a quiet home and be loved and appreciated for who I was. I was just getting to the point where I no longer recalled the sickening feeling of my mother's uneasy logic and mental illness. Not remembering how my mother thought was a milestone for me, and I began to have whole evenings at home where I could focus and read deeply for my own enrichment. I was starting to heal, a process that seemed to make something in Steve and Daniel want to throw me off center, while they constantly quipped and critiqued me for not being centered enough. I was in a delicate phase and I couldn't stabilize it in that house with the many disruptions and slights.

Daniel Kottke, like Steve, always had great confidence in his opinions. They both seemed to perceive the idealized versions of themselves as the whole truth and then evaluate others less generously. I think of it as a little glitch in the programming because I think Daniel, at his core, was not motivated by unkindness. The problem for me in that house was that the guys perceived themselves as the gold standard and me as something corrupted and corruptible. I took it personally, which gave them more to laugh at.

Daniel liked the intellectual traditions that developed from the spirituality of the seventies and for as long as I have known him he has always explored ideas and tried them on, ever wanting to entertain new possibilities. But he could be found laughing at the wrong things and would often miss the full truth of a situation because, like so many science types in the Bay Area, he could be disconnected from the emotional implications of his insights. We were in the kitchen of the Presidio house one day when Daniel said to me, "You were a courtesan in China in a former life!" blasting a laugh in my face and then curling inward like a conch shell, back into his bright, smug interior. I didn't know what a courtesan was exactly, or what he was fully implying. Before the ease of Google, I brooded over the notion. It was a statement of ridicule and got under my skin and stayed there for years. (Now in response to that, I would say my chosen archetype would be more like the four-armed Saraswati: the powerful creative feminine aspect in balance with her consort, the realized male aspect, without compromise or prostitution by either. Just fullness of being.)

Much potential was flowering and flowing at that house—so much vision and promise—but my efforts to speak and be understood were too often co-opted for a laugh. When I told Steve that Kobun had once told me that "Steve has a very deep ignorance," Steve said he considered it a compliment. He was building himself into an enlightened warrior, so instead of heeding the warning, he decided that one deep ignorance wasn't such a big problem in the grand scheme. At this time, fewer and fewer things made him stop and reflect, unless it was about another's failure to think as he thought. Sometimes I would go for days without talking because Steve could turn anything I said against me; my only recourse was silent revolt. This made Steve and Daniel laugh more patronizingly, pretending that they understood. As time went by I began to shrink and disappear (even to myself) in equal proportion to Steve's growing arrogance.

I realize now that we were all expressing the cultural norms of the time. None of us recognized that we were links in a long chain of broken and unresolved issues. I had no models to teach me about the value of the feminine aspect, and neither Steve nor I had models for an evolved male/female relationship. Adding significantly to this dynamic was the male bias of Kobun's Japanese culture. More than once I had heard Kobun say that a really good man runs from women who want to marry him. *And well he should!!* But I never once heard him say that a really good woman should run from men who want to marry her. It seems to me now that the teacher's influence may have been very worse than none at all.

Steve barely made time for the two of us anymore, so I was happy when he surprised me by suggesting we take a walk together. As we ambled along, however, we ended up listing our grievances with each other. Neither of us felt we were getting what we wanted from the other. And it was turning into a pretty lousy walk when, halfway across the school lawn, we were distracted by a compelling sight. There among a row of newly planted trees was a clump of about a thousand bees hanging from a branch, all clinging tightly onto each other like a dangerous cluster of grapes. It was a buzzing, half-flying, half-heavy thing, weighty enough to bend a tender sapling branch down about five inches.

We were riveted.

Neither of us had ever seen such a thing. We came in close to have a look at the mishmash of jillions of tiny repeating insect parts vibrating with their harsh yellow-and-black-colored bodies. The buzzing alone was unnerving. I wondered out loud if they had lost their queen. As fascinated as little kids, we looked around to find a stick to poke at it. We were scared that they'd swarm us but way too curious not to investigate. Steve took the stick and I stood half behind him and with both of us bent over and peering, we got as close as we dared while making ourselves ready to run. Then Steve said, "Okay, one, two, three!" and jabbed into it. Suddenly and anticlimatically, half of the clump dropped to the ground like whipped cement: the bees splattered on the grass, seemingly dazed as they continued to buzz and crawl all over each other. Some flew up to hover and then shoot off. In the rush of shared excitement we finally stopped all the blaming and were quiet. Turning around, we headed home in silence.

In the chaos of the bees I saw a symbol that my world was disconnecting from Steve's. We had extraordinary codes for creativity together, but I would be excluded from his trajectory and he from mine. History unfolds like this. Some of the finest impulses in people go unrealized because of the crosswinds of ignorance, distraction, power abuse, jealousy, bad timing, faulty memory, scarce resources, a lack of confidence, sexism, racism, wrongful ambition, laziness, wars. . . . The list of goof-ups is long. Overwhelmed, I excused myself from him, not wishing to go in the soul-numbing direction he seemed to be headed.

Soon after that walk, circumstances finally turned forever. It was late on a Saturday morning right before Steve left for work, and he and I were in our unfurnished dining room, arguing. His face contorted as his voice launched the harshest, most critical words at me—heavily concentrated explosives in every syllable. I don't remember what the fight was about, only the rapid fire of his dronelike strikes. In my defensive state I separated myself out and studied him as if from the wrong end of a telescope, making his horrible behavior tiny and more manageable through its contracted lens. I thought to myself that he was just meaner than anyone ever needed to be. And then I realized that for me it was over between us. Every cell within me, from the bottom of my feet to the top of my head, knew I didn't have what it would take to withstand any more of this. Normally I was caught up in the blame, but this time I became peaceful because it was over. His meanness had won. There was no contest. I was done.

Once I see something with this kind of clarity, I can never go back, no matter how much I want to ignore myself. And though it would take me time to take all the steps, from then on I was fully programmed to leave. It would be hard to do it because commitment-to-self was not one of the noble metals of my family experience—there were other noble metals, but not that one. So this was where I would stumble toward maturity.

Ten days and fifteen arguments later Steve was chasing me around his car in our driveway late at night. Daniel was out for the evening so we had some blessed space without his sidekick presence. I was both laughing and crying, trying to let the air out of Steve's car tires in a playful and tearful attempt to make him stay home with me. He was laughing too, and crying as he chased me from one end of the car to the other. Suddenly, his voice pierced the air with a cry, "I've never told you what I wanted you to know." I stopped short and let that sink in. It was true; in our last years together we had never understood our love in the same way at the same time, and so the love between us never had been fully expressed.

I received the blow—his vulnerability, our love, and the loss of it hitting me all at once. The grief I felt was so overwhelming, I bent over holding my stomach and wanted to die from the pain. This was Steve all over, always hitting the grief note to accent loss and blame, when continuity of love and kindness could have saved us.

I resisted the idea of actually leaving Steve, but acted on it nonetheless. Eventually I planned to move to Palo Alto, which I thought was a beautiful little jewel of a town well before it was overhauled to become the hub of the computer age and its money. First, I arranged to get an IUD. Once I woke up to how impossible it had all become, I also woke up to a number of things I had not been taking care of for myself. Birth control was at the top of that list.

Our birth control method up to that point was Steve's coitus interruptus, also called the pull-out method, which for him was about his conserving his energy for work. Not reaching climax is a practice from the eastern traditions of India and Japan that is passed between teacher and male student for the purpose of building focus and power—presumably for spiritual growth. But it is also a practice taught in the 1937 motivational book inspired by Andrew Carnegie, *Think and Grow Rich* by Napoleon Hill, which speaks to building power and wealth by conserving one's vital energies. I knew that coitus interruptus was a bogus form of birth control, but until then I'd suspended my better judgment and watched my cycles.

I called Family Planning in Sunnyvale. They would only place an IUD at the end of a woman's menstrual cycle, so I waited until I'd nearly completed a period and then drove down for the procedure. I felt uneasy about the down sides of using an IUD, but it was a better risk than the pill, which would make my body lethargic and fat with the extra hormones. I knew this because I had taken the pill off and on through the years. That night I told Steve that I had gotten birth control and he ridiculed me. Knowing that I had done the right thing enabled me to finally see the pattern: he would continue to demean me for each and every independent thought and action. It was like a disease in him.

After the IUD had been placed, I felt I could be confident after nearly a year of risky intimacy with Steve. I knew I was not going to get pregnant and I was relieved, even giddy, to have that one huge pressure taken care of. Or so I thought. Within twenty-four hours of getting the IUD, I got pregnant. I know exactly when conception happened because Steve was truly kinder that night. He breathed as if he were letting go of everything and he'd cupped my face with a deep sense of real connection in a way he hadn't done for some time. For a moment I relaxed, feeling his full acceptance of me. Love shone that night, and then it was eclipsed again.

SIXTEEN

AN OLD STORY

Within a two-week period, somewhere in early October of 1977, the clock was up on everything. I realized I could no longer endure an intimate relationship with Steve. I got "reliable" birth control as the first of many steps to get out and away. And Rod Holt, one of the first ten employees at Apple, approached me about a paid apprenticeship designing blueprints for the Apples. Steve and Rod saw me as a good fit for the job, and it was, but I was concerned about taking a job like this because I just wanted to be an artist. As a caring older adult offering me a tremendously valuable opportunity, Rod saw my resistance as profoundly misconceived. I told him I would think about it. Then I found out I was pregnant.

It took me a few days before I told Steve. We were standing in the dining room, talking about something else entirely, and I told him: "I'm pregnant." Steve's face turned ugly. He gave me a fiery look. Then he rushed out of the house without a word. That was day one.

I know it's widely believed that Steve asked me to have an abortion. And Steve, himself, has apparently been quoted as saying he had asked me to end the pregnancy. He even actively led people to believe that I slept around. But none of this was true. It served Steve's purposes to appear as the victim of a crazy woman to whom he'd had a slight attraction, but never loved. The truth is that at the beginning of my third trimester Steve shook his head and said: "I never wanted to ask that you get an abortion. I just didn't want to do that." And he never had.

Steve didn't and wouldn't talk to me about the pregnancy. When he wasn't arguing with me, he would hold me off with his tightlipped silence. It would take me years to understand why he wouldn't discuss something so important to both of us, especially since he and I had dealt with this situation five years before and had come to a mutual and comfortable decision about how to handle it. This time, I tied myself in knots trying to work out why he wouldn't just talk with me. What I saw is that after I told Steve I was pregnant, and once he'd adjusted, he behaved with unnatural calm in the face of my panic and tears. If I had just gotten mad, I would have broken the spell, come to my senses, and taken action because clearly I had no way to care for a child. But I didn't even have it in me to get mad because I think I was too deeply affected by his silent abandonment and what amounted to months of his negative projections on me. So I spun between two poles: the pregnancy itself and the chaos that was unfolding around me. I had a sense of there being no place to stand with this.

Steve's silence reminded me what it was like to be around my mother's mental illness, where I struggled to make sense of her insane and cruel behaviors. She, like Steve, lived in a symbolically rich world in which she would perceive my actions in starkly negative terms—things just too terrible to repeat. I realize now that I believed her worst perceptions of me rather than admit that my own mother was so mentally ill. Equally, I came to realize that it was easier to think there was something wrong with me than to see that Steve was leveraging my pain and confusion not only because he wanted to protect himself, but because he was inclined to torture. I looked weak and this would have brought it out in him.

If I had hammered Steve for a conversation, we might have found our way through. But he behaved as if everything was my fault and I didn't know how to push back with the force necessary to match the strength of all his blame. This all took place just before the common availability of DNA testing, so it was difficult to prove paternity. When Steve ran out the door, or at least soon after, I don't doubt that he went to a legal adviser who told him that if he said nothing, then nothing could be used against him. I believe that the motivation behind this was all that was happening at Apple.

Steve was fully aware of the big picture, but I had no way of knowing that Apple would go public within three years and that my pregnancy would have been perceived as a threat to Steve's public image and therefore, the Apple brand. I think they had it pretty much figured out by then that Steve was a wild card and a public relations nightmare. But spin it just right and you could romanticize him as the upstanding, if quirky, genius. Apple was a young company and needed to build public trust. So they created a persona for the gifted, good-looking young man. It was all identity branding and power. It was about money. Done.

Abortion was an option, and an important one. A woman knows whether she has the capacity to care for another life. Adoption was also available. But I went blank. I had no idea of what action to take. And I wasn't eating well. I was idealistic about being a vegetarian when I probably needed some meat. I also suspect I had parasites from India that were affecting my focus as well as my strength and sense of well-being. Added to this was the Buddhist precept Do No Harm that was very important to me. Inexperience. Idealism. Health issues. The flood of hormones raging through my body. I just didn't have the clarity to make smart decisions.

I didn't talk with my father. He knew something about having children and supporting a family so likely he would have been very helpful, but I didn't fully trust his take on things and I think I was a little too private and maybe even arrogant. I didn't want to talk to him—there had been many betrayals by this time. None of my friends had enough experience to help me, either. They were still growing up into their lovely lives.

As time went by I felt more alone and more paralyzed by conflict. I did not want a baby, but neither did I want to harm the little one developing inside me. On top of that, I was having a recurring nightmare, charged with bizarre hostility, where I saw a faceless doctor coming toward me with a blowtorch to give me an abortion. So I went to the Zen master. Kobun, unlike Steve, would talk to me. Kobun, unlike my father, didn't seem full of chaos because he, Kobun, appeared to be kind and intellectually sound. Kobun embraced the situation. He wanted to be helpful and I was relieved to have someone to talk to. Now I see that Steve and Kobun had exchanged roles. Kobun gave me to Steve to help with my enlightenment, and Steve left Kobun to assist with the decision about our pregnancy.

More than anything, I wanted Steve to just talk to me so we could make a decision together. This was our dilemma but instead he blamed me as if it were mine alone. At one point, well into the pregnancy, he told me he felt like I was stealing his genes. He had begun to think of himself as a high-end commodity—despite the fact that he was acting from low-end accountability. I didn't dare imagine Steve wanted to marry me. By all his actions it was clear that he had started considering me an embarrassing inconvenience.

So I threw myself upon the mercy of Kobun for a way out of trouble. "Keep the child!" he said with enthusiasm. "I will help you." Later in the pregnancy Kobun would tell me, "You're not the type of woman who could give a baby up for adoption." I didn't know if he was being manipulative or honestly believed that; I personally had no idea if I could or couldn't give a baby up for adoption. But at least I knew that Kobun had promised his support if I decided to keep the baby.

Kobun had warned in a couple of his dharma talks that "Zen meditation was not to be used for psychological purposes, or purposes unsuited for a spiritual endeavor." This wisdom floated a bit beyond my grasp at the time. Now I understand it to mean that the development of someone's spiritual life will always integrate into a person's psychology and improve character, sometimes in vast ways. But spirituality should never be used to develop personal goals or worldly gain. Such an act empties the seeker of the authenticity that comes from a sincere spiritual quest.

And yet, despite these words, I came to see that Kobun did manipulate situations for worldly outcomes. One day when I was about six months pregnant, he told me that he was using all his inner power to bring Steve and me and "the child" together, but that it wasn't working. If this is true, and it might not be, it's a discerning factor: because any real meditation practice worth its salt is about penetrating to the root causes so that right action takes place of its own accord. Kobun couldn't penetrate the problem. And he was dumbfounded by his failure. He wasn't as advanced as I had thought, or maybe as he had thought.

And he wasn't curious either, because after this admission, Kobun did what so many do when they don't do the work it takes to be thorough and honest: he became glossy with sentimentality, that slippery insincere slope of Hallmark cards, skipped steps, and happy endings. "Let life happen through you!" he said with a whoosh of spirit that had absolutely nothing to do with the pressing realities of my situation. And I thought, *Wow, what a cheesy, manipulating statement!* Later, I told my older sister, Kathy, about this and she said, "I feel like punching him." That seemed about right.

I teetered on the brink of indecision knowing that the day would come after which I would be too far along to get an abortion. I went to Family Planning to have the IUD taken out, thinking this might determine things. Family Planning in Sunnyvale set up an appointment for a very careful procedure of going into my womb, while saving the pregnancy. But I learned almost immediately that the IUD had expelled itself, likely within a few hours of its being inserted. That's why I had gotten pregnant.

Toward the end of the time when I would have had to make a decision about going forward with the pregnancy, Kobun repeatedly told me, "I'll give you money and I'll raise the child until you are ready, or

even forever if you want." I knew that Kobun was romanticizing himself
and his tradition and for this alone I should have taken greater heed. I
also knew, though, that his mother ran something like an orphanage at
his father's monastery, so I thought he was honestly awake to my reality. He told me so many times that he would help me and my child, that
I believed him. But I never got anything in writing. Why would I? He
was the spiritual leader after all, and no one in the spiritual community
ever told me he wasn't as good as his word. No one. The most I ever challenged him was to say, "Kobun! Your wife would never agree to having
my child in her home." It took nerve for me to say this because it seemed
so outspoken to confront him.

I didn't know Harriet Chino personally, but I knew how she would
look at me sometimes—hard and mean. Plus I had heard stories in his
lectures about her tigerlike anger. I suspect that he called her a tiger
because she was a strong woman with goals of her own and because she
yelled at his students to get out of their house. I was idealistic and couldn't
imagine that she might tire of Zen practitioners intruding on their
family life. But Steve often joked about how she disliked him in the
early years. In fact, he told me that she thoroughly despised him because
of his habit of going to their house late in the evenings and waiting on
the sidewalk or in the alley behind their house, willing Kobun to come
outside for a breath of fresh air and a cigarette. However, Harriet's dim
view of Steve must have changed once he became famous, after which
she would ask him to accompany her on social engagements when her
husband was out of town.

Kobun said to me, "If she objects to my taking your baby, *then I will
divorce her*!" Ohhhh, ho-ho, did this statement signal a darkening
turn. And that he announced this with such bravado made me take
note. I felt this was way too cavalier under the circumstances. Kobun
and Harriet already had two small children and I imagine that she was
the main person responsible for keeping the family running smoothly.
Kobun, it turns out, wanted more babies and she didn't. Within two

years she would divorce him and take their children with her to live in another state. As for me, I slowly began to recognize that Kobun was putting me, and my baby's life, in danger.

Rod Holt was still waiting to hear from me about the position at Apple, but I was so distraught that I couldn't get myself to respond to him in a timely way. He was incensed, and honestly, it was never like me to drop the ball about something as serious as a good job offer, especially one that was both an honor and a fit. But I was caught in the head-lights; I couldn't even tell him what was up because it was so personal. In the end, I just couldn't imagine staying at Apple. Steve astonished me when he offhandedly, even naïvely, said, "You can be pregnant and work at Apple, you can take the job. I don't get what the problem is." But I felt so ashamed: the thought of my growing belly in the professional environment at Apple, with the child being his, while he was unpre-dictable, in turn being punishing and sentimentally ridiculous. I could not have endured it.

It must have been around this time that I observed that Steve's pos-ture was that of a brute, with royal ease. "Brute" because he was treating me with a hefty arrogance that leveraged his self-esteem off my despair. "Royal ease" because he now had the power to make anything look rea-sonable and the resources to work it all out effortlessly. He told me as much. "If you give up this baby for adoption, you will be sorry," he said. "And I am never going to help you."

I soon quit the little job I had at Apple and went on welfare and started cleaning houses to make a little more money under the table. I also asked Steve for money a couple of times so I could rent a place, and he tilted his head in a kind of little boy way so that I would feel for him and said, "You know I don't even get around to getting Apple to pay me back for my out of pocket expenses." And at this he pulled his wallet out to show me the blur of his receipts for the month. This was the extent of his answer. He wouldn't even take responsibility for saying no. I am sure that he was advised that if there was a legal case that it would not look good for him to have given me money.

Lifetimes later, in September of 2011, literally a month before Steve would die, I sat with Jeff Goodell from *Rolling Stone* magazine at an outdoor café in Menlo Park, California. He had written several articles about Apple and had interviewed Steve a number of times. Jeff related that he'd read everything there was about the company.

Through the years, I'd learned not to talk with reporters and I had no intention of talking with Jeff until he surprised me in an e-mail by saying that he had also written a memoir and knew what hell it was. I was years into my own memoir at the time, so this got my attention. Jeff also told me that Steve really had liked him. The latter comment may be a standard way to get an interview with the intimates of famous people, but it seemed so utterly naïve and refreshing that I decided to meet with him. Also, I knew by then that in regard to work-related situations, Steve made sure he had great people around him. If Steve liked Jeff and gave him interviews, it meant he was likely a great person. So I met up with him and, during our only face-to-face conversation, I could see why Steve had liked him. I liked him, too.

In our nearly four-hour conversation we came around to Jeff telling me that he had also worked for Apple and that he left right before it went public. I felt a sudden, excruciating excitement to know more. I could hardly believe I was sitting at a table with another person who had the comparable history of having left Apple soon before making what would have been a lifetime's worth of money. In his case, he left it all to go to Lake Tahoe and become a blackjack dealer. I said, "Do you regret it?" That was the only real question I wanted to ask. Jeff casually and confidently shook his head and said, "No, not at all. Not one single bit. Apple didn't have an environment I could thrive in." An oasis of a response.

At the moment of this conversation, the memory of being at Apple and all that gray particulate of computer substance—half-matter, half-blackened energetic discharge—seemed to gather at the table like a miniature sandstorm. Then Jeff said something like, "It would never have been worth it to have stayed there." Jeff was discreet, polite, and so uber-aware of power that I wondered at all the complicated egos he must have interviewed through the years.

It was in this conversation that I realized I had so identified with conventional thinking about the very real losses of my life that I never understood the degree to which I had actually made great decisions all the way through. Jeff said, "The cubicle life, the quality of the air and the light inside the buildings, the overweight people who wrote code late into the night, their poor diets and their bad jokes . . ." He sighed and summarized, "Chrisann, it wasn't a good environment for me." Being in Jeff's presence and seeing the love, the humilty, and confidence he had for his life and family, made my regret melt away into something deeper, truer, and more meaningful. It's what I already knew, but it was so good to hear it in another. Because for all of Apple's religion, it just was never my temple. And to be perfectly honest, I had felt profoundly ambivalent about spending my life in such a place. Even a minute of focus in the wrong direction seems too costly to me.

I sat through three or four Zen meditation sesshins during my pregnancy. I wanted the familiarity and warmth of the Zen community, and the comfort of the nutritious food that was served. I also felt that meditating would help me better understand my circumstances and find a way through. Sitting still was my way to find answers. When I wasn't at a retreat, I ate without joy and grew small. Few people knew I was pregnant until I was about six months along, after which there was no hiding it. I lived in different homes during this time. I always had a place to sleep and cook, but I was basically homeless. I ate only to nurture the child and worried about getting enough protein since I was a vegetarian. My father told me, "You know the nutrients will go to the baby first so you'd better eat well so that you get what *you* need." It's the only time in my life when I considered eating to be a stressful chore.

It was in meditation that I would see my child's essence curling up through the center of my torso. And in my mind's eye I saw that the child had a quality so like Steve that I felt sure I was having a boy. The sex of the child seemed to make all the difference to Kobun, who by this time was becoming a dramatic caricature of himself. He told Steve that he should do more to help me because, he exclaimed, "What if it's a boy?" Little by little Kobun made it clear that, for him, a male child would be of more value. And by association, so would I.

This piqued my attention. The idea that boys and men are more valuable than girls and women is not something I could ever believe. And so in this way the dialogue that ensued about the sex of the child allowed me to see more clearly and brought up the lights on what Kobun and Steve really believed. To me this was something I imagined might be a perception in a country oppressed by fundamentalist religion, but not in a tolerant American society. If this was what they believed, then we disqualified each other; I wasn't in their club and they weren't in mine. If I had to put words to how I felt at that time, they would be, "My God, I am bigger than these two shysters." Steve as boy-wonder genius and Kobun as unfathomable Zen master were promoting a concept of reality that I was deeply stunned by for its total lack of moral vision.

Worse yet, when Kobun would say, "What if it's a boy?" Steve would smile with a big secret confidence and say, "I'm not worried. It's not a boy." I felt incredulous at their little society, and I used it to finally purchase a stark independence for myself.

But who wants independence when she's pregnant?

That spring Kobun taught a meditation retreat in Cloverdale. I signed up and ate well. The kitchen had the sweetest fresh milk from local cows. I drank cups and cups of it with honey and fresh homemade Tassajara bread with butter. The sesshins were a place of rest even though it was a big deal for me to keep my spine straight, given how much physical and emotional pressure I was under. At one of the lectures I remember that Kobun talked about a spiritual kind of logic saying, "To say 'No' is to go higher and to say 'Yes' is to go deeper." He also went on to tell people that tilting your head to left means "yes," and to the right means "no." My dyslexia often makes it hard for me to remember left from right so it could have been the other way around, but what I do recall is that suddenly Kobun burst out laughing and in front of the whole group said, "Chrisann, your 'yes' is everyone else's 'no.'" I took the warning. He was basically saying I had separated myself from the tribe, the sangha, the collective. Basically, he was saying I was on my own.

I drove home with Kobun after that sesshin. There were three of us in the car and we were to drop off the first person, a woman, in the hills around Sebastopol, and then Kobun and I would drive back to Los Altos together. When we stopped to let her off, she invited us into her place before heading home. Kobun accepted. We had tea. Within a short time the two of them had lit up a joint and were smoking some marijuana. I did not join them because I was pregnant. I sat at a distance, smelling the burning marijuana and watching them through a bluish haze.

Kobun told the woman, "Never let anyone who is not enlightened come on your land," at which the woman pointed at me and said, "Well she's not enlightened!" They then talked about me in third person as if I weren't there. I felt bad. The woman had been nice up until that point, so didn't understand the shift. Kobun replied with something like, "Well, she is with me, so it is okay," and then he told the woman how much his mother-in-law would love this marijuana, which the woman had grown herself. Might he bring some back to her? The woman opened a big container and generously raked leaves and buds into a big plastic bag, careful not to break up the dried clusters. She gave him a lot, but Kobun asked for more, and more again. I watched the whole thing with uneasiness because the way he pushed beyond her already generous gift wasn't right. Not to mention that I was stunned, too, to think that his children's grandmother smoked marijuana. She was just a perky, wrinkled, little white-haired old lady with an edge. I couldn't imagine her stoned. It seemed sacrilegious. (My parents were way too fifties to have even considered smoking grass, and for once, by contrast Kobun's behaviors looked childish to me compared to my parents.) Things were becoming clearer.

Eventually it was time to get back on the road and as we were walking to the car, Kobun pointed to a hawk wheeling high up in the sky and told the woman, "Whenever you see an eagle or a hawk flying overhead on your land, you are to know that this is me watching over you and your land." I could see that the woman was beginning to wonder if Kobun wasn't just a bit of a cad, interested in self-promotion to an attractive lady. Kobun had said in a couple of lectures that his wife called him a playboy, and now I was wondering about it, too. I felt embarrassed for both of them.

Finally Kobun and I set out for the drive back to the Peninsula, a two-hour sojourn if we didn't run into traffic. But when we got to the top of the forested hill on the dirt road that led back to the highway from the woman's cabin, Kobun stopped the car and got out and looked back to where the woman lived and laughed out loud, slapping his thighs with both hands, saying, "I have stolen from her! I am a thief!" He laughed and laughed and repeated proudly that he had stolen from her. This was very like the spiritual teachers of the seventies: they were full of the merriment of the trickster. For example, Chögyam Trungpa Rimpoche cracked open the veils for new levels of consciousness in the Western mind, but by all accounts, he drank way too much. For a while these teachers had Teflon-like protection. They used their extraordinary capacities to teach, but also to test and social climb. I guess nobody really understood the ethics in this new game plan of East meets West.

I was dumbfounded. Kobun offended my young sense of idealism because I knew none of this was funny or ethical. I had seen him as the pinnacle of uprightness and I had trusted him. I had reserved all my judgments about him and much had turned in favor of my keeping this pregnancy because he had confirmed that it was the right thing to do and that he would help. But who was he really? Here he had not only just smoked marijuana and "stolen" some for his mother-in-law, but he considered it all hilarious.

A visceral sensation hit me; the stakes were so high, and here this guy was just playing games. What's more, he was letting me know it, too. Everything was in such precarious balance for me and my child and my whole being was starting to recognize the truth. Several more of these booms would drop before I truly woke up under the full weight and awareness of my own circumstances. I would be alone. He wasn't going to help me and by his measurement, I was laughable, too. I really did not know what I did not know, but I was getting quite the education.

Steve wanted to control what people thought of him. That's likely why he started to seed people with the notion that I slept around and he was infertile, which meant that this could not be his child. People believed him, I think, because people wanted a hero. Apple was succeeding, and Steve was brilliant, but mine was an old story, and no one really cared about a single mother. A mother who was married, yes. But a single mother? No.

Steve was succeeding in a big way. And he was growing a big personality. But he didn't have the emotional maturity to manage it. I remember going to the Presidio house after I moved out (I needed to pick up a few things that I had left there), when Steve came home in a hurricane of a mood. He ran into his room and slammed the door behind him. I waited a few minutes before going in and asking what was wrong. He was sitting on the floor and motioned with his hand, but never looked at me. Instead he kept his eyes focused on a lit candle on a low table. He stared at the candle so intensely that I knew he was using it as an aid of some sort. The whole scene was odd, my standing there looking at him in silence over my big pregnant belly, watching the contrast between the soft candlelight and the buzz of his vengeful intensity, not knowing what to do. I thought back to the scene when we were nine-

teen and Steve first asked me what I saw in the candle. Maybe everyone in the world knows about this candle technique but I didn't, and
my guess is that he was using a Hindu meditation technique for con-
trolling his infantile outrage. It seemed to work, because the longer he
looked at the flame the more his anger was dispelled. It also seemed like
there was a weird allowance for my presence in the room that night,
too, a negligible disturbance he maybe even wanted, because despite
the hurricane, he did not ask me to leave.

Later that week I met up with a friend at one of my birthing classes
and she told me what had happened to have aggravated him so. Lori
was a secretary at Apple, and when she saw how Steve was behaving toward me, she had offered to be my birth coach. A smart, capable woman
a little bit older than me, she just wanted to help. Lori explained that
Apple had moved to a new building and Steve had slipped in fast and
had taken the best office. It was the corner office full of windows and
high views and so should rightfully have gone to Mike Markkula, Apple's then president. Apparently there were words. I had never represented enough power in opposition to Steve to enrage him like that.
For me it was a new Steve.

Lori was my eyewitness into what I would never have otherwise
seen, bringing a more balanced view to what was really happening with
Steve. Through her I understood that he was just as bad at work as he
was toward me. Lori told me that there was a company-wide meeting
about getting health insurance. During the meeting, Steve kept harp-
ing at the agent who was describing the policy choices, saying to her,
"It's an inferior health insurance company if it doesn't pay for pregnan-
cies if the couple is unmarried." Apparently it went back and forth between the agent and Steve many times until finally, the agent said in
disgust, "If it's your baby and you're a human being, you'll pay the bill."
Lori told me that it finally stopped the repartee because the comment
had hit the bull's-eye in Steve's fancy-pants, tricked-out hypocrisy. If
you didn't know the whole story, this exchange would seem forward-
thinking, heroic even, on Steve's part. But the opposite was true.

Lori had told me another story. On February 24, 1978, Steve's twenty-third birthday, the Apple executives had gotten Steve a huge funeral wreath with a ribbon draped over that said Happy Birthday Steve!!! It was a joke, of course, but Lori said that when Steve walked into the office and saw the funeral wreath in his name he stopped dead in his tracks. He was wide-eyed. Slack-jawed. Skin white as a ghost. I knew this quality in Steve. His response was so personal and dramatic it must have spoken to that big symbolic world inside of him—the closet mystic. Was it a chilling reminder that his life wasn't going to last that long? Lori told me that it choked her up to see it because even though Steve could be so awful, that quality could flip into a kind of extreme vulnerability that made you willing to run and trip over anything to help him be okay.

In the complexity of all he was and all he was becoming, I had always given Steve room to be changeable. I believed in him, as almost everyone did, because some parts of him were so extraordinary that he was always worth the effort. So when I was seven months pregnant and Steve very tenderly asked me, "Would you like to give birth to our child at the Presidio house?" I considered it. Even after everything, I still hoped for decency as the way through. I thought he might have, finally, come to his senses.

But after about three weeks of serious consideration I knew this baby's and my well-being were all my responsibility. I could not risk trusting him. I knew the child's safety made having the birth at his house out of the question. I played it straight and told him, "You know, I've really thought about this but I don't think it's a good idea to have the birth at the Presidio house." I had planned to go on and explain more, but as usual Steve interrupted the flow of real communication: "What are you talking about?" He was indifferent and distracted as if he'd forgotten he'd ever suggested it. Then he said offhandedly, "Oh that, okay, no—not a big deal." The casual response mortified me in the moment, and haunted for me years. Now after all this time, I know that if I had said, "Yes, I would like to have the birth at your house," he would have also asked, "What are you talking about?"

Winning was always losing with Steve. The more he protected himself, the more callous he became. The more callous he became, the more power was within his grasp. The more power he had, the more money he made. The more money he made, the more he was applauded. This equation didn't ever really change—it all just got bigger. Because I had no worldly power, my recourse was to witness. Witnessing would end up being the source of my power.

SEVENTEEN

PERFECTION

I don't think babies should be born in hospitals unless they or their mothers are at risk, but when the birth house I had selected burned down, it looked like a hospital was my only option. I was in my eighth month of pregnancy but oddly confident and calm. This was around the time that Robert and Abha and their children had just returned from India. They were staying at Steve's for a few days before flying to their home in Oregon. That's where I went to visit them, and that's where they saw how Steve's and my relationship had disintegrated. Decent and good people that they were, they invited me to their farm for the birth. I accepted with delight and relief.

Two weeks before the baby was due, I drove to Oregon so I could settle in. Once I got there, Abha and I began the process of finding a midwife and/or an obstetrician. We were looking into adoption, too, as I was still considering that option. We had plenty of time. Or so we thought. I had been warned that having extra energy meant labor was coming and to lay low and save it up for the birth. Nevertheless, when I got my own little boost I decided to bake some bread. It had come on so early—only two days after I had arrived—and was such a subtle boost that the significance was lost to both Abha and me. I drove to the health food store in town to get some flour and the other supplies I would need.

Seventies health food stores were of a different order than the big bright Whole Foods of today. With dark wood and pungent aromas, they seemed like outposts of a changing culture where customers were like adventurers claiming a new frontier. That day I was enjoying my little shopping trip and thinking about the bread I was going to bake, when suddenly I had this odd feeling. I went to the bathroom to discover my plug had broken. This was it! The rush of excitement ran through me like a wild river. I thought I better find a phone and call Abha when, by pure outrageous chance, she walked into the store. I excitedly told her what was happening and we left the store and drove back to the farm in our two cars.

The baby was coming two weeks early and we had nothing in place. But babies don't wait. Abha made a few calls and then we got into her truck and drove back into town to meet some doctors. Every bump produced a contraction. I was in and out of ridiculous levels of pain while we searched for the address of two doctors who had a one-room birthing center in Sheridan. We were interviewing each other—the doctors worked as a team—when a woman walked in whose baby had been born the week before. "These two clowns are great," she told me, and at that all three started joking about how they watched the football game while she was giving birth. Judging from the banter the woman didn't seem to mind. But, I sure did. What kind of woman would have allowed this? I signaled to Abha that it was a no-go. I cut the interview short and we went back to the farm where she called everyone she knew for the name of a suitable midwife.

Robert took it upon himself to call Steve, whose secretary got him a reservation to fly up that night. In the meantime, however, I discovered that if I stayed quietly by myself I could rest without contractions. This gave Robert the impression that I was in false labor. He called Steve to say that he didn't think the birth was imminent, and Steve canceled his reservation. But by 5 p.m., my contractions were coming two and a half minutes apart. Robert called Steve again, but it was too late to get another flight.

By early evening Abha had found a midwife team that was willing to come to the farm. They asked her to have ready a new shower curtain and an unopened bottle of olive oil, home birth basics. By 7:30 the midwives climbed the stairs to my room, where we all introduced ourselves and set up for the evening. Besides the midwives, Abha's friends— about six women with loving faces and warm smiles—came with diapers, baby clothes, a changing table, bouquets of flowers, and candles. It was truly a miraculous coming together. Robert was the only man present and he was photographing the birth, also holding up a mirror so I could see what was happening.

In birthing classes I had been taught to breathe and push, but as my real-life contractions increased that night, this child was coming out so fast that soon it wasn't a matter of pushing, but of stopping the expulsion. I had no idea this was even a possibility. I was starting to panic. "Slow it down!" the head midwife said. But I couldn't. Then she shouted, "Slow it DOWN!" Now I really was panicking. Sensing danger, I searched the women's faces for help. One set of eyes after another. Nothing was helping. I couldn't stop the speed of the delivery, until suddenly I locked into the assistant midwife's eyes and found what I needed. Whole worlds of information passed between us wherein some sensibility in her clicked into me and I suddenly was able to slow everything down. After that the waves of labor moved forward more safely.

Through the mirror I could see the child's head crowning, bigger and bigger. The pain was incredible when suddenly it was over and my baby slipped out into the world. The midwife held her up, turned her carefully, then lay her on my stomach. The women whispered in awe, "Ohhh. It's a girl! It's a girl!" My newborn found her own breath, after which the midwife cut the cord. That's when the world began for my daughter and she began for the world.

I was wonderfully surprised. I could have sworn I was carrying a boy. But in the instant I realized that my child was a girl my heart sang with a flood of pure joy and gratitude. In that blessed moment of recognition I was finally able to acknowledge I had wanted a girl so much that I didn't dare admit it to myself in case it was a boy. A healthy child is a blessing and I'm sure I would have been overjoyed with either a boy or girl, but this was the Christmas I had wanted. Robert wrote down the time of birth on a piece of paper and added the Sanskrit symbols for "Jai Ram," the English equivalent being something like, hallelujah to God on the highest.

May 17, 1978, 10:38.

My daughter looked different than the babies born to my mother and to my friends' mothers. My family had blond-haired newborns with tiny little noses, but this one had such a crop of pitch-black hair with a large distinctive nose. Also, the back of her head was elongated like that of an Egyptian princess. Her fingers, translucent, moved in slow motion, like they were sea anemones. I gave her cheekbones a little massage that first night and watched as she leaned in to it. She liked massages! She weighed all of 7.5 pounds. I both loved and liked her immediately. The midwives asked if there was any chance I'd had a venereal disease and I said "no," so they didn't have to put silver nitrate in her eyes. Hospitals usually carry out this procedure because of the possibility of blinding, but it can mess up the bonding between mother and child because the child is blinded by the drops for a period of about three to five hours. Here my baby could see me and I could not stop looking at her. And throughout it all I kept thinking: *I know nothing!*

Nothing was ever more clear to me than the fact that I didn't know anything about the total perfection of my baby's tiny sweetness. Here I was a new mother with my newborn daughter. And with that realization came the understanding that my own parents must have been the same when I was born. *Oh, they were as I am now—awed and inexperienced.* I knew my child was a hero to have been born to Steve and me. I would watch her sleep in amazement, feeling dismayed and teary. For what purpose did she come into this situation? I never felt sorry for her, just a glowing, true admiration. I knew she was courageous from the first day.

Steve had made a huge deal about his not being sure it was his child. But when Robert, one of his closest friends, looked deeply into her face and said, "Well, she sure has his vibe," I didn't care about the comment one way or another. I was just so dead tired of being called a liar and of the implication that I didn't know who my child's father was, when I'd known and said I'd known all along.

That night, whenever the baby or I made a sound, Robert got up and came inside the doorway to ask, "Are you okay?" and "Is everything okay?" He was so solicitous, so urgent about our welfare. I had torn in the delivery and my nipples felt like screaming fire engines of pain because they were raw from the nursing, but I would assure Robert that everything was fine. I was so surprised by the sense of responsibility and passionate care that this man had toward me and my baby. I could see that he had been deeply affected by her birth, too.

Steve didn't call. Not a word for three days. I was utterly bereft. Outraged, too. I don't know if he was distracted or cowardly or both. Robert called him in the middle of the third day and nailed him for his despicable behavior and it was blessed to hear. Steve had turned into such a golden boy by this time that no one came close to having the personal power and moral authority over him that Robert had. I listened from the guest bedroom with our daughter in my arms. Steve flew up the next day.

He stayed for three days. On the first night he came up the stairs and into the bedroom where I was sitting holding the baby. He sat next to me on the Japanese bed on the floor with our backs leaning up against the wall and I started crying. "I just don't know what I'm going to—" I couldn't even finish my sentence before Steve cut me off. "You're clean and dry, so you're fine!" he said sharply. Then he walked out. This was such an extremely odd response that it startled me out of my fear and sadness. Later I would understand that birth patterns replay over generations. Perhaps the Jobses had said this to Steve. "I was too frightened to love him" were Clara's simple words to me. I can imagine them saying to Steve, "You're clean and dry, so you're fine. . . ." and left him crying. Many adopted kids believe that they deserve only to have their basic needs met. I often felt that this was true of Steve and that, ironically, it had flipped in him and morphed into his enlarged sense of entitlement.

It was different at the Friedlands when Steve was there. He was persuasive and oh so capable of rededicating the emotional territory to the low hum of his negativity—the result of his own irresponsibility. I don't know what he may have said to Abha and Robert, but I felt that when Steve arrived he brought a cloud of darkness with him. It turned out to have been a very good thing that he had not been present at the birth.

It was on Steve's last day that Abha pushed us both outside: "You two have to decide on a name for this child. She's already six days old!" So Steve and I walked out into the fields that surrounded their house and laid out a blanket. We sat under an open sky with a baby name book and our sleeping child between us. Steve liked the name Claire. It seemed like he had arrived ready to suggest it. I didn't want it. Claire was too close to his mother's name and I wasn't going to honor her in this way.

"They *are* different names, you know?" he said gently.

But I couldn't go along with him. "They're close enough to be the same, so there's no way."

We continued to look through the book. We both really thought "Sarah" was lovely, but my sister had just given that name to her little one, born six months before. We went through a lot of names and nothing seemed quite right until finally I remembered a name from high school I had always liked.

"How about Lisa?" I suggested. This name seemed so bright and beautiful I could hardly speak the words fast enough.

Steve said, "Oh yes!! I like that!"

We looked up the meaning and found "Light of God." We liked this, too. Eventually we settled on Nichole for a middle name. "Nichole" has a smooth sense of classic, time-honored beauty, and this fit our child.

Even as a newborn, she was truly beautiful.

Lisa Nichole Brennan.

And later, Lisa Nichole Brennan-Jobs.

Over the next month, when I started to doubt our choice of name, I discovered that Steve was extremely attached to keeping "Lisa." This was especially strange because he was also publicly denying paternity. The inconsistencies were really too much to keep up with, but I was too exhausted to do anything but adapt. Daniel Kottke called and told me I ought to get some money out of the name because Steve would pay to keep it. He knew more than he was letting on, but I considered the concept of leveraging money to keep my daughter's name distasteful in the extreme. I had no idea that Steve was naming a computer The Lisa.

Later I understood that he had wanted to name our daughter Claire not because, as I had thought, it was close to his mother's name, but because he wanted to name the next Apple model "The Claire Computer." The idea here was to project some kind of idealized feminine saint in association with Apple and himself because he fancied himself another St. Francis. St. Claire is considered the patron saint of TV in Italy because she had visions. While on the one hand it feels unexpected to connect a saint's particular gifts to technology, it's sort of perfect, too. St. Claire was a cloistered nun and a clairvoyant with a capacity for "remote viewing," so in a way the camera, the TV, the computer, and the smartphone really are perfect associations. Taken a step further, if people didn't have the extraordinary vision and intuition to see the future, then this technology could never have been created. Visions have been around way before technology. And yet visions helped pave the way for technology itself. The Claire would have been just a fabulously great name for Steve's computer. He should have used it.

It was Steve's weird fantasy to try to merge biology, mythology, and technology, as if such things don't have laws of their own. It would seem he was trying to graft everything together for commercial purposes, and also to strengthen his own idealized mythos. Who knows, perhaps he was even attempting to compete with me by trying to birth something in a parallel universe where biology is equal to technology. A computer equal to a child? This made me think of all the men who had tried to infuse life into inanimate objects: Geppetto and his Pinocchio. The Tyrell Corporation and its Replicants. Frankenstein.

Why Steve wanted to use our newborn's name, while denying paternity and dishonoring and abandoning both of us, was a question I couldn't answer then. The truth was so horrific it was sort of good at the time that I couldn't see everything that was in play. To be clear, Steve didn't have my permission to use our daughter's name for his computer. And he never asked. He just appropriated the name Lisa and, like so many other things, hid it under the radar of my comprehension. I later understood that Regis McKenna had his team work with Steve to come up with a suitable acronym. Steve claimed at the time that it meant "Local Integrated Software Architecture." But we both knew the truth. All this monstrous chaos would extend further when Markkula at Apple took Steve off of The Lisa to put him on the team to develop the Mac. Steve then competed against The Lisa, eventually killing it.

During the month I stayed at the Friedlands' house I still hadn't ruled out the possibility of putting my child up for adoption. I felt a love toward my child that was both tender and fierce, and I didn't imagine that giving her up for adoption would be easy. But I wanted the best life possible for her, even if that meant a life apart from me. Abha and her friend took me to visit a woman in the area who was the head of an adoption agency, and while we walked around the woman's home she told us her story. She said that she had given birth to two children who were fully grown but she and her husband had gone on to adopt seventeen others. Seventeen! She had adopted many babies and kids who were harder to place. Kids who were considered too old, who had special needs or were mixed race. One child had not been placed because of a birth defect. Another, from Vietnam, ran crying whenever he heard an airplane overhead because he had seen his family and his whole village bombed to smithereens. Each child had a story.

This woman and her husband had built separate dorms for the girls and the boys in their house, which were painted chalky pink and blue with little bunk beds. I was glassy-eyed to see this wonder and happy that the children had their home and each other. But meeting this woman didn't bring any clarity to me about whether to put Lisa up for adoption. I knew that Steve would hate me for the rest of my life if I gave Lisa up for adoption, but I was checking out all the possibilities. Kobun's words seemed less and less of a gold standard as time passed. It seemed possible that Steve would hate me but what drove me on at this point was, of course, more about love for my daughter and what would be best for her. I thought it was odd for Kobun to have framed things through the idea of Steve's importance and his hatred. It was a manipulation below his station. I don't recall Kobun ever advising me for my well-being. Or my daughter's. It was always all about Steve.

In the Bay Area I had gone to an adoption agency when I was about seven months along. The head of the agency had talked with me in her office saying, "You have no right to keep this child because you have no way to take care of a baby and you don't seem mature enough. Look at yourself," she demanded. "You are not capable of managing this!" She was incensed.

I like people who say what they really think even when it is difficult to hear, and I later went back to continue the conversation with her. However, on the second visit I was told there had been an emergency and that I had to see someone else. Disappointed, I went to the information desk to schedule an appointment with another counselor when I saw the head of the agency carrying a tiny newborn baby on her arm. She looked like a speed walker, rushing down the hallway and curving swiftly before she ducked into a small room and out of sight. The dewy-eyed child's head was planted in the woman's palm, and its legs straddled over her forearm with the diapered bottom against her elbow at her hip. I wondered why she didn't hold the child to her heart. Then about four women came running after her like a gaggle of geese. They looked like a cartoon of self-important little busybodies. I felt I was seeing through the curtain into the gap that divided the birth mother and the adoptive mother and I didn't like it. Since that time adoption practices have developed to humanize the process in the same way that birthing practices have been humanized, but back then my head swam in sorrow for the child and in protection for my own. I found myself as judgmental of that woman as she had been of me. Funny how that works.

I made another appointment with a new counselor at the same agency. This woman was much younger than the head. She seemed clearer and more respectful in her approach with me. She didn't have a preconceived judgment about what I should do, and her questions were so astute that I finally felt that I could, with her help, work out my next steps. I felt she could help me understand what it would mean to me and my baby to adopt or to be a single parent. She was a gifted counselor.

My relief was enormous. This woman had a clarifying effect on me. I could focus in her presence. I knew she could help me, step by step, to get through this process in a coherent way. I was hopeful and happy when I set up a second appointment, but she called to tell me that she had decided to leave the agency to be with her own kids. I pleaded with her; wasn't there some way that she could still work with me? She had been so unusually helpful and I knew no one like her. She reluctantly gave me her home number. Yet within a month's time I found there was no way to schedule consistently. She was busy with her kids and kept canceling. The one person that I'd found to help me think it through fell out and away beyond my reach.

After a month at Robert and Abha's house, I was becoming a strain in their lives. It would have been too much for anyone. Their house wasn't that big, so Robert ordered a teepee so we would all have our space. It was truly generous of them to say I could stay on their property, and I tried to imagine living in a teepee with a newborn. But my sister

Kathy called when she heard about it: "You need running water, a kitchen, and a washer and dryer near at hand. Please come down and live with us for a while." She and her husband and their child had a home with enough space for Lisa and me. I knew it was the right next step.

When I drove back to the Bay Area on my way to Idyllwild, I shared the driving with a woman who was traveling around with a tape recorder interviewing people who had been close to the guru Neem Karoli Baba. She was collecting stories for his biography and had come to Robert's house to interview him. Robert and she were old guru buddies and she was a savvy earth mother type, impressive for all the right reasons. It was good to drive with her. A few years later *Miracle of Love: Stories about Neem Karoli Baba* would be on bookstore shelves. Remarkably, it was on the way up to Oregon for Lisa's birth that I gave a ride to Ken Kesey's secretary. I had serendipitously traveled with two women, up and back, carrying small tape recorders who were directly connected to two significant counterculture influences of our time. What are the odds!

I stopped over for two weeks on the SF Peninsula on my way south. I didn't stay at my father's house because his wife was concerned about "the baby peeing on the furniture." So I stayed with Bert and Betty Wilder whose children, Dave and Camille, had gone to school with my sisters and me. Steve came by to see Lisa and me during my stopover. He was used to people not liking him, but he managed to come when the Wilders were out doing errands and so avoided their glares. Not that he ever cared much; it was more of an issue for me that he was so disliked.

That day Steve asked me if we could go for a walk, so I strapped Lisa to my front. And within fifty feet of the Wilder's front door Steve's body slumped in wild agony. His head hung down in shame. He was deeply sincere. He looked at me from an oblique angle and said with a heavy, heavy heart, "I am really sorry. I'll be back, this thing with Apple will be over when I'm about thirty. I am really, really sorry." A promise to be back in six years moved through my body like a deep, aching river. Everything in me wanted to hear him say this. This was the most real I had seen him in a very long time. It was the first decent response to what had been happening for almost a year. I felt strengthened by his acknowledgment, disarmed.

Yet in the next ten seconds and four steps, Steve lit himself up in a super cartoony way and began to tell me about a flowering tree that was in his front yard and how beautiful it was. I observed the emotional roller coaster and watched his crazed showmanship. Here was the inspired maniac. At a loss for any words that could possibly matter, I managed to say, "STEVE, I lived at that house, you know I—lived—at—that—house. I know what the goddamn tree looks like. Why are you talking like this?"

He responded with a glossy sigh.

It was all so strange, this weird loss of memory. It was as if Steve had created a fictional state in which he didn't have to concern himself with responsibility or reality, as if simply not remembering could give him a way out. This odd behavior seemed to me to be all about a lack of connection and an inability to string together shared experiences that made him somehow unique. His sentimentality and inspiration gave him no-stick accountability. It was a way out. Disconnecting from the simple shared experience of the flowering crape myrtle tree that grew in front of the house that we shared, he was in essence telling me that my experience didn't count for him: that Lisa and I did not count, that he did not recount, and that he was not accountable. And that was the point.

Kobun used the same methods. During the two-week window of my being in the Bay Area before leaving for my sister's house, there was a night that my father and his wife took care of Lisa so that I could go to the Zendo for the Wednesday night meditation. I had not seen Kobun since Lisa had been born, although he had called a day after her birth to express his best wishes. At the Zendo that night I practiced the forty minutes of sitting zazen and then listened to the lecture and had tea. When it was all over and everyone was outside putting their shoes on, Kobun asked me if I would be coming to the next Zen retreat that was in about two weeks. My jaw dropped. Who would leave a five-week-old baby to sit a meditation retreat? He had young children at home—how could he possibly think I would leave a newborn for seven days? My mind raced and I felt a weak breathlessness, but I managed only the obvious: "I have Lisa to take care of." My heart felt like it was contracting with his betrayal. He didn't ask how Lisa was or how it was going for me. It was as if the last nine months hadn't happened. I looked at him closely to make sure he knew who he was talking to. But it was like the many dreams I'd had about him, where he held a mildly frozen smile with what seemed like an intentional fog over his eyes. Here it was again, the refined aesthetic of the misty cloud-covered mountain peak. It was pure irreproachable indifference. After all that Kobun had offered, it turned out that in the end, he would never be helpful to me in any way—not memory, not money, not babysitting, not food, not even a baby gift, and not in defense of me and Lisa with Steve.

The truth is I think Kobun taught Steve how to be unaccountable.

Lisa must have been twelve when we met up with Kobun again. It was at Steve's Woodside house, where she and I had gone for a swim. From the time that Lisa was eight until she was about thirteen, Steve and I had what was, for us, a relatively decent balance in our working together. I had kept the door open and when Steve got kicked out of Apple he did find his way into falling in love with Lisa and returning to a friendship with me. It was never easy between us, but it was workable and sometimes very enjoyable. We would share birthday parties, major holidays, dinners, and some NeXT events. Mostly it was like family downtime, with the significant people in our lives.

At Woodside that day I discovered that Kobun had moved into Steve's house with his girlfriend, Stephanie. They had come from Taos, New Mexico, where, according to Stephanie, they had one bathroom to ten people. At the Woodside house it was more like ten bathrooms to one person. Steve was living in Palo Alto at this time, so Kobun and Stephanie had the whole place to themselves. They sort of took care of it, too.

When we got out of our car, Kobun walked over to us across the huge green lawn from the big backyard. He had on his beautiful traditional Japanese "casual" clothing. I was always curious about how Kobun dressed because there was such beauty to it. His informal wear was what he worked and relaxed in, and that day I noticed that he had leather shoes on, too. Normally, when I saw him, he wore his formal Japanese robes and had the crisp white socks with a tailored indent between the toes so he could fit perfectly into his sandals. I could tell that the leather shoes were very old but had been beautifully cared for and shined for years. Kobun knew how to take care of things and had a rich sense for things themselves, something I had very much enjoyed and admired about him.

On that sunny afternoon we greeted each other with wide smiles. It was always special to be around Kobun and I was surprisingly happy to see him after all these years. Standing there talking, I remembered to tell Kobun that Lisa had been studying Japanese. I thought he would be delighted to hear this because he, of course, had a deep abiding love of his country and language. Kobun's eyes opened when I told him and he turned to Lisa and said, "Since you can speak Japanese, you can be my secretary." I was standing about five feet away when it registered that Kobun had made this proud determination, this opportunity to serve the worthy master. But for me it was as if Beelzebub had reached for my daughter's hand. The thought of this man and his notions influencing Lisa caused my psyche to blow. The implications were clear.

Lisa would be nobody's secretary, least of all this guy's. And though I didn't want to be rude to Kobun (in fact, hated to be so), there was no way I would let him anywhere near my daughter. And no way would I smile and pretend it was okay. Taking a giant step between then, I said, "I am sorry. Lisa will absolutely never be your secretary!" I was smiling as I said this, but I was intense. Neither Lisa nor Kobun acknowledged what I had said, they just ended their conversation as nicely as it had begun—as if I had said nothing, as if I wasn't standing awkwardly between them. Lisa, at twelve, was often mad at me for embarrassing her, but this time she never said a word.

Within a month Lisa and I were again visiting Steve's Woodside house and I saw that Kobun had set up a large multilevel altar with pictures of all of Steve's relatives. Here he had draped beautiful cloth on some long boards, and placed candles and incense cups and bells around the framed images of family members. I didn't look closely at the photographs because I felt it was private. At the moment, it was enough to grasp the broad stroke of an ancestor's altar in the cavernous living room.

I remember being surprised by the number of photographs on the table because I wondered who all the people could have been. I never knew Steve to have a big family because I had never met, and rarely, if ever, heard about grandparents or aunts and uncles. Maybe these were people who had died. I wondered about Clara and Paul and Steve's biological mother and father. I wondered about who was included and who was excluded. To me, that altar implicated the wiggy rat's nest at the heart of all Steve's complexes.

I knew it was intended to honor the ancestors and the living relatives but it felt embarrassingly large and cluttered and very unlike Steve. My first impression was of generosity; that Steve gave Kobun the room to be and act as Kobun. But, I also felt a bit scandalized because I felt it was gross with a sense of pandering. It was just a feeling I had about it but it was clear and strong. Was Patty Jobs on the table? And what about Lisa? Would she be honored in the panoply of hosts and decedents? Steve had a designer's concept of DNA whereby he insisted on picking and choosing family and identity as might fit his moods. Because once he had made himself into one of the most sought-after men of the centuries, he could be precious and despotic about who was in and who was out. And *when* they were in and out. I've wondered if Kobun had adapted that altar to fit Steve's charade or if Kobun used it to needle him. I regret that I hadn't looked at it more closely.

●   ●   ●

There was another evening that year, in mid-October, when I again saw Kobun at the Woodside house. There were a number of us for dinner: Lisa; Kobun; Kobun's girlfriend, Stephanie; Steve; Steve's girlfriend, Tina; Steve's sister, Mona; and my boyfriend, Ilan Chabay. Steve's cooks had created a sublime ravioli made from wheat ground that day, and just-picked garden vegetables for the stuffing. It was a dinner that melted in the mouth, and the setting itself was so old-world beautiful, with at least twenty squat candles of different shapes and sizes lighting the long wooden table. This was Tina's artistry, I was sure.

After the meal everyone lingered at the table over water and wine. A gentle fire flickered in the huge fireplace and we were all enjoying the deep fall and the chilly promise of winter in the air. It was then that Kobun threw out a number of testing insults at Steve, like the old wife. My nerves jangled with the breach. Kobun was a teacher and a guest. Why this offense? A tenuous discomfort permeated the room. Steve held his tongue. Kobun, glinting and sly, sent out several more demeaning little remarks. He wasn't behaving like a master who saw through everything and spoke on behalf of the group; rather he was speaking like someone who had been jilted, ignored, and cast off. It looked to me like Kobun was using the persona of the Zen master to settle a personal score.

I don't remember Kobun's exact comments except one—something about making a computer being no different than growing a bigger potato. I had by this time heard the analogy twice, the first time in one of his lectures, and both times wondered if I was missing something. It would be like Kobun to expand out into simplicity so profound that it sounded weak and stupid. He was trying to put Steve in his place, but it wasn't working.

Later that night I talked about it with Tina when we snuck off to share a cigarette together. She had seen it, too. We discovered that both of us had witnessed the same behaviors on several other occasions, separate from one another. Neither of us liked it. We felt it was degrading for everyone within hearing. At home that evening I spoke about it with my boyfriend, and he said, "Yes, and did you notice also that Kobun never directly answered a single question anyone put to him?" Ilan, a scientist with a Ph.D. in physics, had taken his contact lenses out and was eyeing me through Coke-bottle glasses to see if I understood how obvious it was—and how serious.

If my life has been about studying power abuse, then this night watching Kobun and Steve was truly the night of all nights of my erudition. Kobun, acting out of blinding pain, had not resolved his issues with Steve and so had addressed them in a group setting. Kobun was drinking too much during this time, and there were stories. I also noticed he was extremely disregarding of his girlfriend, Stephanie, that night and in general. She, an accomplished musician, acted ditzy, as if she couldn't think for herself around him. This behavior was not unlike what I had fallen into right after I got pregnant with Lisa when I couldn't think for myself. Whatever on earth Steve and Kobun had going, that night it had risen up between the two of them.

Here was the teacher with a capacity for insight way beyond all of us, and yet he had stepped out of impeccability. For what? And why wasn't Steve more loyal to Kobun? I didn't particularly admire either of them by this time. Later I understood that Steve was jealous of Kobun's capacities, and that he didn't want to share the spotlight. For his part, Kobun had taught Steve many things, one of which was to ignore people. Steve turned that teaching back on Kobun, and Kobun was not happy about it. So it all started with Kobun.

That evening, observing Kobun's behaviors, I had the feeling of being angry with him on behalf of Steve, his host and most excellent student. But within hours I thought better of it. The chewy hidden center inside both Kobun's and Steve's power was never something I could stand up for, because both regularly exploited people. So when it came down to the two of them, Steve won by doing nothing and owning everything, as Kobun spun out of control with challenges that had all the impact of a spitwad blown from the lofty heights of the peanut gallery.

I was living in Paris in August 2002 when I received an e-mail from a friend telling me that Kobun had died a sudden and tragic death. In a bizarre accident, Kobun's young daughter from his second family had fallen into a lagoon while he was giving a retreat on the property of one of his students in Switzerland. Someone rushed in to tell him she had fallen into the water and Kobun immediately ran out of the building to jump into the lagoon to save her. From what I understand, they were found four hours later downstream, the child wrapped in his robes, both dead. No one in any world would want such a thing to happen, but I do wonder if in the struggle to save his own beloved little girl's life, Kobun came to recognize the value of a daughter?

EIGHTEEN

THE REALITY DISTORTION FIELD

Idyllwild, California, is tucked away in the San Jacinto Mountains, just above the Palm Springs desert. A quaint resort town with a small-town feel, "Mile-high Idyllwild" has a couple of private art schools and a summer music festival. The local newspaper is called the *Town Crier* and the residents once elected a golden retriever to the position of mayor. I was relieved to arrive there with baby Lisa in June of 1978, and not just because the air was high-altitude fresh and the town had a creative hub-bub. I was there to be with family, and family was what I needed.

My sister Kathy picked me up from the Palm Springs airport with her husband, Mark, and their baby, six-month-old Sarah. My father and his wife drove my car and theirs with all my things, which included a small English-style crib for Lisa that they had found through the want ads. It felt good to arrive at Kathy and Mark's home, a wonderful 1930s state-built home for the forestry department service people. (Kathy was a ranger and her husband was a forest firefighter, and a writer, too.) Kathy's house had that particular kind of clean, well-cared-for look that comes after years of good maintenance. Their neighborhood was in the middle of town, a beautiful spacious area with large grassy lawns, outdoor clotheslines, and covered porches. It was like Mayberry.

Kathy and I are half sisters and nothing alike, but our natures are complementary and we've enjoyed a rich, collaborative friendship throughout the years. The five months that Lisa and I lived with Kathy and her family were full. We shared our great enjoyment of cooking—and eating, of course—and every evening, after the children were fed, we'd have engaging conversations over sit-down dinners with Mark.

But I had long days by myself when everyone was at work. I was depressed, in shock, really, from the events of the past year so I just sort of floated as I cared for my little baby. There had been so many terrible incidents with Steve; the sheer number of them seemed to indicate that I deserved to be treated badly. I knew in my heart that I didn't, but at the time I lacked the knowledge that a man who treats a woman badly is simply out of integrity with all life. Now I believe that my whole life has been about the work of understanding not just this, but how love is bigger than cruelty. Back then I felt shattered and numb by Steve's contempt and abandonment.

I tried to hold everything together, to understand my emotional life, and get organized to make things happen, but it was all too much and the ground was falling in under me. It was like I was living a life on several levels and struggling to come to terms with each one. I was tuned in to the immediacy of daily life with Lisa's little sweetness and her back-to-back needs, trying to understand whether I should place her for adoption. Nothing was more important than working through this. Besides this I was coping with the dynamics of living with my sister, and dealing with past issues connected to our mother. Then there were the larger issues having to do with Steve, and what he was and was not doing. Pressing in on all of this was the fact that I had precious little money.

I took care of Lisa's needs. That came first, of course. I loved her and loved playing with her. We would cuddle and I would hold her close to me. I enjoyed her sweetness, but there was no way I could tell how my own unhappiness affected her. My days were filled with dullness, dread, and delight—the three *D*s that constantly darkened me and lit me up. Kathy worked during the weekdays. When Mark wasn't out fighting fires for the national parks (he could be away for weeks at a time), he'd either be writing at home or at the library, or working out at the gym. Sarah went to a babysitter during the week, and I'd putter about at home with Lisa, and also walk around town with her strapped to my front in a baby cozy.

In the evenings, Kathy and I made dinner together while the children sat side by side in little seats that we had placed on top of a big chest in the kitchen. These seats put the babies' eyes just above the level of the countertop so they could take in what we were doing. Talking, laughing, and playing music while we made dinner we'd sometimes pick the children up and dance. Because they were different ages they balanced their bodies differently when we danced with them. Sarah used a swimming motion to readjust her self so that she was always perpendicular to the floor at every move. But Lisa was so tiny that I'd cradle her in my arms—holding her closely and then outstretching my arms to sweep her around the room. I held her head stable when I did this, and she would flow with the movement and look around in twinkling wonder. "Twinkling wonder" pretty much described Lisa at this time.

When Mark came home he'd join in the mix, sort of like a friendly, visiting dignitary. Mark said that he was going to be the next great American novelist and I, for one, believed it. I still have never met anyone as intelligent as that man, nor do I recall knowing anyone who read as much as he did. Mark read books by the foot, covering a vast array of subjects. He just ate them up, claiming that a true intellectual doesn't have preconceived notions about what is important, but is interested in anything and everything on its own terms. I loved this information and like many of the things he said, it has served me well over the years because I really like the idea that everything is worthy when you know how to look at it.

Mark brought home some great science fiction books during the time I was there and they left their stamp on my imagination. I still wonder as to the plights of the characters in those futuristic scenarios.

Also tucked into my memories of those days were his arriving home and playing the first Bruce Springsteen album I'd ever heard, *Darkness on the Edge of Town*. Was I surprised by that music.

Springsteen wrote songs that were evocative of an earlier America, yet heralded a new vision into the future at the same time. Songs like "Candy's Room," "Racing in the Street," and "The Promised Land" contained within them a passion for an America coming of age and for American life. The ache and vibrancy in these songs is so alive that it turned me inside out with a kind of urgency I had never felt before. After the Vietnam War, which for many in the sixties and seventies was synonymous with the betrayal by American leadership of Americans *and* the world, I was struck by Springsteen's love of country. Fresh, and beyond any false nationalistic sentimentality, his were the songs of the dream and promise of America, sung back into the blood of youth. Give that man a medal.

If weekdays in Idyllwild were about domestic life, weekends were about the great outdoors. Saturday and Sundays we'd all hike in the hills with our children strapped to us—Sarah on Mark or Kathy's back and Lisa on my front. Kathy knew the best trails, being a ranger, and we'd walk together under the pines, smelling their resin in the light fresh air while trekking deeper into the woods. We followed the most beautiful paths next to rivers, and up onto rock outcroppings. There, under brilliant clear blue skies, we'd enjoy the views over the top of the deep dark evergreen forests to the distant horizons. Having small children is about being in small warm spaces, but this was its opposite and I'd hold Lisa's little face cupped in my hand as I walked and she'd seem very content. I could tell that she liked it when I was happy because she would look up into my face and mirror my excitement.

Life could be bright and interesting when I lived at Kathy and Mark's, but there were no real conversations about what I was going through. We were, each of us, under thirty, and my situation was over everyone's head. How could they understand? My life was so out of balance that I must have seemed like a sinkhole to a lot of people and so we just stayed at the surface of it all.

I wish I'd had a therapist to help me mine the darkness, but that was beyond my resources. So I got up every morning and worked my way through the days without design, except to care, hoping something out of the ordinary would happen, something to move me into a happy flow so I could forget what I was so alone in grappling with. It was at this time that I bought a handbook of crystal identification at the local bookstore. I had so little money that it really was an extravagance, but I had to have it.

The book contained photographs and precise drawings of naturally occurring and idealized crystal formations, along with descriptions as to where the crystals could be found on and in the earth. I just loved this book, and would pore through the pictures to look at all the crystalline shapes that were so beautiful and perfect. As a child I had always had gorgeous rock collections and so I suppose that studying these pages was an extension of that original love of the mineral world. But it was different, too, because looking at the idealized geometric shapes offered me something strong and beautiful, something more than the day-to-day difficulty that I felt. The artist in me couldn't get enough of looking at them. But as I realize now, it was at this time when I felt buried by Steve's negative versions of who I was, that the shapes and the way the crystals caught the light reminded me of natural bright elegance and wholeness—the poetics of inspired survival. Indeed they were a precursor to the artwork I would begin to do right as Lisa left for college.

During the days in Idyllwild I loved to watch Lisa and the little searching movements of her nose and hands and feet. She was like the movement of water at its surface: perfect wiggly contentment. People watch fires and TV and even aquariums but a baby's face? I had no idea that her endlessly nuanced expressions would be such a constant draw for me. Sometimes I would hold her upside down by her little legs because I had discovered how she delighted in seeing her environment from different angles. Her cheeks would fall around her eyes and she would have the most sublime smile as her head turned slowly to marvel at the upside-down world. Like me, she enjoyed variety and movement.

I'd also sing to her—made-up songs and musical scales—and I'd repeat words and sentences in a singsong way to keep us connected and amused. For her part, Lisa would gurgle sweet babbly baby noises that sounded to me like the equivalent of an abstract painting, having all the colors but no real form you could understand. Until, one day, to my utter astonishment, I realized that her sounds weren't arbitrary. She was imitating every word, song, and tonal repetition with absolute precision. Suddenly her world opened up to me and I understood that she heard and repeated everything I shared with her. This mother and daughter call-and-response pulled the shades off my sadness every time. It was a wonder to me that my tiny baby could pick up so much and then turn it back around and talk to me with it. This is where the everyday mundane suddenly became magical. I had a magical child.

The one thing she didn't repeat was this gravelly sound I made at the back of my throat when I got her out of bed or changed her diapers. I only kept making this sound because she was so amazed by it. She would look at me with laughter in her eyes, and she'd be riveted. It was as if this was the most remarkable sound in all existence and she was really impressed with me for being able to do it. I mean *really impressed,* as if I had insider knowledge and was passing the codes of the universe on to her. And who knows, maybe I was.

The first time Lisa smiled at me she was three months old and it broke out in thousands of rays like sunshine over a new world. Things were moving forward.

For Halloween that year I came up with costume ideas for my sister, her husband, and myself. I love to come up with costumes that express a person's essence. While I don't sew them, I tuck, fold, rip, cut, paste, pin, and tie materials into place. I was happy and breathless doing this, my hands moving in advance of my thinking. It was pure play. We had so much fun that day and Mark and Kathy kept saying, "Gawd, you really should be making a living at this." I made Mark into the black and white man with the golden tear, an image I connected with Steve. They were quite alike, Mark and Steve. Both were off all charts intelligent, angst-ridden, and dramatic. Mark started with a top hat, but I did the rest by adding a cape, and painting a black-and-white checkerboard on his face. A golden tear at the corner of his eye was the finishing touch. I made my sister into a nun, a Mother Superior with massive folds of mauve and white cloth that she had around the house. She wore no makeup at all. As for me, I painted my face white and covered myself with a transparent mosquito net. I was a ghost. No kidding, right?

We drove to the party leaving our children with my sister's babysitter, a caring, trustworthy woman who had children of her own. This was the first time I had given over my daughter's care to anyone outside the family, having only left Lisa once with my dad and his wife for a couple of hours, and with my sister now and then to go to the store. It revived me immeasurably to be able to go out, and that Halloween I felt the blessed helium of my freedom. Shy from having been so homebound, I hesitated in finding my way into party mode, but with all the corn chips and salsa, the sangria and the music—with all the dancing and laughter—I was just starting to have fun when the babysitter arrived with Lisa beet red and splotchy from nonstop crying. The sitter had tried calming her for three hours without success. And since no one at the party was answering the phone, she eventually drove Lisa to me. Lisa bawled even harder when she was handed to me, because my face was unrecognizable covered in white paint and netting. So Kathy held her as the Mother Superior that night and Lisa finally stopped crying. Oh, the will of her, to cry for three hours straight! Up till then I'd never let her cry for over a minute or two. It broke my heart to see her in such distress, but Mark repeatedly reassured me that there had to be a history of hurtful repetitions before a child could be scarred. He kept saying, "Babies are resilient. She's really, really, really okay."

●   ●   ●

When you have a baby, you need resources. Since babies are physical, you need physical resources. But when I mentioned the need for money to Steve and Kobun, they both responded as if I were a nuisance, a buzzing bee bothering and below them. It's hard to fully describe the effect they had on me because they spoke with silence—by ignoring me—more often than with language. But I remember.

I had been in Idyllwild about six weeks when Daniel Kottke called. He told me, among other things, that a number of people were asking Steve why he wasn't just giving me any money, and Steve apparently was saying, "She doesn't want money, she just wants me."

I was overwhelmed when I heard this—especially because even Daniel, who should have known better, seemed willing to believe it. How could they be so wrong? The realities of nursing and caring for my small baby took all my time and attention. And the lack of every kind of resource made me depressed. In the mix of this and more, Steve was very low on the totem pole of my personal wants. I was insensible to that kind of longing then; my nervous system was so battered in response to Steve's meanness that I was too closed down to even think about him in such terms.

Later I wondered if Steve was offended that I wasn't pining for him. It certainly would be typical of him to make statements that ran the direct opposite of the truth. The real truth was that I didn't want to mess up Steve's trajectory because, despite everything, I was excited for him and his potential. I love my own creativity and I extend this kind of joy to others—Steve included, Steve especially. It wasn't about stopping him from where he wanted to go. I just needed money. This was just another of his deluded and distracting comments.

My mind searched to understand this new injustice that was being passed around—that I only wanted Steve. While I was living in the shadows, I was being cruelly examined under the most dishonest light. Steve was somehow making himself out to seem not only desirable, but principled when, in fact, he was saying "No, I am not going to be responsible to my child or her mother."

I had no one in my corner, so I worked hard on being in my own corner. Listless at first, enlisting much later, because it is nearly impossible to do well without a tribe. It would have made a huge difference to Lisa and my happiness and to Steve's well-being had he been held accountable to his humanity. But nobody I ever heard of questioned it. Well, perhaps there was someone. I don't know if it's true, but I was told after the fact that Mike Scott at Apple repeatedly said that Steve should just give me money, while nearly all other top executives advised him to ignore me or fight if I tried to go after a paternity settlement. (Curiously, years later when I painted murals at the Ronald McDonald House in Palo Alto, Mike Scott was the only person from Apple whose name I recognized on the donor tiles.)

It was very hard to imagine and accept that, at a time when I had no voice, Steve was using his against me to silence me further. He even told me and others that, "If I could just help Lisa without helping Chrisann, I would be happy to supply money." This was the beginning of his working to split apart my daughter and me. I think Steve villainized me because, in his twisted logic, he unconsciously believed that if he couldn't have a loving committed mother then he didn't want Lisa to have hers. He wanted Lisa in his club.

Years later, after Steve got kicked out of Apple, he apologized many times over for this behavior. He said that he never took responsibility when he should have, and that he was sorry. He even told me, "It wasn't Kobun's fault. It was all mine." (Hmmm, I always become suspicious when people in positions of power claim to take all responsibility. What does it really mean to say such a thing?) But then Steve also said that he loved how I parented so much, he wished I had been his mother. He was in my kitchen and I had my back to him when he said this, and I thought *Whoa, that's a piece of information.* That day I could see why I was impressive to him. It wasn't that I was a perfect parent. I'm a human being with plenty of foibles. But I learned as Lisa grew to pay close attention to good parenting and teaching, to make sure she was thriving, delighted with life, and truly happy every day.

But Steve's contrition didn't last. He may have appreciated my mothering Lisa eventually, but after he returned to Apple in the nineties, he went on to reenact the same hateful odd behaviors toward me.

Through the years I've watched how Daniel has alternately admired Steve, and felt scandalized by him. I've come to recognize that Daniel and I shared some of the same dynamics as we watched Steve become more impressive. And the most interesting thing to me about Daniel is that he sometimes had the most revelatory insight into Steve's changes.

When I was pregnant and still living at the Presidio house, Daniel came home one day after work and told me, "Steve is winning at work even though he's going against everything I've ever been taught was right and good." Daniel doesn't remember saying this, but I do. In fact, I bet that over the years I've had about ten important exchanges with Daniel, of which he has no memory. Daniel's memory seems to slip between insight and being overly sentimental when it comes to Steve. That particular statement at the Presidio house made a big impact on me, because it was the first time I saw Daniel really trying to figure out what was going on with Steve. Also he repeated it several times.

I listened deeply to Daniel each time he said it, because I could feel his incredulity. Yes, like everyone, Daniel seemed to doubt what he was actually seeing. But then I observed how carefully worded and worked out it was. And I also saw that Daniel had to think down to his core to understand what laws of humanity were being so profoundly trespassed.

He said something about how the ideals of human behavior and good character that his parents and professors at Columbia taught him, and that all great classic art exemplifies, were opposite to the values that are advancing Steve. Daniel was dismayed, and I was impressed because I knew that what he was saying was true and perfectly discerned.

He also said, shaking his head, "It's shocking because the worse he becomes, the more success he achieves." Daniel was watching how Steve operated at work. I, of course, didn't see this part of Steve's life, only how he was behaving toward me. I was always trying to understand

Steve, and to that end looked for whatever wisdom about him others had. I had no words or logic for how horrible he was increasingly becoming. All I knew was that Steve wasn't acting the way people were supposed to act.

I later understood that Apple's marketing agency had promoted the concept of a massive genius figurehead for the company. Big wink to Regis McKenna. Steve was their boy, when in truth there were many people who built Apple. One of them, Jeff Raskin, was quoted at the time saying that what was happening to Steve was sad because "Steve believed his own press." I was always looking for foundational wisdom on Steve and this statement by Raskin seemed right.

Daniel also told me that people at Apple had started talking about Steve's "reality distortion field." When I heard this, I knew immediately that the phrase was perfect. I could hardly believe someone had been able to identify such an amorphous quality with absolute accuracy. And I marveled that three simple words of such scientific and poetic brevity could get it completely handled. The term "reality distortion field" contained the notion of wizardry, and the idea that Steve had some kind of dubious talent that suggested something of an alien power.

So I wasn't alone in noticing it.

My own experience was that Steve had a recontextualizing force field around him, like a conceptual miasma that bent meaning whenever you got within a few feet of him. The reality distortion field may have been invisible, but it left an impression on your actual senses. And it was so new and so distinctive that someone—I don't know who— was compelled to give it a name as a way of dealing with it.

Various publications have said that Steve wasn't ready to be a father. The truth was that neither of us was ready to be a parent, but Lisa came into the world anyway. Still, people evaluated our roles—and the significance of those roles—quite differently. It was that old double standard, a worldly distortion that says a mother has primary responsibility for the child when it's blatantly obvious that children need both parents, in whatever way they can show up well.

Steve wasn't ready to raise a child and neither was I. I needed my own free life and lots of time to grow up. I was a very young twenty-four-year-old when Lisa was born and it was way beyond me to deal with the limitations that her tiny existence imposed on mine. Still, it was in Idyllwild that I arrived at a form of logic that I could rely on, a logic that led me to the conclusion that I would keep and raise my child.

At that time it was hard for me to think anything through clearly, but once I did, I never got lost in the crazy cycles of worry and indecision again. It went as follows: I accepted that I was nowhere near having the experience or wisdom to know if I should keep my daughter or give her up for adoption to a couple more financially fit and emotionally ready. So my backdoor logic ran that if I couldn't understand whether adoption was right or wrong until way down the road, then I had better not risk letting my own child go. I thought that holding her close—as terribly difficult as the circumstances were—was better than understanding, years later, that losing her was too profound a loss to bear. Or worse, never even understanding how profound a loss it was because such an act would have amounted to killing something in me, and in Lisa, too.

It was a fragile kind of logic but it was a starting point. Though there would be times within the first years of her life that were so hard that I would briefly consider adoption again, acknowledging how much I didn't know saved me from losing her until I was able to gain the knowledge of her true value to me, and mine to her. Beyond this and bigger than all the rainy and sunny days, between my unhappiness and the times when things got easier, my mind might not have always understood, but always my arms knew to hold on.

She was mine.

I was hers.

Years later, when Lisa was in her thirties (about ten years older than

I was at the time of my decision to keep her), we talked about it. I told her that while the situation had felt impossible, I'd decided to keep her, even before I could see what it meant. Given how hard it was, I had worried through the years about whether or not I had done the right thing. Lisa listened deeply, and a week after that, I felt the delight that all parents come to know when my daughter called of her own volition and told me she was really glad I'd kept her. She told me that she had thought it through and she knew it would have been very hard on her if I had let her go.

With that I felt as if Lisa had some kind of self-knowledge that I knew nothing about; not in her or in me. I wondered how she could arrive at such a conclusion. I didn't understand it. But I believed her. We both knew how difficult it had been to endure Steve's many faces, so having this discussion helped us see that we had more than survived it. We really love, like, and enjoy each other. And sometimes I think that Steve's absence was a very good thing given his Tourette's-like cruelty. Still, back then when Lisa was just a baby, the situation was pretty much unbearable on a daily basis and for years my child had a sad and unfulfilled mother—the one thing Steve could have taken care of.

Kathy and Mark's generosity had saved the day. They gave me wonderful memories and the stability to take the steps I needed to keep my daughter. When Lisa was seven months old the winds of change blew through Idyllwild and I knew it was time to move on. With my car stuffed and my sweet little darling in her bucket car seat strapped in next to me, we hit the road and I drove up Highway 1, the scenic route, next to the Pacific Ocean and returned to the Bay Area where I knew people and would live for the next few years.

NINETEEN

DARK TIMES, BRIGHT MOMENTS

I was proud of my sweet happy little baby and I wanted to show her to Steve's parents. Paul and Clara loved their son and so, I reasoned, they would want to see his daughter. So when Lisa was still only one month old and we were staying at Bert and Betty Wilder's house on my way down to Idyllwild, I drove over to the Jobses' house. Paul was doing some yard work when I arrived, and he stepped out of the garage with a rake just as I was walking up onto their lawn.

Hello!" I said, holding Lisa in her baby blanket. "I've brought your granddaughter for you to see."

Paul was gruff. "She's not my granddaughter."

He was such an idiot. So I flipped it. "Well, of course Steve was adopted . . . still, as this is his child I thought you would consider her your granddaughter. But I understand."

Paul grumbled something that I couldn't make out. It wouldn't have mattered what he said. Nothing could have excused his poverty of spirit. I went in the house and sat with Clara as she held Lisa. She was distant and polite. The whole thing was awkward.

Later, after Clara died and Paul had recovered from her death, he became the most sought-after bachelor in his community of senior citizens. It was Betty Wilder who told me this. (She was the mother of some friends of mine, and I had actually lived at her house a number of times.) Betty also told me that Paul had told anyone who would listen that the day I had brought Lisa over he'd run me off with a rake. Such a deceitful boast. And so dreadful.

Then when I returned from Idyllwild I was staying at my father's house for a month as I looked for a place to live. Knowing I was there Steve came over to my parents' to get the painting I had made for him that long-ago summer when we were seventeen. My father and his wife had already left for work and I had slipped into the bathtub with Lisa, so I didn't hear the doorbell. It was my sister Linda who answered the door. And it was Linda who told him he couldn't have the painting. She was outraged when she told me about it and, really, outrage was the best and only response. "How dare he come over here and ask for anything!" she exclaimed, adding, "Chris, I told him if I gave it to him, it would have been over his head. And then I told him how dare he come here and ask for anything!"

Hearing the way Linda responded to Steve's slouching self-interest reminded me of who I was long before I had collapsed under the weight of everything. It did my heart good.

Our next address was Oak Grove Avenue in downtown Menlo Park. Welfare payments were $384 a month and the rent was $225, so the shabby little rental was all we could afford. It may have been small (some four hundred square feet), and the little patio may have been made of porous cement, but I had my own door to shut and a place to call my own.

I considered it an incremental improvement.

Lisa and I lived in the stucco apartment for three years. I felt unsafe in the beginning because I didn't have a car or even a telephone, as it would take me months to save up the money for the deposit that was required in those days. But I was one street off downtown Menlo Park, so I had an easy walk to a grocery store, Peet's Coffee & Tea, and window shopping. In this way I started to branch out and build a community.

The old woman who lived next door told me that the owner of my house was waiting for her to die so he could buy up her property to build his office complex. She hated him and "his type" for it, as she would say. Sure enough, within a year she went into the hospital never to return, and Al, my landlord, did buy her property. It would eventually become an office complex, but first it was flophouse for immigrant Chinese.

My new neighbors would play mahjong late into the nights. I would listen to the clicking of the granulated game pieces when I left the windows open on hot summer evenings. The sound captured my imagination and washed my mind like ocean waves. I still don't know what the game actually looks like or how it's played, but the ebb and flow between the completely silent moments in which fate hung in the balance and the crashing roars of laughter or disappointment that followed kept me engaged for hours. Sitting in a rocking chair next to the window I would hold Lisa, listening in my loneliness, and cry for hours while she slept in my arms.

The days were monotonous, a lifeless routine that backed up on itself and created a gray world. I'd put Lisa in her high chair for a meal and she'd look at her food with worry because there was never enough money to buy a variety of good foods and she didn't like what I gave her. I had so disconnected from the flow of my creativity and lost so much that one day I noticed that my hands, once so full of energy from my art, had become dull and lifeless. I shrugged with a sense of, *Ah yes, this, too, is gone.*

The finer perceptions that come with happiness and maturing were so impossibly locked down due to poverty that I just registered the change and surrendered to it without tears. I have worried that I missed too many hours of happiness in this life. But far more than that, I have been haunted by what I wasn't able to give to Lisa during this time, because surely our beleaguered circumstances had an effect on her. Still, like children all over the world Lisa had joy in her, and she'd pull me outside to take her for walks on beautiful days, unroll reams of toilet paper in play, and sing songs with her tongue moving back and forth to wiggle the sound as it came out of her mouth. All of this made me laugh because she was *so* sweet.

And we just kept going.

I had heard that in Tibetan culture, if a child is going to be wealthy and powerful in his or her adult life, that the community will surround that child with less than ideal circumstances so that he or she matures knowing both worlds and will have the heart and generosity of both experiences. I like this idea. It makes sense to me.

I sang her all the songs I had taught myself in my teens. She loved my rousing versions of the Beatles' "Rocky Raccoon" and some of the jazzier Joni Mitchell pieces, along with Hindu chants that I had collected in India. And once, only once, I sang the folk song "Tom Dooley," and my tiny child looked at me like I was nuts and with such serious question in her face as to why I would deliver such a sad message that I never sang it again.

About four months after I had moved into the house on Oak Grove, Daniel called to warn me that Steve's attorneys had blueprints of the Presidio house. They were trying to make a plausible case that I could have had men coming through the window from the front bedroom of the house and so argue that someone else could have been Lisa's father. He also told me that Steve and the lawyers assumed Daniel's buy-in to make a stronger case against me. Daniel was inclined to align with Steve in most cases, but that day, because of the rush and panic in his voice, I heard how the dishonesty of this undid him.

Daniel tells me that he doesn't remember this call or any attorneys with blueprints of the Presidio house, in fact he's glowered when I've brought it up with him. But I remember. How could I not? I suspect that Daniel doesn't want to remember some of the ways he was so helpful to me because he so wanted to be one of the guys—to be in Steve's club. But he lacked the guts for such base motivations. Stuck between his true, well-founded ethical convictions and his desire to belong, I can only imagine that Daniel simply lost his memory to avoid the stress of his conflicting imperatives.

When I found out about Steve's newest assault I was so jangled I couldn't think straight. It just broke me into pieces. I didn't know why he was suddenly trying to be more damaging when I was minding my own business, trying to do the best for *our* daughter. Again, this was all about Apple going public. The attorneys must have figured out that the best way to protect their boy's image would be to make me—and Lisa— look like illegitimate heirs. There was plenty to go around, yet for this they sold their integrity and their manhood. We were just building up for the Reagan years, a period in which greed was amplified and in which single mothers were vilified. It all fit.

After finding out what Steve was doing I called him a couple of times. During one of a number of terrible phone calls between us, I gathered all my strength, and standing in the kitchen at the end of a long stretched-out phone cord, I yelled at him, saying, "You know that I did not sleep around! And you know this is your child!" To my surprise, a deep well of silence seemed to pool on the other end of the line. Maybe he heard me. Had all the hype around Apple filled him with the horrendous justifications? After that argument I never heard another word about his wanting to drag me over the coals. I wondered what more I could have accomplished if I had put my mind to it, though it would be a great mistake for me to think I could have been responsible for maintaining Steve's conscience by yelling at him. There was just way too much moral failure.

Not long after that conversation came the availability of DNA testing that could prove paternity up to 94.5 percent accuracy. This was the game changer. I had from the beginning claimed that Steve was my daughter's father on the welfare forms, so welfare went after him to take the test. The State was bigger than Apple at that time, so Steve had to do it.

I was surprised that our blood tests had been scheduled for the same time. So Lisa, Steve, and I waited together in a dim, windowless waiting room in some county building in San Mateo. Lisa strained to get out of her stroller so I stood her up against the vinyl couch I was sitting on, and she quickly curled around and took off on her little hands and knees. I moved fast to run after her, bending over to catch her up in my arms. After that I kept Lisa in my lap playing little games with my keys to keep her attentive. The place was institutionally clean and institutionally filthy all at the same time. I didn't want her touching anything. I saw Steve register how immediate and tuned into her I was when I ran after her. I knew him so well that I could tell he was surprised at my speed. He had been projecting quite another picture onto me to keep himself comfy and connected to the justifications.

Steve got called out of the room first and then Lisa and I were led into a small room where we sat on an examination table. They took my blood first and then Lisa's. Lisa, still so small, wailed and struggled against my arms when they stuck the needle into her. As they couldn't find the vein, they poked the needle into her again and again, searching. I was ready to smack the nurse. Just then, I looked up and saw Steve peeking through a tiny window of the mud-colored door, flitting his fingers to wave hi. He was his typical charming and clueless self.

The DNA tests established paternity and directed Steve to pay $385 a month child support (which he rounded up to $500), as well as return to the state all back payments I had received from welfare. Apple went public a month later. Steve was worth millions.

Through some new friends, I was recommended for a waitress position at a Palo Alto restaurant that showed art films and had live music on the weekends. The New Varsity was the closest thing to a "scene" in Palo Alto, with the exception of the Brazilian dance club in Whiskey Gulch down by 101. Both are gone now.

I had unlimited access to art movies in my new job. I drank espresso and worked with interesting people my own age, some of whom surprised me with knowledge that has stayed with me throughout my life. One waitress, a Ph.D. student at Stanford, told me about her work as part of a team that was trying to figure out how DNA was packaged. And then there was the man from Holland, a musician, who had played with Leonard Cohen. He wrote me a year after I had left The New Varsity to tell me that in all his travels through the United States, he had never met anyone with as much soul as I had. This was an oasis of recognition.

And, oh, the movies. I saw so many, including two of the most defining films of my life. *One Thousand and One Arabian Nights* fascinated me for its deep transformational logic. Here was a film that showed how consciousness could work through generations of seemingly unrelated people and events to bring about the next evolutionary steps. I believed this—it's how my mind naturally thought—but nothing in my education had prepared me for it, so I was really surprised to see it in a feature film. *Meetings with Remarkable Men* was the other movie. The life story of the mystic G. I. Gurdjieff, this film deepened my sense of the Middle East and Middle Eastern mysticism. In all, a rich addition to my trip to Afghanistan and Pakistan in 1975.

Later the first Apple store in Palo Alto would be established right across the street from the movie house. And after The New Varsity closed down, it was sold to Borders Group, the now-liquidated book and music retailer, where the dark interior was painted in bright colors. Even though the space was filled with books, it felt to me like a soulless business in a soulful building. After the Borders nationwide bankruptcy, the old movie house sits empty, facing the recently vacated Apple store. (Apple moved up the block to a new location.) They now look like two big, dead Cyclops-eyed buildings looking at each other. Things change.

It was during that time at The New Varsity that a friend gave me Shakti Gawain's book, *Creative Visualization*. A seventies classic, this book explains how to use imagery to create out of the thin blue air. Thin blue air was all I had, so the book held great appeal to me. After reading the book I made myself drive around in my car with a pleasant smile on my face and I became a happier person and more organized because of it. Even my waitressing skills improved. And because of this, some joy broke through and gathered in my life. I had more energy for playing with Lisa and thinking about next steps. I now understand how important it is to generate happiness in as many moments as one can manage because no matter what the circumstances are, happiness is what moves the mountains.

On Saturday mornings Lisa and I would go to Peet's Coffee in Menlo Park. Saturday was a day of regulars: everyone talked and laughed together at the church of caffeine. The barista always managed to pour my cup for free. He knew that even 75 cents was a lot to me and, thanking him, I'd accept it. At around one o'clock things would break up and people would get on with their days except that some of them, myself included, would move over to the park across the street, many of them to play or listen to music all afternoon. This was my social life and I looked forward to Saturdays because they were reliably fun and interesting. The coffee boosted me out of the sadness, and the conversations and connection to people would keep me amused and thinking all week long.

Sometimes at Peet's I would see people point me out and whisper something like, "That's Steve Jobs's ex-girlfriend and that's his kid." On one Saturday morning a woman approached me while I was standing in the middle of the room because in those days Peet's didn't have chairs. Lisa moved from her stroller to my hip, and then someone swept her up to play with her while I talked with the woman. The woman was a little older than I was, also in her twenties, with brown hair. For some reason, I remember how conventional and attractive her clothing was, a flower-print blouse and a thin, brightly colored sweater. She may have told me her name but I don't recall it now and I wouldn't recognize her if I ever saw her again. Her approach toward me was direct and she told me without a moment's hesitation, "I was in the office when Steve and his attorneys all celebrated because he'd gotten off by paying you so little."

Her face twisted and she repeated, "They all congratulated themselves. They literally celebrated!" Then she added, "It was so disgusting it made me ill. It still makes me ill." My mouth must have hung open a little as I listened. Few people ever took initiative on my behalf, but it just took this one moment of her anger for the frozenness around me to thaw. I didn't think anyone knew or cared what Steve had done to Lisa and me, but this woman did, and with a kind of fierceness that for once seemed right. Just seeing the human face of dignity woke me up. I was so deeply hurt after being treated badly for so long that I'd stopped looking at it because I could find no way out. Yet how quickly the fullness of life turned when someone spoke the truth and cared!

Fast-forward six years when Lisa was nine, after she and her father had grown to know and love each other. By this time Steve was no longer at Apple and had become humbled and more like his former self. (I have John Sculley to thank for that because his action to get Steve removed inadvertently made a difference to the rest of our lives.) It was in that window of time that Steve and Lisa decided to get her birth certificate straightened out. At nine, Lisa went from Lisa Brennan to Lisa Brennan-Jobs. Steve told me that he could hardly believe that she wanted to take his name. Very plainly relieved and honest, he said, "I am just so happy that she does." I was touched by his surprise and glad for both of them. I was curious, too, and I would try to imagine the conversations between them that resulted in the decision. I saw Lisa speaking power to her father from her full-on little girl authority, and Steve meeting her power and sweetness with his honesty, each claiming the other as family forever.

William Fenwick of Fenwick & West was the lawyer Steve used to fact-check and change the birth certificate. Though he is a corporate attorney he did this work as a favor to Steve because of the history they shared in regard to my pregnancy and Lisa. Fenwick called me and in-troduced himself and said he had a few questions he needed to answer in order to get the facts straight on the birth certificate. At this time he also said, "You have an incredibly lovely and impressive daughter. And you have done a very nice job with her." I said "Thank you" but held my reserve. I didn't need kudos from people like him. I knew she was lovely and impressive. And I knew I was a good mom. Still, I was concerned. How had this man met Lisa without my knowing about it?

After Fenwick asked his questions, I decided to risk asking him some questions. For years I had decided that if I ever had a chance to talk with any of the men who were around Steve when Lisa was born I would do so. "Why, Mr. Fenwick, didn't, you, as an older man, advise Steve to do better for Lisa and me in the beginning years?" I added something like, "Steve was young, he needed the advice of older, more mature men. Why didn't you say anything to him to help him grow up and take appropriate responsibility?" William Fenwick proceeded to tell me that when he found out that Lisa's eyes were brown that he had a talk with Steve about just accepting responsibility. He said he was proud of having done a good thing and it was why Steve had asked him to do the legal work on her birth certificate. I knew what he was indicat-ing. Chris, whom I had met at Duveneck Ranch, was the only person Steve could identify to target and pin the paternity of his child on. Chris had blue eyes, so Fenwick had done a service to Steve to call him to accountability.

Carefully, building my case, I then went on to ask him about when Apple went public and the attorneys had celebrated because Steve had gotten away with paying me so little child support. I told him about the conversation I'd had with the woman at Peet's. I had definitely as-sumed that he would have been a party to that gathering. Fenwick's voice broke with baffled shock and he said, "Well I was never at such a meeting. And I never would have celebrated such a thing, either." The tone in his voice was honest. I believed him.

Yet, because I thought I might never have another chance to talk with him, I pushed on, "Mr. Fenwick, do you really think five hundred dollars a month was an adequate amount of money for any woman to raise a child much less Steve Jobs's child?" He fired back, "You could have gotten your own attorney!" He spoke fast, harsh, hard, and defensively, and I suddenly understood that I had stepped into his mean sandbox. I could hardly speak because ten thoughts hit me at once. I was unable to parse through them quickly enough and pursue questioning. We soon got off the phone.

Perhaps William Fenwick believes that the law is an equal playground and that a young single mother could be a match for Steve and all the moneyed interest that surrounded him. But that was not the case. Moreover, Steve's advisers failed him, too. To all the men who thought they did a good job by protecting Steve, I want to know, was there some point to keeping him infantilized? And even now, I ask, what is the enlightened response in me to all of this? What will bring me strength and grace in the face of such useless, mindless, wasteful collaborations for power and position when the memory of our daily unmet needs still haunts me?

In 1980, after the paternity was established and Steve was sending an automatic transfer to my account once a month, one day out of the blue he came over to my house on Oak Grove to speak to Lisa. Lisa was not yet three. He sat on the floor with us and then proudly announced to Lisa, "I am your father." It was like some kind of Darth Vader moment. Then he waited for a response with a big, slightly fake smile on his face. I knew he was trying to do the right thing, so I watched, not knowing how to help. Lisa had no idea what he was saying and I was baffled by his stance. The Prodigal Daddy, come home. "Ta-da, here I am!" and, "This is what I look like." "It's me!!!" He literally said, "I am one of the most important persons of your life."

I looked at Lisa and then Steve and then Lisa and then Steve again. After which I was doing the equivalent of hitting my forehead thinking what a fool I'd been. Here was the world genius and the complete village idiot. Suddenly I understood that the person I was longing to save the situation didn't have the basics of emotional intelligence, much less a real conscience. He was somehow just blank and theoretical.

As he spoke to Lisa, Steve presented himself as the big bright shiny balloon that was all too easily popped and gone because if anyone said the wrong word, Steve could just walk away. He would suffer nothing if the environment didn't suit him. I felt so unspeakably heartbroken watching as Lisa, mute and shy, took him in with her soft eyes. She only knew a few words and had no idea who this Mr. Glad Rags was. He wasn't looking in wonder at her and saying anything like, "Hi, little one, who are you? You're so cute! Let me look at your sweet little hands. What is your favorite toy?" My mind spun because he was so outside of anything I knew how to help with.

Eventually, after not getting the applause he had somehow expected, he then asked if we could go outside. At the moment of the request, I understood that my living room was so lacking in beauty that Steve could not bear to hang out in it any longer. Standing in the outer yard next to his car he shared a few more hyped-up words with me and then was gone as quickly as he had come, speeding off without a care in his little black Porsche. It was shudderingly weird. I wondered if the visit was another one of Kobun's "encouraging" ideas? Here I was living in poverty and Steve didn't know or care about anything except that he found things unpleasant to be around and wanted to move away from them. I told Daniel about it in the weeks that followed and he would have forgotten this, too, if it weren't for the fact that it was because of him that some version of it ended up in the made-for-TV movie *Pirates of Silicon Valley.*

Steve never came by again.

When I think back on all this now I wonder at Steve's not being more invested in Lisa; I think it was because he did not provide me with enough money. Lisa and I were very valuable to him but he didn't know it. There are many men who in a backward kind of logic seem to care only for what they pay for and invest in. As there was so little invested, he did not know to care.

TWENTY

MACHINE OF THE YEAR

I met David one Saturday morning at Peet's Coffee in Menlo Park. I didn't realize that he was drop-dead gorgeous, but I did notice that his eyes were full of light and honesty and the perfect amount of mischief. David was a world-class rock climber and a creative force. And though he was less complex than Steve, they both shared some kind of elemental power and a desire for the straight-up climb. I fell deeply in love with David. Lisa and I moved to Tahoe City to live with him in 1982.

David had a nice house with a short walk to the north side of the lake. The sweet-smelling pines and the clear air of the higher altitude were renewing, and David was glad to provide this to us. Lisa was three and a half when David and I met, and he welcomed her with pure delight. There was great potential for us as a little family. David had a clear passion and delight for my daughter and they bonded in many ways, but after a while I found myself uneasy about his parenting. Everybody carries their family's unconsciousness around with them, their family patterns. Steve and I had our own complicated histories, so I wasn't exactly judging. But things had been pressing in on me for a long time and I was worn down. Not having resolved my own history, the thought of dealing with David's was too much to handle. I believe that David and I had the potential for a terrifically good marriage and that

Lisa would have thrived. But I lacked the experience to figure it all out. When things grew uncomfortable between us I fell into fight or flight mode. After a lot of fighting, and too many impossible silences, *flight* won. Lisa and I left Tahoe after a year and moved back to the familiar surroundings of the Bay Area.

It was while David and I were still together that Michael Moritz of *Time* magazine approached me for an interview. I thought of this as an opportunity to tell the truth about what had happened with Steve. It would be my first big interview about him. And my last. Moritz was a serious guy, an intelligent writer type, bristling with ambition. (He would later become a major venture investor at Sequence Capital.) Moritz was professional and personable enough and I think we talked for about three hours. At the beginning of the interview Moritz told me he felt that there was something really off about Steve and that he intended to get to the bottom of it. Anyone who knew Steve knew that something was off, so I believed him. I told Moritz my story as his questions rolled out, and at the end of the three hours I remember him looking thoughtfully and saying, more to himself than to me, maybe I'll call you "Charlotte Broils." There had been some discussion of keeping my real name undisclosed for fear of Lisa being kidnapped. Moritz's comment was a nod to this, and also to how burned I had been. Hence, *charbroiled*. It was clever and insulting and it gave me some idea of how others saw me.

The interview hadn't been as glamorous as I thought it would be, more a combination of exhausting and alarming. Moritz's questions were uninteresting to me, like a drill. There wasn't anything creative or revelatory about our exchange. Years later I was told by another reporter from another big business magazine that the outcome of the article would affect Moritz for years, because he'd had no idea what it was to have gone up against Steve. Now that was revelatory.

In January of 1983 *Time*'s "Man of the Year" issue was on the newsstands. Except that "Man of the Year" was turned into "Machine of the Year." I was in Tahoe when my father's wife called and warned me that the article was "a bit rough." Nothing could have prepared me for what I would read, though. I'm not sure what else may have gotten stuck in Steve's craw, but I imagine Moritz had fired a gotcha question at him about why he'd questioned the paternity of his firstborn.

I imagined that Steve's response was vicious and contemptuous: "28% of the male population in the United States could be the father." But actually I don't know whether he said it in hatred or if he was cool and collected. What I do know, however, is that applying a number like "28%" to such a question is exactly how Steve worked. Steve had long before figured out that numerical detail fascinates the mind. And he was like a magician: good at creating distractions.

In that article Steve had also said that he had named the Lisa computer after an old girlfriend. This of course was a fabrication. He had no old girlfriends named Lisa. It was typical of Steve. He had taken poetic license over the edge. Now he was just lying. Before the article was published I'd been living in some kind of an illusion, telling myself that Steve appreciated all the work and love I brought to raising Lisa. She was almost four when the issue came out, and despite all evidence to the contrary, I still believed in Steve's basic goodness. My daughter had this effect on me.

After I read the *Time* article I was hit so hard that three days went by where I was hardly able to speak or focus. To have been treated dishonorably by Steve in a national publication was so incomprehensible to me that I just went blank. I must have retreated to some place inside myself to work it all out. I don't really know how I got through it, only that after three days I came back with all the love and laughter for Lisa and David I had before.

Steve had the deepest impulse to refine everything he touched, as if the act of refining was in and of the total law of his being. So it should be no surprise that, along with all else, Steve refined hatred into the coldest and most controlled inhuman indifference. Steve's ruthlessness was so stunning that people often endured repetitions of his cruelty in order to understand what was happening so that they could figure out how to get out of the way. Also, I suspect that he used people's suffering as an energy source for himself.

In the days after I recovered from the *Time* article I realized that I was frightened not because I was afraid *of* him—but that I was afraid *for* him. And it made me frightened about the world, too. How on earth, I wondered, could he not know what was important? How could he not know what was real? He seemed to have become a binary automaton of left-brain thinking: yes-no, one-zero, black-white, love-hate. Nuance was gone. Emotional reflection, complexity, and context were gone. What *did* he care about?

Some years after the *Time* article came out Steve was voted one of the "Top 10 Worst Bosses" in the United States. A great weight was lifted off me when I learned this. I mean I floated for a few days in wonder. I had always thought that I was alone in what I had endured. More to the point, I kept forgetting that I *wasn't* alone because being in the sights of Steve's hatred was so disorienting, I crumpled under the weight of it unable to think or remember anything. But here was evidence that many other people had seen it.

Despite his genius, Steve made a huge miscalculation his whole life: he believed that hatred was a legitimate force in the world. And because it gave him such unassailable power, he used it and didn't doubt it. Moreover I think he mistook power for love because it made him feel bigger and better. To my great disappointment, he died before figuring out the mistake.

Later I confronted Steve. "Why did you say twenty-eight percent of the male population could be Lisa's father?" I asked. "And that I would name my child after one of your old girlfriends?" "Moritz lied," he said, unblinking.

If Moritz had lied, what had he lied about? It took me a couple of weeks to realize that it was Steve who was lying. I had spent just a little time with Michael Moritz, yet I knew telling the truth was a big part of his professional legitimacy. The magazine's, too. I came to think that even if Moritz had misquoted Steve, or lied in some way, it would not have been on those statements. Besides this, Steve did have a sense of decency when he was in the right, and if he had been misquoted he would have called me the moment the magazine issue came out to apologize. He would have done something about it, too. But this did not happen, because Steve had lied. And he'd lied because he didn't want people to see who he really was.

There was another aspect of that *Time* article that shocked me, too. It was winter when I was sitting on our warm waterbed in Tahoe City poring over it for the first time. I looked at the beautiful pictures with some wonder as well as alarm to see Steve in his big Saratoga house with his Japanese meditation pillow. There's one image in which Steve is sitting in an upright posture with a small Japanese cup in his beautiful hands. The room is sparsely furnished and luminous, lit by a Tiffany lamp. It was materialism so sublime that it looked holy. The images sent shock waves through me. Steve was building and promoting a commercial image of himself that implied the sacred. And this alerted me to the fact that he wasn't connected to it.

It's a brilliant marketing strategy to imply the sacred in a product. For sophisticated buyers, the sacred dimension enfolds sex—and a lot more besides. Take, for example, the name "Oracle" for a business. It's a name that taps into the message from an elevated level, the divine feminine, the illuminated truth, the higher calling, the riddle of the ancient mariner's song, and the longed-for mystical connection. When the sacred is used to promote material goods (or an idea or person, for that matter), an alchemical flash point is created that gets rerouted into image, exquisite design, cool products, and buyable beauty. And all that taps into the cachet of exclusivity. In this way the idea of the sacred is used to promote image-based identity, and though no real connection has been made with the soul, for a moment the aura of mystique wafts into our lives like the cool winds of heaven—until we need more. And we always need more.

I kept that issue of *Time* for many years, but after this I didn't pay much attention to Steve's career again. Once we started to cooperate for Lisa's benefit, I learned to self-censor my interaction with the public side of Steve because it could set off a chain reaction between us that could produce nothing but harm and destruction. I hung back and assumed a role of silence: Lisa was my priority and so was my own sanity. If Daniel Kottke called to tell me that this or that reporter might like to talk to me, or if an article, a TV show, a magazine, a newspaper, or a book with Steve's face on it happened to be in front of me, or if someone who had no idea of my connection to him mentioned his name, I would consider it like the *I Ching—purposeful chance* where I'd take note in a precise, but mild way. Mainly and with few exceptions, I felt that the world and the worldly did not care about love or kindness, just more toys. And if I did happen to want to test the water and talk to a reporter (they usually ended up giving me as much information as I ever shared with them), I would sometimes mention that I thought Steve was going to wake up at some point again. Well, at that point the reporter would look at me as if I was just plain stupid. How could anyone be so naïve?

The last of the chain reaction set off from that interview with Moritz came by way of Lisa. When she was nine and in the fifth grade, Lisa was a petite and extremely coordinated little sprite of a girl with a very bright and good nature. One day, for no apparent reason, she scrambled up the built-in bookcase in our house and snagged the copy of *Time* that I had kept on the top shelf.

"Where did you get that?" I asked, when I saw it lying on the couch.

"I found it!" she said, then added, "and I read all of it!"

She announced this in short fast high notes that told me she was proud of herself and that she was nervous and out of her depth, too. She got super speedy and alert because of how intensely I questioned her.

"I climbed and got it up there," she added, pointing to the upper shelving, like a confident little elf.

Lisa wasn't a mischievous child. It isn't a trait anyone would associate with her, though I liked it in her on the rare occassion I saw it. Incredulous, I suddenly realized then that she was such a good reader that she now had access to her father's world. I just stood there blinking and thinking *How was that possible?* Was she an intuitive like him? That magazine was placed so high up and away among my collection of about four hundred books and magazines with only its slim, worn, and stapled spine facing out that even I could barely reach it. My mind spun and I beat myself up wondering if I should have thrown it away. She was too young for such things. And I had no idea how to talk with her about it either.

TWENTY-ONE

FAMILY TIES

In the spring of 1983, I was inspired to send Steve a photograph of our four-year-old wearing a huge pair of black glasses with a big plastic nose attached. Lisa was funny and cute—they made her look like Steve—so I photographed her and sent a print to him with a note saying, "I definitely think she takes after you." It must have made him laugh because two weeks later he sent me an extra $500.

I used the money to move back to Menlo Park and rent a room in the house of a friend. A month after that, Steve came by to take us to see his new house in Woodside. This was about a year before he was kicked out of Apple, when things were not going so well for him professionally. He was kinder. We drove in his road-hugging Porsche to downtown Woodside, and turned left onto Mountain Home Road. From there we took a sharp right and drove through an ancient stone gate onto the long driveway of Steve's new property. Altogether it was classically picturesque in an enchanted way, as if we were entering Cocteau's *La Belle et La Bête*.

The Spanish-style mansion, situated on seven acres, came with the rich history of old-moneyed Woodside. Steve walked us through and showed us everything: one musty room after another, including one that held the biggest concert organ on the West Coast. He stood near the door and watched as Lisa and I sat at the organ to play some music

and then peek behind the false paneling to see the hundreds of pipes
that mounted the wall and produced the sound. The pipes were identi-
cal, but scaled to size (from miniscule peeping to massive booming)
and as perfectly intricate as insect bodies. The dining room was next,
then the living room—an enormous ballroom space with huge gaping
Citizen Kane fireplaces. It was magnificent elegance from another time
and place, fantastic in the current one. The ceilings were about twenty
feet high and the echo of our steps was weirdly poignant. I could feel
the strange gravity of the large hollow interior spaces press on my senses.
And I saw that day that his mansion had an etheric overlay of Steve's
plain and empty warehouse sadness. He was still the same Steve.

Eventually we walked out to the side yard to look at the swimming
pool, a cool oblong of aqua surrounded by a lip of uneven cement. It
seemed to float without rhyme or reason in the middle of a sea of dense
green crabgrass, with no delineating fence or pathway. The three of us
arrived at the pool's edge to look in—it's a natural impulse—and there
we saw a thick carpet of dead worms at the bottom of the pool. It was
so completely awful and fascinating, this mass grave. We couldn't help
but look. Subdued and sort of sad, Steve said, "Well, I've just bought it
and so I haven't had time to clean it."

Which meant *get it* cleaned.

The next morning when Lisa woke up, she shouted that she'd had a
dream. "Mommy! I saw all the worms in Steve's pool turn into dragons
and fly up into the sky!" "Wow!" I said as I marveled at her. I was so
impressed and I told her so. "That's amazing, sweetie." And I meant it.
Lisa's young psyche had picked up on something in Steve. I wondered
what it must be like to have a sense like this about your own father. Lisa
and I had left town when she was three. Now that she was almost five
and more her own person, she knew things. She could tell me about
them, too. I smiled into her eyes, and as I petted her hair, I thought: *Yes,
sweetie, your daddy can turn dead worms into dragons that whoooooooosh
up into the sky. He is not very nice, but he is special, and he is yours.*

·   ·   ·

After returning to the Bay Area, Lisa and I moved five times in two and a half years. I worked increment by increment to get Steve to give me money so that Lisa and I could live with strength and decency. There was every reason for Steve and me to join forces for the greatest outcome for our daughter. And though sometimes he gave as easily as fruit falling into the hand, more often he was harsh, demeaning, and unconscionably stingy. But still I returned to work with him to improve all our lives: Lisa and my material well-being, and Steve's heart and soul. I didn't know what else to do.

Each house we lived in was an upgrade, due to Steve's providing small but increasing payments, until we came to live on Rinconada Avenue in Palo Alto, where we would live for ten years. At last Steve was coming closer to covering our real expenses. I am quite sure that it was his failure at Apple that brought him around to reflecting on doing better for Lisa and me . . . for a while.

Within the first four months after returning from Tahoe City, Lisa and I moved three times as I tried to establish a safe and happy environment for us both. We moved from Los Trancos Woods to Menlo Park to East Palo Alto. I used a friend's address so I could place Lisa into the Palo Alto school district midyear; I chose the alternative public school called Ohlone. It was well known that the Palo Alto school district was one of the best in the nation, yet I soon found myself alarmed by the school's approach to early childhood education. Until this time, I'd had no idea that I had such strong feelings about education.

Ultimately it came to this: I never questioned my child's intelligence and ability to learn, but I did question the emotional tone in the classroom and the school as a whole. And I didn't like what I saw. So, at the end of Lisa's kindergarten year, I placed her in a Waldorf school for her first grade. I always felt it was important to choose a school that reflected my value system, so I chose Waldorf because its stated goal is the protection of the emotional life of the child.

After a week at the Waldorf school all the toughness that Lisa had built up to protect herself from the hurt at "the best kindergarten in Palo Alto" dropped off of her. At her previous school, the "best kindergarten teacher" was paying kids with bright shiny toys to get them to read, and this was creating competition. Lisa, who by nature is extremely competitive, wasn't ready to read and so had started to become mean to the weaker kids in the class because she felt so bad about herself. I saw Steve in this behavior and it alarmed me: they were both so good at competing. However, once Lisa was at the Waldorf school, she became the sweetest, softest, happiest little first grader. This was the school that promoted awareness for the integrity of the whole child, where love and respect was fostered in the classroom and on the playground. It was such a good environment that Lisa and her friends didn't like breaking for vacations because they didn't want to be apart from each other.

Within a few months of Lisa's entering the Waldorf school, Steve had finally increased the monthly money so that we were able to move into a nice apartment in Palo Alto. It was so solidly built and well laid out that it felt like a home. My spirits were uplifted and I had a new sense of safety and overall well-being for us. Still, I often didn't have enough money for food, rent, and Lisa's private school, much less furniture and new clothing.

When I returned to the Bay Area from Tahoe I found freelance work illustrating for a magazine and also on a book about the English colonization of China. We had moved around so much that getting a full-time job was problematic, because I never wanted to leave Lisa for forty hours plus commute. I considered Lisa to be my job and added outside contract work doing illustration when I could find it. I also cleaned houses so I could bring in extra money, control my hours, and be there to pick her up after school.

One day Steve had his secretary call to ask if I would be willing and able to bring Lisa to an Apple event. It cannot be overstated that when a man puts money into his family, he starts to take an interest on a number of important levels. The invitation told me that Steve wanted Lisa to be a part of his life. I wanted to respond to his efforts so that he also felt respected and connected to Lisa. I took her out of school for the day and we went and sat near the front of a ridiculously large auditorium filled with Apple devotees to watch the opening. The presentation was overwhelming for Lisa, seeing her father on stage like that. And a new experience for me, too. Steve spoke so rapid fire that it felt as if I'd have to unfold my ears into two big dish antennas to capture it all to match his mind's extraordinary acceleration. There wasn't a wasted syllable or a missing beat in service to the logic of his presentation. It was an exhilarating river of pure content. No wonder people were so excited about him! Later when Lisa was older she told me how disturbing that day was for her. She felt it was too magnificent for a little girl to see her father like that. I would not have known better then. In many ways over the years I took actions to connect them to each other with the best intentions, though things didn't always turn out the way I'd hoped.

It was a wonderful feeling to have the Waldorf community to return to after the Apple event. These were lovely people and many were very thoughtful, old-soul types who wanted to hear how it went. I remember being happy that Lisa was being so thoroughly cared for, that we had a community, and that I was no longer alone with my situation. I could share things, and these people were interested and interesting.

Soon after, Steve called and invited us for breakfast at his Saratoga house. It was a Saturday morning and I picked up berries on the way. Walking into his house, I was overwhelmed by the beauty and spaciousness. Beauty feeds me, but Lisa and I had been living so close to the stressful line of barely making it that my insides seemed to expand to acclimate to the beauty I had not experienced in a long time. This was the house I had seen in the pictures in *Time*. In Steve's mind, it was very simple: he was entitled to all wealth. We were not. I numbed myself to keep my rage in check. It was easier to push down than to confront him. Standing in his kitchen, I pointed to his espresso machine and made a distracting comment to help me stuff my sorrow. He said, "I am never going to use that again!" Indicating that Steve on espresso was a very bad idea. Whew, I could imagine! He then showed us the rest of his expansive two-story house. He'd had a sauna put in and talked about how very important it was for him to relax. His casual indifference to our needs made me feel like we were the orphans.

After a breakfast of berries, nuts, and homemade bread with jam and fresh-squeezed orange juice, we all went for a walk and Steve began excitedly to tell me that he had found his mother. And once he had found her, he discovered that he had a wild red-haired younger sister who was a writer living in New York. He put his hands up around his head to show how big the sister's hair was and I pictured something like a deep red Afro.

I got so caught up in what he was saying that we stopped walking. The conversation required all focus. Since we were standing still, Lisa tried her hand at climbing up the twelve-foot embankment that rose up from one side of the paved road. We were in the shade, and the embankment led up to someone's backyard in the wealthy Saratoga area. The sun behind the leaves up on the embankment made it look like a stained glass window of nature. I could see why she wanted to get up there. Lisa herself was only about forty-five inches high and could only get up four or five feet, before she'd peel back off to try it again. It was a noble effort. I held my arms out to guard against a possible tumble as Steve continued with his story. He told me that his sister's name was Mona. I thought it was a beautiful old-fashioned name, and it told me that their mother had poetry in her. But to me it was also like "mono," as in one child. I've wondered since what she would have named her son had she kept him. Surely not "Steve" with all those electrified es.

Steve told me that his parents had married after he'd been adopted. As he kept on with his story, I hardly had time to consider what that must have meant to him. The forward movement of a narrative has a way of minimizing the deeper realities. In recounting this conversation now, the grievousness of his loss nearly immobilizes me. How can he find a way to live with such knowledge and the particular sense of abandonment it must have generated in him? There were journalists writing articles at that time about how the hyperactivity in Silicon Valley was connected to the avoidance of the feelings around death. I think, in Steve's case, it was more like the avoidance of the feelings around birth and the mother. Maybe it all comes down to the same thing.

Steve was smiling and turning his hands in the air as he related his tale because now he had relationships with these two people, the mother and the daughter. I was incredulous. "How did you find your mother in the first place?" I asked. For as long as I had known Steve it had been such a giant issue. Now that he stood on the other side of it he told me that he had just called the doctor on his birth certificate. It was simple and straightforward. I wondered why he had not done it before.

When he called the doctor, who was by then retired, Steve told him he was Steve Jobs and asked if he could tell him who his mother was. After he had explained everything, the doctor apologized, saying, "I'm sorry, son, I have delivered hundreds of babies, I just don't remember you." And then, just like Steve, Steve said, "Look, I'll give you my contact information. Please take it and if you remember anything, anything at all, just write or call me." The doctor agreed to do so and took it all down and they said good-bye. (This was all before e-mail!)

Steve was animated and he spoke as if opening presents, the next more fantastic than the last. And all the time we were talking, Lisa was making runs for the top of the embankment with a confident little smile on her face at each try. Her attempts were worthy and reflected well on my former mountain climber boyfriend, who had taught her how to do it the right way, because not only was Lisa charging for it, she was applying skill, too. She aimed high, trying to get to where it was bright and beautiful; it dazzled me, too.

He went on to explain that the doctor had written him a letter the moment they got off the phone: "To Steve Jobs in the event of my death . . ." it began. In it, the doctor explained that he did know who

Steve was and that his mother had lived with him and his wife during the last months of her pregnancy through to the delivery. The doctor revealed the mother's name and signed and addressed the letter and put it in his top desk drawer. That night the doctor had a massive stroke or heart attack (I don't remember which), and died. And Steve got the truth of his history.

Whoa! My mind jammed with so many thoughts we just stared at each other silently. Eventually I asked point-blank, "What did you do, kill him?!"

A little part of me wondered if he was lying about it all because how would I ever know? I couldn't quite get a read on his expression, but it didn't seem as if he was lying. Maybe the doctor was only waiting for Steve's call, I reasoned silently, so that he could move on. In general, things like this did happened around Steve, and honestly, they happened a lot. Certainly his fast rise onto the world stage had some shenanigans behind it, but this was going too dark and too far. I was left with the disturbing question of what it might be to even innocently interfere with his trajectory.

Steve was always clear that he never intended to meet his biological father. He was afraid the man had weaknesses and would try to use him for his money. It was like Steve to have hunches and even pure clairvoyance about people and circumstances. But his comments about his biological father also had the quality of a bugaboo to my tired ear. Steve had a precious sense of himself and it was exhausting. The word "untouchable" comes to my mind: Steve as the golden boy who thought his own father was unworthy of him. It's well known that Steve's birth mother put him up for adoption because her father didn't like Steve's biological father. Steve's biological grandfather didn't want his grandson, either. Funny how that kind of pattern replicates itself.

I found out later through written accounts that Steve shook his biological father's hand, while both were unaware of the truth of who they were to each other. It was in the father's restaurant, which Steve frequented, that respect between them was formed. He'd just found his way to him. I like to think that Steve and his father recovered some of the missing peace through that handshake.

That day in Saratoga, Steve shone when he talked about his biological mother, "My mother is like a grad student!" He must have told me this about fifteen times, which made me suspicious. I find that when people repeat messages they're trying to numb the real truth of what they're facing by overwhelming the mind with the verbal repetition. Or they are trying to give their own self a message they can't or don't want to hear yet. I didn't quite know what it all meant to him, but as I had always considered the Jobses more like grandparents, I can imagine that the contrasting liveliness of this intellectually youthful woman must have been terrifically impressive to Steve. Continuing brightly, he told us that his sister Mona Simpson's book, *Anywhere But Here,* had been on the bestseller list for twelve weeks.

This truly was a fractured fairy tale of magnificent proportion.

Later that week, as soon as we had a spare moment, I took Lisa with me to Printers Inc. Bookstore in Palo Alto to find Mona's book. I couldn't afford to purchase one, so we sat on the floor poring over Mona's black-and-white author photograph. A connection had been made to the lost family. I don't know what it meant to Lisa, who was by then six. She was just getting to know about this thing called her own father. But we sat excitedly together and I narrated my thoughts as I worked to find Steve in Mona's face. Lisa was so cute as she pointed things out with me. We talked about the fact that Mona didn't have an Afro as Steve had implied. Because of Mona's freckles and her big bright crystalline spider-lashed eyes I could not see any resemblance. "They don't really look alike," I shared with Lisa. But a few years later Mona, Lisa, and I took a trip to Montana and there, talking late into the night with her, after Lisa was asleep, I finally did recognize her jaw and the upside-down look of Middle Eastern lips to be exactly like Steve's. It took a darker room for me to look past the coloring and into their shared bone structure and lip contour and finally see their resemblances.

• • •

Lisa was going to the Waldorf school when the story of Steve's firing from Apple hit the newspapers. I remember that the parents at the school were so sympathetic and scandalized by the raw facts of Steve being ousted from the company he'd started. "Poor man," they exclaimed. "This is just not right! It's just not fair!"

I had two thoughts on the matter: that Steve has always been remarkable in his capacity to capture people's hearts (not the least of which was my own), and that if he was as terrible to the people at Apple as he was to Lisa and me, he probably deserved what happened to him. I was impressed with Sculley for managing to do it. But I kept these thoughts to myself during that time. I wouldn't have known how to speak the whole complex truth of who he was, and no one was listening anyway. I knew even then that I was dealing with a huge cultural bias. This is a man's world and the Waldorf school was no different than anywhere else. And so it was with the Waldorf parent body that I was learning to listen without comment. Compassion is such a refreshing and wonderful thing, and since nobody could possibly have imagined how awful Steve was, I would just nod to the lovely sense of care directed toward him. This school was at heart a wisdom society and these people had taught me to listen and so when I was at my best, I stayed silent and held dual realities in appreciation of kindness for its own sake.

Not long after he left Apple, Steve sold the Saratoga house and moved permanently into his Woodside home. This brought him closer to us, and with more free time, he spent more of it with us and as a result saw where he could help out more.

Steve confided to me, "It was terrible going to work every day right before I got kicked out because everyone hated me." He then told me that Sculley had gone around talking to people to get a consensus against him. Hearing him speak like this made me empathetic toward him; he was honest and I could feel how hurt he felt. I silently pictured all the work Sculley had to do to sow the seeds, group by group, to get the people on board to agree to get rid of Steve. Yet this is what Steve had done to me, except far, far worse and when I was pregnant with our child. I wondered how he could be so stupid as to assume blind loyalty from me when he had none for me.

Over the next year, I observed that Steve wore his failure with so much grace that my memory floated back to the poem he had hammered to the side of the door when we were living together in the summer of '72. He wrote something about pain causing our senses to rise, and for years I would return to those words. I didn't really understand what he meant because I had been dulled by everything Steve had put me through, but I think for him, pain was transcendent. This was the imbalance between us. He took too much and I should have taken more.

It was a little past a year since we heard of Mona's existence that Steve brought her over to meet us. After that began a very long relationship where Mona worked to do well by me for Lisa in many ways. But there were little betrayals that didn't so much diminish my affection as sharpen my curiosity: what did these two brilliant sibs have going on that was so problematic for me?

Both Steve and Mona had public lives, and when they spoke, they sometimes created impressions that weren't true. When Mona wrote about the mother in her novel based on Steve called *A Regular Guy,* people believed it was me. The mother images in Mona's books tend to be horrendous, and because she'd captured Steve so well, people assumed that under the thin guise of fiction, she had also captured me. Many of Mona's books play out the theme of abandonment, particularly by the mother. It's tricky, because a writer has to be able to write her fiction, but that book has shadowed me and my daughter with a false overlay.

At that first meeting, Mona stared at Lisa and no other word can describe it better than that she drank Lisa up into her huge crystal blue eyes. I was actually a little uncomfortable with it but censored my impressions because I did not want to even consider disliking her. Instead, I imagined how many years and shifts had to have taken place for all of us to be in one room together, and what it must mean to the three of them to be meeting after all this time. That day began the literary aunt's attentions on my daughter. I saw Steve quietly beaming and very still, like a true guardian. Mona seemed to be the aunt of all aunts and she poured her affections and gifts and sparkling thoughtfulness into my child's life, and in this way I felt so much more supported and happy. It seemed like the good was winning.

After this, Steve and I began looking for a house to buy for me so that Lisa and I would have appropriate stability. However, every house I found and liked, Steve would either not like or be too late to make an offer. He seemed lethargic about coming through for us. I can imagine that he may have had to deal with a lot of uncomfortable feelings whenever he acted in our behalf. There were many Steves and most every one of them took an enormous amount of effort for me to deal with. His remove could feel impossibly unending and disregarding, and I really did not know how to work with it. Indeed there are many Chrisanns who found it hard to work with him for all kinds of her own reasons. So it was in this way that we ended up following the line of least resistance and I rented a three-bedroom home in old Palo Alto from one of the parents at the Waldorf school.

It was a house that I truly liked, there was something about it and we were very happy living there for years. Steve hired Tom Carlisle, his interior designer for NeXT and the Apple stores, to freshen the place up. Tom was excited about a peachy-rose-colored paint he had just discovered and wanted to use. He told me that it changed colors on the walls as the sun moved across the sky every day. So I said, "Let's use it!" Amazingly, he was right, they did, and the changes gave me a new understanding of how the sun shifts color throughout the day. He also had the wood floors refinished and stained white and all the old faucets and light fixtures, plugs, and light switches traded out for new. In the end Steve said, "It's too chichi," and this being so, made it perfect. I was happy. This was the first time I had felt as if materialistically things were lining up in an appropriate way. Steve also hired his organic gardener and the gardener's assistant to make the landscaping beautiful in a way that the house still benefits from today. Within a year of moving in, Steve bought me an Audi, and finally he increased the monthly support he sent us. I still remember the happiness in my body from this time of new things that made our life better. Beyond better.

TWENTY-TWO

TRACTION

Things were different after the power cord between Steve and Apple had been cut, but I don't believe much good would have taken place without Mona. And we were all the better for it. Like families everywhere we had our skirmishes and hurt feelings, but all boats rose in a tide of natural affiliations and shared goals. We were family, no more and no less than the obligations of blood. I believe that Steve, in his core, had always wanted to do the right thing; Mona helped him do it. I had an ally who did something few could: help rebalance things between Steve and me so that Lisa could thrive.

Mona got to thinking about how to improve Lisa's and my situation like any woman would, by addressing the obvious. I sort of remember her telling me that she was going to help, but still it surprised me as it happened.

In the beginning there were many obvious things to be done and it all must have seemed like low-hanging fruit to Mona as she set about, one by one, to put things in order. She was thoughtful in a woman's way and she got the details right. First she talked with me about getting Lisa into therapy with a male child psychoanalyst so that my daughter would have a long-term relationship with an emotionally mature father figure. At the time of this conversation I knew—she knew, we both knew—what kind of father Steve was and was not. Things needed to be augmented so that Lisa would have the best possible advantages in life. Mona also suggested that she would look into a therapist for me and ask Steve to pay for both of us if I wanted. What a boon! I said, "Yes!"

Lisa was in third grade when I took her to the first appointment and that night after the session she asked with her sweet belligerence, "Well, what if I don't want to see him again?" I told her, "Then you don't have to. It's your call, sweetie." It was a moment of pure bliss for me to give her all choice in the matter. Her little face curled into satisfaction and self-ownership. She warmed to the idea after that and always loved going to see her therapist.

It amazes me now how quickly and deeply my psyche was able to figure out whether or not I trusted this therapist with my eight-year-old. In short order, my instincts laid out a very precise map of who he was. He and I did not agree on everything, but in the balance of all things I found him to be professional, insightful, trustworthy, and a person of great kindness. Because federal law mandates that the parent of such a young child is to be included in some of the sessions, I had direct and regular contact in which I saw how he was with her. It was in this way that I discovered that they played checkers and chess, walked to the local shop to get ice cream, and didn't actually do much of anything except play and talk. Sometimes I thought he was a little too kicked back for the money Steve was paying. But when I joined in on their sessions and witnessed firsthand how free Lisa was to be her most lively authentic self, I knew he had to be remarkable. Like many parents, I navigated by my child's joy and so understood people by her reception of them. He was pure gold.

As Lisa got older we endured more of Steve's unconscionable behaviors: from not showing up for prearranged dinners and dance recitals, to being seven hours late from a trip and not calling me to let me know, to kissing Laurene in front of Lisa while telling Lisa how beautiful Laurene was, when at the same time he was telling Lisa she herself was not beautiful . . . this is only the tip. It was then I discovered that in addition to this therapist's ability to free up my child for her happiest little self, he also possessed a near surgical ability to cut to the bone of truth about Steve's behavior—without harming Lisa's relationship to herself or with her dad.

It's not for me to share the details of those sessions, but suffice it to say they bolstered Lisa's self-assurance because her therapist's anger was clean, quick, and discerning. He presented a fiery cleansing flash to the full Steve Jobs catastrophe. In my whole life, I will never forget the times I witnessed the therapist addressing Steve's contemptuous, smarmy betrayals with an immediacy that seemed to slice through the air like Blue Angels. His words were the technology of excellence in the future of war: strikes so precise that there could and would be no collateral damage. The sheer severity of his insights sucked the air out of my lungs and gave me wild wonder into what it is to speak the most precise, searing truths without doing harm. Because I would look at Lisa's expression in the midst of his comments and to my utter delight and relief she would sit serenely, in all consideration, protected. The truth was so good to hear that I felt blessed, blessed, and blessed again.

As we were beginning to feel stable and thrive, a sense of urgency moved through me and I started to think I could go to a four-year college. It was such a happy exciting feeling, like a thousand Christmases all at once. *Oh my God,* I thought, *I can.* I can lead a fulfilling life. I can make money. I can be part of the world through my true gifts.

The year before, I had brought my portfolio to a group of children's game designers in Palo Alto, called Grey Bridge, to see if they might be interested in hiring me. The cofounder and head designer told me that I had the nicest portfolio anyone had brought in a long time. I wondered if he said that to everyone. My portfolio consisted almost entirely of some illustrations I had done for Art Canfil's book *Taipan*. It was a computer game in the context of a novel about the opium trade during the English occupation in China. I did about eight highly rendered pencil and ink drawings to illustrate this horrific, yet fascinating, history. I had other images in my portfolio: a painting of a Persian rug that turned into a bee hive that turned into a computer circuit board with bees buzzing all over the surfaces and honey pooling in the circuits; a woman falling, in multiple sequences, naked, Eve thrown out of the garden with ethereal fall lines. The cofounder and I talked about how the Art Center College of Design in Pasadena, California, was the best commercial school in the country. It's where he went. At the time I thought, *Oh, God, I wish I could go to Art Center.*

So it was from this and the fact that the circumstances had so improved for Lisa and me that I decided to apply to the Art Center. I drove with Lisa down to Pasadena to interview and showed them my portfolio. I was accepted two months later. A diploma from the Art Center was carte blanche for an interview and quite possibly a great job with any number of the top design groups in the country. Steve was giving me about $2,500 a month, and with the addition of a student loan, I figured I could make it work. I could finally get some traction going in my life.

But Steve begged me not to move so far away. He said, "Please don't take Lisa away from me. I'd really like to see her on a regular basis." He wasn't dramatic, just persistent. He made sure to bring it up each and every time we saw one other. Eventually, between his clear, repeated requests and the fact that the school had warned me that I would have to work an eighty-hour week, I came down to earth. There was no way I could put my daughter through that much hardship.

I had always given Lisa a lot of attention. She thrived with it. I don't know if she was high maintenance or if all kids need as much as she needed, but I knew it wasn't right to leave her with babysitters or in school too long. She wasn't on my schedule. I was on hers. Back then people talked about having "quality time" with your kids as a way of managing two-parent careers, but I never felt Lisa and I shared quality time without a large quantity of time. Maybe others could, but I couldn't. As Lisa's welfare was by far the most important thing for me—and this included Steve's having easy access to her—I put my own requirements on hold, once again.

In the end, I was accepted into the California College of Arts and Crafts, an art college in Oakland. I transferred my credits from Foothill College, so this put me into my junior year. Though clearly this school would never give me the training, financial advantages, and cachet of Art Center, I felt peaceful and thrilled to have a plan that could work for everyone while I built into the next stages of my life. When I asked Steve if he would be willing to pay my tuition, he gave me a happy *yes*. Steve was making things easy now and I loved him for it. And it seemed to me that helping in this way put a hop in his step, too.

It was during the first year after moving into the Rinconada house that I wanted Lisa to go to The Nueva School, a private school in Hillsborough. It was about forty minutes round trip from Palo Alto. I kept pushing for it, until one day Steve and I had a big argument over how wrong he felt it was for me to keep changing Lisa's schools. *Whoa,* I thought, *he is actually concerned about her in the right ways. Duly noted!* But she wasn't thriving at the local public school and I couldn't leave it that way.

A majority of people believe that the most important time to be paying for private education is in the older grades, such as high school and college. But I feel that if you have to choose, early childhood is the time and place to put the resources to work. That's when children's hearts and minds are wide open, when they're creating pathways of meaning for the rest of their lives. (I've also wondered if people regard higher education as being the more valuable place for resources because, historically, it is the time when the men take over the teaching.)

My impression of the environment at the public school was that it was structured to dumb down the children and the teachers. Not just intellectually, but also emotionally. For example, I observed that the children and teachers were rarely willing to meet one another's eyes, which was in marked contrast to the Waldorf school, where the first order of the day was to greet each child with a little handshake and direct, loving eye contact. Lisa was starting to harden and think like everyone. I was extremely uncomfortable about it.

I wanted a school that addressed each child's individuality. Knowing the great influence Lisa's childhood environment would inevitably have on her long-term personal relationships and work life, I kept hammering Steve for a change. I needed the money to pay for it and I saw his buy-in as the direct route to my goal. I knew Steve and I shared many of the same creative and educational values for Lisa. I had every hope and intention of turning it around.

Eventually Steve saw what I saw.

Alarmed and exasperated after Lisa spent a year and a half in a public school, he called one day and demanded, "What is happening to her?" indicating that he had, at long last, understood that Lisa was being disconnected from herself. I jumped with a rush of joy. "This is what I've been telling you! And this is why I've been asking you to help me get her into Nueva."

Bingo! Steve heard me and got it together to speak with Bill Atkinson about the school. Bill was on the original Mac team and had a child at Nueva. Bill raved about the education there and so it was in this way that we placed our daughter into a top private elementary school in the Bay Area.

Nueva's approach to education was to take care of the children's growing hearts and minds in delightful and challenging ways. The subjects were so well conceived and presented that all the children were met with excellence, as well as deep regard. Addressing each student's uniqueness meant that every child received the admiration of their teachers and peers for their own giftedness, and in this way learned to truly appreciate the gifts of others. This was my idea of a good environment, school and otherwise.

I felt Lisa and I were upheld every day by this school. I am happy to say that long after Lisa graduated from college, she called me from the various homes she was living in all over the world, to tell me, "Mom, Nueva was my Hogwarts! I do not know how to thank you enough."

So it was in 1988 that Lisa was going to Nueva and I was going to art school in Oakland and both of us were in therapy. We had a nice home and a new car, a gardener and a house cleaner. Steve had also generously paid off the student loans that had been following me around for years. It was a completely appropriate turnaround and everyone was happier. I was enjoying Steve, too.

It was also during this time that Mona had a conversation with Steve about just giving me a financial lump settlement. But this is where it stopped. "No way," he said. Mona and I rolled our eyes when she told me and we discussed that Steve's withholding this eminently right action was a way of remaining too attached to me. It further implied that there was something that he was not explaining. Understandably, Steve was a man with attachment disorder. His withholding was a form of intimacy through control, which fit the history. I also suspect that I was caught in the crosshairs of some very pernicious negative female projections, which confused me because I took it to mean I was at fault.

With so much in order, Mona suggested that I move everything out of my bedroom and turn it into an art studio, and get to my real work. Our home had three bedrooms; the master bedroom, the largest, was at the back end of the house, away from everything. Having my own working space was top on my hierarchy of needs and Mona was completely right to have suggested it. But the master bedroom didn't have good ventilation, and it had been freshly painted and newly carpeted. I loved that she was thinking in my behalf and appreciated her goodwill toward what might be my professional life. But I couldn't quite see converting that bedroom into working space. Oil painting is toxic and unavoidably messy; the notion of turning it into an art studio felt as impossible as jumping on furniture with muddy boots.

Within the year, however, I set myself to the task of clearing out the detached garage, which was loaded with wood debris the owners had left behind. I had it sheetrocked and my father and I patched the roof. I put up track lighting and my friend Avi, a house painter, kindly painted it for me. Twenty steps away from the house, plenty of room to make a mess, big enough to hold classes, a wide garage door to keep the place aired out from the toxic materials, and close enough to hover for Lisa's sense of Mom being nearby, I had the best working space imaginable.

It was also at this time that my father gave me small amounts of money on an irregular basis, money I was to use to hire an attorney to force a financial settlement with Steve. I think two things happened for my father to step in this way. First, it may have been that because of Mona's involvement to get things right, he woke up. My father was sort of a follower. But it wasn't just that. I was more stable and in a stronger position, so perhaps my father perceived me as finally being able to confront Steve. My father had always wanted to do something about the situation with Steve, but while Steve was at Apple, he was untouchable. Once I had that cash, I started interviewing attorneys in San Jose, but nothing ever worked out because after Steve had gotten kicked out of Apple, he made sure to give me more child support than was required at the time. Long story short, I never found an attorney who had the creative power or interest to establish new legal precedents for my situation with Steve.

It seems my whole life was about moving toward what I felt was right before my mind understood the *whys* and *whats* of how everything worked. I didn't think, I didn't analyze, I didn't strategize, I did not manipulate. I was a person who operated out of emotional impressions that drew me into action. I picked my battles with Steve and I now think I should have picked more of them. I should have leveraged my not going to the Art Center into a cash settlement. With so much in place I was finally able to care for Lisa and myself in ways I saw fit. Both of us stable and safe. Lisa thriving in her new school. I let it be. I was thirty-five years old and just catching my balance from the earlier years. And I must have I figured I had more magic beans at the bottom of my pockets since I still didn't know enough to think and plan and negotiate for my financial future.

I used to go roller-skating all over Menlo Park in the early days at Oak Grove. This was 1979 and I had the classic skates with the big orange wheels. In the beginning skating was a near-death experience; I didn't know how to stop and the roads vibrated my eyes so much I could hardly see. But once I somehow got past that stage it turned to pure happiness. I found that no matter what, no matter when, where, or how, skating turned into a three count. It was a waltz rhythm and I was always humming "The Blue Danube," changing from left to right on the first count and elongating the last count with a prolonged glide, 1-2-3——1-2-3——. The rhythm and motion were addictive. The more I skated the more I wanted to skate. The texture of movement under my feet, the air in my hair, and the freedom of all things speeding by was happiness itself.

In the beginning, I'd go next door to the church parking lot when Lisa was napping. There I'd practice twirling. The momentum of the fast spiraling turns would lift my arms outward in graceful lifts, and then I'd flip around fast to stop on my toe guards. It was as if the air were my dance partner.

I fell a lot in the beginning but it didn't matter, I loved it and was proud of my various scratches and bruises. When Lisa was awake, I'd put her in her stroller and we'd fly together. Much later, when Steve discovered that I had skates, he wanted some, too. So it was on a bright Saturday early afternoon, when Lisa was old enough to have her own skates, that the three of us went down to the Palo Alto Sport Shop and Toy World and he bought a pair for himself and Lisa (both with those big orange wheels), so that we could all go skating together.

On weekends we'd go up to Stanford or across old Palo Alto to Caffe Verona because they had the best soup, pasta, and cappuccinos. After some time, Tina, Steve's girlfriend, joined us. And Mona after that. Mona was neither as coordinated as me nor as recklessly bold as Steve, and I remember the unspeakably sweet look of her on skates as like that of a grinning schoolgirl. Tina looked like Daryl Hannah in *Blade Runner*, tall and athletic, sweet in all her magnificence. Eventually, Lisa and Steve started to go out for hours on their own. It could have been at one of our skating outings or at a dinner together or just a time when we were all hanging out talking, when Steve said that he would take Lisa one night a week when I was at school in Oakland. Every semester I stacked all my classes because I didn't want to be far from Lisa more than two days a week. Babysitting was always an issue, so Steve arranged his life so that he could take Lisa every Wednesday evening. He wanted to be a dad and this seemed like a fabulously great next step for all of us. Lisa was nine years old. It would be the first time Steve would take responsibility for his daughter on a regular basis and he wanted the chance to do it, like a real father.

The logistics ran as follows: every Wednesday, one of Steve's secretaries would meet Lisa at the bus stop in Menlo Park right when she got dropped off at about 3:45. The secretary would take Lisa to NeXT where she would hang out until the end of Steve's workday, doing her homework and generally being cute and precocious in what was otherwise an adult's world. Steve would have her around and she could see him in action in his work life. So every Wednesday Steve had his own take-your-daughter-to-work day. I was flipped-out happy about their being together without me. I never knew what those afternoons looked like exactly, but I trusted the situation because even if Steve was occupied, and just a bit of a new clueless parent, I knew his secretaries to be very conscientious people.

One day Lisa let me in on a little scam she had going at Steve's office. She and I used to draw the sculptures at the Rodin Sculpture Garden at Stanford University, and there was a day she'd gotten me so involved in her drawing by asking good questions that I'd abandon my own piece to do more and more on hers. As I was teaching her how to draw and working away, it occurred to me that I wasn't working on *my* drawing and so laughingly I complained. It was then that the light descended. With her little face looking brightly into mine she told me, "Mommy, this is how I get the secretaries to do my homework at NeXT!" "What!" I said. Then Lisa said, "I tell them that they are really good at how they think about my homework." I laughed, unable to hide my admiration of her audacity. I knew she had natural leadership qualities when, at age five, she made it possible for the girls to play in the boys-only sandbox. Now I was seeing that she had figured out how to motivate the adults around her without anyone really noticing because it was so fun to help Lisa.

I was thereafter aware of how much time I was working on her drawings, as I played the edge of her very real and remarkable reception of what I was showing her with the fact that my little darling simply wanted to lay claim to a better drawing. It was all in good fun and it wasn't long before I recognized that the collaborations between her artistic awkwardness and my skill resulted in better, far more interesting drawings than anything we ever did individually. Lisa helped me loosen the grip on my all too factual renderings and I helped her tighten her artful lack of dexterity. We were well matched!

After work, Steve and Lisa would go home to his house and they would make dinner and eat and then watch a movie on the VCR from his bed. Then she would go to sleep in her own bed in the room next to his. Mona had bought Lisa a beautiful bed for Steve's house and made a nice room for Lisa. On those nights Steve introduced Lisa to all his favorite movies, *Harold and Maude* being one of them. It was something marvelous between father and daughter and I was so delighted by Steve's sharing his love of movies with her. Lisa and Steve liked to kick me out of their world, and eventually I found that they would only get me involved if they were having a problem in their relationship. At those times I would help them come back together and then they'd kick me out again. A form of success, I suppose.

There's a hormonal balance like a wash that comes over women when we know that good is happening for everyone in our sphere of care. I can barely describe the exquisite feeling I had of all being as it needed to be because Steve and Lisa were entering into the world of the normal day-to-day stuff together. I was happy for Lisa, happy for Steve, and happy for me. Yet for every next level of complexity there would be new devastation, so I can only say that I'm glad I was young and of good health.

After what was probably a couple of months of Steve taking Lisa on Wednesday nights, there was one evening when my class was canceled due to finals. I drove back to Steve's house to see if they wouldn't mind my joining them for dinner. There were no cells phones then, so I just drove the forty-five miles. It was night, but the front door was always open at the Woodside house. When I stepped inside, I heard their small faraway sounds in the kitchen. Simultaneously knocking and walking in, I sung out, "Hi! Do you mind if I join you?" Both looked up surprised to see me, after which Steve, with a confident smile, motioned me in to sit down. "Yes of course, of course, come in, come in! Have a seat."

I cozied up to explain what had happened and to watch their interactions and Steve's cooking. The whole scene was charmingly animated. I hadn't been a part of these nights and felt something close to bliss at being included. But in that awkwardly shaped and horribly lit kitchen, my heart sank. Steve was teasing Lisa nonstop about her sexual aspirations. She didn't know what any of it meant, and her face was blank with pain and confusion. He was ridiculing her with sexual innuendos that she wasn't old enough to understand. And of course she couldn't understand why her father would talk to her this way. Steve was joking about bedroom antics between Lisa and this or that guy. It was so off. I could see that Lisa was in shock.

I will be clear. Steve was not a sexual predator of children. There was something else going on. I haven't studied psychology so I still have difficulty framing it, but my sense is that part of Steve's fractured emotional development resulted in a his ludicrously fetishizing sexuality and romance. And this, in combination with the fact that he was often obsessively looking for ways to disconnect people from their natural confidence. Well, imagine the scene. . . . I never saw Steve organize around such behaviors, it just happened at times, reflexively. He was on a slide whistle between human and inhuman. He wasn't conscious of the behaviors because, really, how could someone be so awful? I don't say this to excuse him, it's just the stunning fact.

My sadness is beyond telling and sadness is not quite the word for what I felt: damage, betrayal, stupefaction. They come close. I was blown through and vacant and really had no breath to call it anything. I simply wanted to move my body between them, to hold Lisa to my heart, and get her the fuck out of there. Yet I couldn't even do that because Steve's behavior had a paralyzing effect on me, too. But I knew I wasn't going home without her that night. I changed the subject, dinner was served, and after that I gently suggested I take Lisa home with me since I was already there. "That way, Steve, you won't have to bother getting her to the bus stop."

I felt very bad for Steve. Somewhere in himself, he knew. I could see it all over him.

No matter how incomprehensibly off Steve was at times such as this, afterward I always forgot. Later when my highly respected Ph.D. psychoanalyst was taken aback by yet another story I told her about Steve, I got mad at her saying, "How the hell is it that after all I have told you that you are shocked by what he does!" and with a wide-eyed, near loss for words, she said, "I am a human being, one never gets used to it with him." It was balm to my heart to hear her speak these words because they helped me understand my own experience and to forgive myself.

After this I didn't stop Steve from being with Lisa. I did my own calculations, slowly: Steve and Lisa liked and loved each other and there was every reason in this world and the next to support their being together. I would have been like a wrecking ball if I had tried to speak out about it because anything I would have said or done would have created a big mess. It would have damaged what was good. So I decided to take their being alone together on a case-by-case basis. After that evening, I tended to join them or stay home when they were together so I could go get Lisa if she called. She knew to ask me to pick her up if she felt uncomfortable about something in Steve. Steve always gave her a choice in the matter so it was never a problem for him. They both knew when it wasn't working for them. In the end, I found another place for her to be on Wednesday nights where she felt cozy and cared for and I think it was a relief for him to stop. He never asked why I had changed the arrangement. It was as if there was an unspoken agreement to slide over it.

In traveling the forty-five miles across land and water to the school in Oakland there came a time in the early spring of 1989 when I started to be concerned about what I would do if there was an earthquake. Both Steve and my boyfriend were often out of town on business so I could not assume their help in the event of an emergency. There was no perfect solution, so I transferred to San Francisco Art Institute in the fall of 1989 so as not to have a body of water between me and my little daughter. That October, right after I had transferred, the Loma Prieta earthquake rocked the area and broke the Bay Bridge between San Francisco and Oakland for months. I had finally anticipated a problem in a timely fashion.

The new school had a fabulous history and views of the San Francisco Bay that included Alcatraz and the Golden Gate Bridge. I felt a great romance at being there. I was older than most of the undergraduate students by ten years and I soon discovered that I drew better than nearly all of them. Kids would approach me smiling to say, "Wow! You actually know how to draw." I was so surprised, even irritated that they didn't. What kind of art school was this!? A few other students were even jealous and behaved badly toward me. I wondered if I had made a big mistake in transferring. On the other hand, it was a gift to be ahead of the game because it gave me some extra time to learn to write. I really needed to make money, and writing was a weak point for me. I needed better communication skills so I could market my art. But I had other reasons, too.

In the beginning I wanted to broaden my own academics to understand what paintings were really saying over time as a way to understand the forces behind culture and social movements. I wanted to understand my own era, I wanted to understand how women were framing the issues compared to men. I wanted to understand the subversive instinct, in myself and in artists like Goya and Manet and even Monet. Simply put, I wanted a dialogue in myself for understanding my creed as an artist. My hunger for this cannot be overstated. I studied writers Linda Nochlin, Camille Paglia, Lucy Lippard, Walter Benjamin, Fredric Jameson, and Frank Stella, who all gave me the handles for art and social analysis that fed my intellect. And thus began my wide arc toward my left brain. I took drawing, painting, and etching classes but my core tussle was in getting myself to put words onto the page for the ideas that mattered to me.

In the beginning I went blank with real terror when I had to write a paper. My mind scattered and I felt utterly undefended as I worked to surface even single words out from under the bottom of the oceans of my perceptions. Instinct alone told me to walk around the house on the days I wasn't in class and talk out loud so I could hear myself and be present in the body to take words and sentences from speech into writing. Talking out loud in a big room by myself was alarming but also revitalizing. I have heard of other dyslexics learning to write in the same way.

As I walked and talked out loud to myself, I held a pencil and paper in my hands to capture the words and sentences. Often I had the feeling that my mind was a fast river, so fast that I could only participate by sitting quietly and watching on the bank. Eventually I thought to turn on National Public Radio in the background to bring an influx of ambient language into my mind so as to kick-start word fascination while I focused on this or that school topic. By half listening to the random conversations on the radio, I was able to tap into a confident parallel stream of talking where more and more individual words caught my attention like shiny fish and helped my deeper self fly up to where the mind could sparkle them into wordy shape.

In analyzing it now, I feel that the intense promptings to write were the beginning of an urge in me to get both hemispheres of my brain, image and language, to balance, relate, and work together. And it is as interesting for me to think of letters as pictorial forms as it is for me to think of paintings as documents of information like written reports.

Later I put these promptings and skills to use with a job in an emerging field called "graphic recording." In the late nineties, I started to visualize information for corporations. It was a new kind of work and by using colored pens on huge sheets of paper taped to the walls, I tracked and captured words as well as visualized content as it flew around the room during corporate meetings. Graphic recording was the art of the iteration, and by God, thanks to Steve and my learning to work together, I knew something about the art of iteration! As many companies in the Bay Area were hiring, I started getting jobs and more experience. I was fabulously well paid for what I privately thought of as "corporate graffiti." Most people who did this work came from an organizational development background and then learned cartooning techniques, but I came from the opposite end, moving from a fine arts background into learning about the organization of information. I was sort of the Jackson Pollack of graphic recorders and I could not believe I was being paid so well for something that was so outrageously experimental and fun. There were particular groups and companies that really liked how I was approaching it and they kept rehiring me. I also did summary maps for weeklong company offsite meetings. These allowed me to bring greater image-making skill and mythology to crystallize the visions that the companies were creating for themselves at the retreats. Years later, the group at Hewlett-Packard, for whom I had worked a lot, told me I was one of the best graphic recorders they'd ever had. I did this work until the dot-com bust in 2001 when companies returned to a meaner and leaner focus again because of the economy.

Steve came by one day to pick Lisa and me up in his little black Porsche to go to a party at his girlfriend's, Tina Redse's, house. With Lisa buckled in on my lap, Steve drove the three of us to the little town of Pescadero, about an hour west of the Bay Area over the small mountain range and down to the coast. I was enjoying the ride and feeling the lovely pull on my body as Steve took the fast curves in his low car. Halfway through, as we were just getting near the skyline, Steve started to tell me how it was that Lisa had two thirds his genes and only one third of mine. I don't know if I'd caught him in an especially inspired state on a day when we just happened to be together or if Steve had been planning for this brilliant conversation.

For years I had seen people tune Steve out because he would at times pull for a concept of reality that was just so off that one dropped into patience waiting for it to be over. Sometimes there would be the noble soul who loved the art of debate and so took time with him to argue the points and laugh and give him a run for his money. But this was never, ever my forte, I just found it annoying, until I really thought through what he was saying at times like this and then it was just outrageous. Okay, I said to myself at the point of this particular conversation, I know he really, *really* likes and admires Lisa so much he can hardly believe she is his, and this is his lame expression of it. In a convivial manner, I lightly implored in an offhanded way, "Come on Steve, she's not more you than me." He was pleasant and enthusiastic but kept going. It was his mental habit to cajole during this kind of conversation. I tuned out because I did not want to dip into his logic or bear up under the implications. Also, I knew that if I had paid close attention there was a good chance I was going to get my feelings hurt and then I'd get mad. He was making me invisible by percentages, again. For most of the ride I was sort of batting it away like a persistent fly while I diffused my awareness by massaging Lisa's little hands (she loves massages), breathing in the fresh scents of the redwood trees and with the ocean air that was stronger as we got nearer to our destination. We were going to a party on a beautiful afternoon and I was predisposed to being happy.

When we arrived, Steve parked about three hundred yards away from the house and as we all got out he continued his line of thought. It finally dawned on me how long this frigging conversation had been going on. It was likely that he felt badly; if anyone had more influence in our child's life it would be me because of all the work and time I had put in compared to him. So as per his usual method of dealing with feelings of insecurity, he flipped this into his having the dominant genes. It was also typical of him to plant a suggestion, intending it take root in my sad sense of disempowerment. The truth is, Steve never had to worry because once he and Lisa had come into each other's lives, she lived as much in his conscious and unconscious as she lived in mine. She was like blotting paper, she soaked us both up because she came from both of us. He just did not know how love worked, and I think he simplistically/primitively thought in terms of owning more shares.

When we walked into the house that afternoon, Steve found Tina and I remember being really relieved that I didn't have to deal with him and that conversation anymore. It was the beginning of my friendship with Tina. I adored this woman, and Lisa really liked her, too. She was a shiny, lovely person who worked to keep her heart bright and open, and in time she was someone, I came to discover, who had a fabulous sense of humor, which helped me deal with Steve. I did not know then that Tina and I would be good friends for years.

A bunch of people at the party were standing in the kitchen when Steve and Tina leaned up against each other, propping themselves against the counter, and started making out. They would do this a lot, at my house, in restaurants, and I could never quite wrap my head around how public they were about their intimacy. I steered Lisa out of the kitchen and into the living room, where she ran about talking and playing with everyone. My daughter has a bright, innate sense of friendship with all beings great and small; it is just the way she is. And as I sat drinking a beer and eating chips, I watched and enjoyed her interactions with everyone that day. Tina and her friends and family always felt like family to my heart, and they had a beautiful sense of childhood and were playful with Lisa. Steve never brought the genes issue up again.

TWENTY-THREE

THE PATH OF THE HEARTH

I think Tina believed if she could just love Steve enough, he would be okay. For my part, I think I was too exhausted to care about Steve with such earnestness anymore. We did like each other in many ways, but I no longer had the illusion that I could bolster him up or save him. There was just too much history between us; I was backed up and closed down. I was done. We sort of existed side by side, for Lisa's sake. What I now believe is that Steve and I were well matched, but it would have only been by telling the deepest truths that we could have had a real relationship. In the end, I don't think we knew how to be honest enough to be responsible to love. I guess that's what it all came down to.

Tina's father died when she was young, but she had a strong mother with a tremendous spirit who had escaped Nazi Germany during World War II. Ruth was very real and one day asked her daughter, "Tina, why are you with Steve? *He doesn't even see who you really are!*" Ruth was angry with her daughter for wasting time with Steve. But Tina was also a keen observer, and told me a number of times that it was the result of watching how Steve parented Lisa—and how he treated me—that she knew she would never marry or have children with him. Still, when Kobun encouraged Steve to propose to Tina, there was a flutter of activity.

Tina and Steve had broken up and she was beginning a relationship with another man, but because of Kobun's influence, Steve walked back into Tina's life and asked her to marry him. Despite her awareness and all of her misgivings, I saw her consider it—all the hope and the bright possibility. Tina confided in me to some extent. She told me how Steve had driven to her house in Pescadero, and how awkward it was for her new boyfriend to leave the house because Steve had suddenly arrived with his proposal. Tina was discreet about the details but I got the picture.

It was during this window of time that I drove with Lisa to NeXT to meet up with Steve. It was on a Saturday afternoon and except for Steve's Mercedes, the parking lots around NeXT were completely empty. When I drove up I was surprised to see Tina. She and Steve were talking to each other next to his car. They seemed upset. I parked, with the nose of my car pointed to the south, and suddenly I gasped: in the parking lot one over, crashed and crumpled, was Tina's new car, totaled. That day, we canceled the plans and Lisa and I left. Tina later explained that upon getting into her car after a fierce argument with Steve, she accidently put it into reverse and accelerated backward, crashing about fifty yards over a six-foot embankment on the south parking lot. She was okay, but she told me the incident made her realize that she couldn't endure a life with Steve. She would end up killing herself, she said, whether by "accident," as in accidentally driving off a road, or worse. She ultimately declined the marriage proposal and they separated for good.

Tina shared two insights with me that still boggle my mind. In the late nineties she told me that Steve shared with her that I was one of the most creative persons he had ever met. Why oh why didn't he tell *me* this? She also told me, some twenty-five years after the fact, that while she was dating Steve there was a moment in which she understood that his and my coming together would have created the deepest peace inside Steve, which is what she wanted for him. I believe this to be true. I had my own sense of it, and now I feel that the most radical piece of insight I have ever understood about Steve and me is that—it was our souls that matched, not our neuroses. Moreover, not only would our coming together have created the deepest peace in Steve, but it would have done so in Lisa and me, too. But this was not to be. The closest we got was when Steve came over a few times to the house on Rinconada and happily said, "You know, it's like we are married!"

Indeed.

Tina contributed to my understanding of myself in a number of ways. She told me many times over the years that it was through me and my example that she learned the value of the feminine way of doing things, something she never thought highly of before. For years I wondered what she could possibly be talking about, but then another woman I knew told me the same thing. Eventually, it dawned on me. They were talking about *the path of the hearth*. There used to exist religions that connected women's homemaking to a sacred dimension—from cooking, cleaning, and making things feel good and beautiful to raising children and loving men. What could be more sacred than a home?

About two years after I moved into the Rinconada house, in 1987, I started a new business. It was inspired by a dream I'd had in which I was at Steve's Woodside house where I saw a set of intricate carvings of the story of Beauty and the Beast. The dream eventually got me wondering about developing fairy tales in huge mural format as a business for children's environments. I couldn't shake this idea after it had landed, so I began figuring out how to do it. Eventually I was in full swing. I began making huge stenciled fairy-tale murals that made whole rooms into storybooklike experiences for children to walk into. I made all my own designs, hiring artists to assist when I needed extra help. I made them for homes, but mainly for pediatric environments such as hospitals, doctor's offices, and Ronald McDonald House. I worked locally and also had some big installations in L.A. and in Boston. It was a business that would allow me to work commercially, retain a fine arts sensibility, and provide excellence in children's environments for families in crisis. Eventually I got to the point of making all the murals in my studio on huge gessoed canvases that I would roll up and FedEx to clients to be hung like extremely expensive wallpaper. Everything was done with the love of layered paint and colored patterns, with textures you could run your hands over. This was the opposite of the infinitely replicable computer-generated image; I wanted children to feel the hand and the aura of the original. I worked to make my murals playful and daring and sweet, like childhood. I knew at the time this was not my real work, more like a placeholder with stacked purposes. It allowed me to work at home late into the night while being within earshot of Lisa. It gave me flexible hours and was hugely important in providing me with years in which to develop my color and form awareness, while making money. It was a lot of work but it was gratifying and fun, especially when I had enough work to hire other artists to help.

After Steve and Tina broke up, he was single for a while. It was then he started to come over to my house on weekends to sleep on my couch in the middle of the day, even when Lisa wasn't there. I thought this was odd but fine until I realized he wasn't talking to me during these visits, just sleeping and then leaving. I didn't like it. I said, "You know, if you are not going to talk to me when you're here, then please don't come over." I felt he wanted to soak up my creativity and the warmth of my home, but didn't value me enough to talk to me. It all pointed to something but I didn't know what. I had a mix of impressions as I watched Steve walk out the door and down the sidewalk to his car. Peering beyond the screen door, I examined my feelings about having basically thrown him out. He looked back at me with a kind of squirrelly hurt pride, but also as if I was the loser. I didn't feel like a loser. I also didn't like throwing him out but I felt he was using me without acknowledgment. If he had had the manners to greet me, talk a bit, and say good-bye, I would have made space for him but he came and went like a thief and it hurt, deeply. I did a lot back then to leverage everything for the common wealth while Steve tended to the amassing of his own uncommon wealth. Beyond this, in the logic of fairy tales, it was like the taking of the rose from the garden in Beauty and the Beast—it looked like such a small thing, but it wasn't.

And then Steve met Laurene Powell. Within a week of their meeting, Steve took Lisa and me out for dinner and told us he had met, in his words, "someone special." He met her at a talk he'd given to the Stanford Graduate School of Business, a talk that he had almost canceled because he was so tired. But he was unbelievably glad he had gone, he said, because he'd met this woman and it seemed like a big deal. Steve gave us the details about how she sat in the front row and then waited for him at the back of the room until after everyone had left, leaning back on a chair and looking intently at him.

"Is she pretty?" Lisa asked.

Steve laughed and threw up his hands. "I really have no idea," he said. "I can't tell."

We showed our happiness for him because he was happy, but I think Lisa and I were also both a little uneasy.

What would it mean?

We would find out a couple of months later.

Lisa and I sat on the floor in the dining room—I was helping her with an art project. I like sparse furnishings and we never had tables big enough for some of our sprawling projects so we just spread out on the floors when we needed it. I loved the floors at the Rinconada house—since Steve had them redone, they were white stained, clean, and without scuffs, and with a little wiping down were like the best tables ever. At this time, I think Lisa was making maps on poster board to learn every country in the world. It was a part of the Nueva curriculum to learn all the countries and their capitals. I always helped her when it came to building things because I liked showing her how to use the right art materials and I loved thinking about content and aesthetics with her. That day we had colored pens and pencils, X-Acto blades and cutting board, tape and spray mount all over the floor as we sat legs straddled and hunched over our work. Lisa's petite body was so cute when she was focused and working like this.

When the knock came, I shouted "Come in," and Steve ushered Laurene into my house. She walked toward me fast and certain, as if she were a model on a runway. When she got within four feet, she struck a pose. She placed one foot in front of the other, before turning them out at gracious angles. She elongated her arms and opened her hands, turned her head to the side, and then looked down at me sitting on the floor with a slight smile on her face.

I was confused.

Why was she modeling for me? Was this what the next generation of Stanford girls was doing? I don't remember anything about the conversation, just the pose and my getting a sense that the world had changed. *Maybe even gone backward,* I thought. This kind of finishing school presentation was precisely what my generation had rejected. Here was a different kind of woman and I was trying to understand what the behavior meant in the mix of everyone being polite at a first meeting. I think I must have looked a little like a flashbulb had gone off in front me—bewildered. Whatever her motivation, I decided that she was very sweet and courageous to present herself as she did.

After that I saw their relationship grow and I came to feel that Steve had met his match. She was ambitious and tough enough for him. I remembered them stopping by right after they had raced in their two cars down the freeway. They were laughing and full of vigor. She'd won, and oh did I love to hear this! Later I found myself very impressed by Laurene's cool-mindedness and negotiation skills when Steve had a run-in with a surly waitress. It was right after their son, Reed, had been born and all five of us, Lisa, Reed, Laurene and Steve, and me had gone to Il Fornaio in Palo Alto for breakfast. Things got off on the wrong foot and Steve was in a power struggle with this older big-boned waitress who wasn't going to let him boss her around. The waitress was in the wrong but Steve was being vicious. The whole thing was ridiculous. Laurene was very cool and narrated what the misunderstanding as it was happening. Her reasoning seemed to help tone down the tension. Right before they became engaged, someone in the group—Mona or Fin Taylor, Tina's cousin—eventually named it. In sharp and utter contrast to all of us, Steve especially, Laurene had no quirks.

There are stories that Laurene had arranged for or anticipated (I am not sure how it came together) Steve's talk at the Stanford Graduate School of Business so she could set up that seemingly fateful meeting. I only found out about this years after the fact. And Laurene claims that they are untrue. But when I first heard about there being a question it was by way of two different people, both women, independent of one another, who sought me out to tell me that there was some kind of setup. One was at the event and the other had a close friend at the event.

Once I was told this I sat with the knowledge deep inside me for a couple of years. I couldn't grasp why this woman who wanted to marry Steve shouldn't marry him—especially since he came to want to marry her. And why had my friends who attended the event been so incensed? Eventually, in 2005 I decided to call on my friend Michael, to ask him what it meant.

Through the years I have called on Michael for his perspective on many things. More often than not, I am relieved and enlivened by what he says, and to have his wisdom and great aerial view of human life. When I told him about what Laurene had allegedly done in order to meet and marry Steve, he laughed with a low and long-drawn-out chuckle. Slowly he said, "Well, you see, love is something we commonly believe is given to us, a gift from something bigger than ourselves, providence or from God, if you will. But if such a thing is manipulated from the level of worldly ambition, it is of a different order." I would think on this for a long time. I liked that he had framed love as being outside the worldly spheres of ambition.

Throughout history, there have certainly been many different kinds of marriages. And you could argue that if Steve wasn't going to be more reflective about how he treated people (and if he wanted to be married), then he was very lucky that Laurene walked in. Moreover, if she chose herself for him in the way that some people have indicated that she did, it all points to her being a match for Steve. I assume that he eventually heard about all of this and I always wondered what he made of it.

Laurene knew how to take care of herself. Though, by her own admission, she was not a warm person, I saw in her a capacity for self-interest that I consider to have aspects that are admirable and ahead of their time in terms of women's empowerment. I came to feel that she was uniquely suited for Steve. Her thick bones, goal-oriented focus, and levelheadedness all told me she could handle what he could mete out. I didn't *not* like her. In fact, I found it easy to care about her. Not long after they married, she came to my house unexpectedly and sat with me on my porch and told me why she loved him. I believed her, but wondered why she was telling me.

I now understand that it might have been strategic. On another day, she followed Steve through my living room enthusiastically telling him, "What a good father you are!" Steve was a pretty poor father, anyone could see that. And anyone could see that he wanted to hear good things about himself even if they weren't true. Laurene was willing to do that for him.

Within about five months of their going out, Steve asked me if I would have them over for dinner so I could get to know them together. It was to be a sort of welcoming dinner. But the request bothered me and I hung back. Parenting, especially single parenting, is exhausting. I didn't have the extra money and I was often very tired by evening, after a full day, doing my own work, driving Lisa forty miles to school, and cooking, having dinner, getting her into bed with stories and conversations. I was usually done in by 8:30. Why couldn't he just take the three of us out for dinner so we could talk and not have me work so much? Slowly it dawned on me. Steve was attempting to recast the roles to fit his newest narrative. This time it was with me as his mother, which would have made Laurene into my daughter-in-law. In that scenario, my having them for dinner made sense.

I felt insulted and thunder rolled inside me.

Was everything going to be a big awful lie again?

I didn't have them over for dinner nor did Steve and I talk about it. I didn't even try to bring it up because I knew better than to try and manage that conversation with him. It would have amounted to nothing but another horrible argument so I just let the whole thing drop, incomplete as per our usual.

Through the years Steve and many of his promotional people, including marketers, attorneys, and biographers, and the collection of people he had around him, worked in a number of ways at different times to publicly define me as an inconsequential person who was a hanger-on and a whack job, who got pregnant so that I would have access to Steve's wealth. But I am not motivated to deceive. In fact, intentional deception absolutely terrifies me. I make for a very poor trickster and I am far from having the glossy finish of a player. The law of my being is that I only derive strength after achieving transparency into the truth. And so how strange then is it that I have been publicly vilified for exactly what I would not do and what Laurene successfully did do to become his wife? Steve respected power and Laurene had earned her place next to him by doing exactly as she had.

TWENTY-FOUR

THE WATCHTOWER

In 1998, Andy Herzfeld of the original Mac team, with his wife, Joyce McClure, invited me to join them for a Bob Dylan concert at Shoreline. I jumped at the chance to see "Grampa Dylan" as Joyce affectionately referred to him. It was one of the most powerful performances I've ever witnessed. The sound that amplified out of Dylan's four-man band was impossibly huge. It blew my mind. And when they played "All Along the Watchtower," it seemed to gather the winds to whip up a storm out of nowhere. It was music as invocation with Dylan in the role of shaman. The memory of that night and that song has stayed with me all these years for one simple reason: Steve lived inside each and every song-temple Dylan ever wrote—perhaps that one most of all.

That evening we sat in Woz's box with around twenty other people. Woz! I hadn't seen him since before Lisa was born. At intermission when he found out that I was present, he turned around and looked at me from the front of the box, stunned. We stared at each other for a very, very long time. I remember all these happy people trying to get me to go up and talk to him, "Come on up, come up here. Sit next to Woz and talk to him." But I pressed back against my chair at the farthest corner of the box. It was the weirdest scene: Woz's stare was so intense that I just couldn't move or speak. It had been nearly twenty years of world-changing history since we had been in the other's company, but from the way he was looking at me, I felt that he had some idea of what I had been through.

Much later, in 2006, I heard Woz on NPR's *City Arts and Lectures.* Among many things, he told his personal story leading up to the founding of Apple. I found it touching and also very interesting to hear how his personality and creativity wove through Apple's history. I always knew that Steve expected to be famous, but I never thought about what it all meant to Woz. In the vacuum of any real knowledge I had assumed many things, yet as I listened to the interview that day I heard a surprising story and felt a puzzle piece click into place. Woz said that as a child he wanted to be an engineer like his dad. He didn't have aspirations of fame and fortune. He just loved his dad and wanted to be like him.

When Woz designed the first personal computer prototype Steve said something like, "Hey! We can sell this." But from that interview I understood that Woz was reticent about being a founder of Apple and that Steve actually had to talk him into going into business with him. Steve needed Woz because even though Steve was proficient with technology, Woz was the technological genius. The way I see it, if Woz had made a different choice—as he almost did—Steve would have found another Woz. Because above all else, Steve was driven to move ahead, to become famous, and to make his mark. (As to that other creative genius, I believe that Steve was somehow informed by Dylan's love of playing with amplification. Steve was certainly an amplifying genius.)

Back to that 2006 interview. It was by way of Woz's careful discretion that I understood even more of what went on when the interviewer mentioned a line in Woz's book. It was something about how he (Woz) would rather be the guy who laughed than the guy who controlled things. The interviewer asked if he was referring to Steve. "No," Woz said. It was just a "general philosophy."

Sometimes people don't say things because they understand too much. Sometimes they stay quiet because they don't understand enough. Sometimes people speak before they really understand. And sometimes they don't because they know no one is listening. But it's all part of history, this speaking and not speaking.

My history with Steve is so easily misinterpreted that I haven't talked with the press very often. Society has assumptions about the type of woman who would claim that a powerful man like Steve is the father of her child—no matter that he *is* our child's father. It's just never been worth it for me to confront that stereotype.

The histories of women involved with so-called great men occupy a shabby territory in the public's mind. And so it was when I had no voice and little to protect me that Steve leveraged this misanthropic confusion to avoid responsibility (as if responsibility were a bad thing). It was that simple and that obvious. No one cared, so I held my silence and worked to keep my child safe, and later, to bring her together with her father. I was operating out of a mother's instinct because I lacked the ability to do battle with Steve and all the moneyed interests that surrounded him. Lisa and I really suffered and should have been protected by law and by community. But we weren't. Instead I learned to lay low and to study what was so right—and so profoundly wrong—with him for over thirty years.

The Apple cult was all about being hidden, but Daniel Kottke became a willing source of information about Apple and Steve (and about me, too). I feel that Daniel spoke to reporters before understanding his own relationship to the truth. But he speaks so well and was so available that many reached out to him. What a boon for the reporters. Steve purely hated him for it. I believe that much of what has been written about the Apple history has Daniel's perceptions stamped all over it. We live in a time of multiple narratives. That's a good thing because the collective wisdom is served by hearing different sides of a single story. I'm all for it, even if I'm still figuring it out for myself.

Daniel was one of the first thirteen full-time employees at Apple, but the only one of the first one hundred who did not become a multi-millionaire. After it was clear that Daniel wasn't going to get a fair shake, it was Woz who later made sure that Daniel got stock in Apple. And I heard Steve ridicule Woz for it.

Daniel used some of his stock to buy a Victorian house in Palo Alto. These days his house is filled with stuff. A lot of stuff. Daniel collects things he feels are interesting and important. It starts out on his front porch and moves to the entryway just inside the door. It goes up the stairway with piles on each successive step and down the hall of the ground floor, into the rooms and out into the backyard. Tall shelving is lined up and filled to overflowing in all the rooms, and blocks the light from the windows. To get through the house you have to move through pathways, negative space that has been sculpted between the valuables.

Daniel's home feels to me like the storage basement of an old museum or library. I don't think he suspects he is a hoarder because he thinks of all of his things as extremely valuable. Over time, as the collectibles and the dust gathered, I began to understand something was wrong. Daniel's house seemed to have turned into a holding pen for the lost idealism of the sixties and seventies. I feel Daniel has chased that idealism over the years, but has never been able to put things together, to clarify and organize. It's as if he's the curator of a lost time capsule, maintaining his collection and a loyalty to something he still doesn't understand.

When you talk to Daniel, his expressions are cultured; his words are intelligent and credible. He projects big bright architectures with clear, gracious interiors. But when you see his house, you notice that things aren't as they seem. I find that what Daniel projects and how he actually lives—what he says and what he understands—are as disjunctive as Steve's visionary clarity and his inhumanity.

People love Daniel and I remembered why when I saw him back in August of 2010. Daniel and I had dinner together and our conversation led us to his wanting to share some information in a book he had, so after dinner we went to his house to get it. The house was many times more stuffed with things than the last time I'd visited, some seven years earlier. It sent a jolt through me. I sat on a couch, where things fell in on me just from my weight pressing in on the cushions. I wedged my feet between the seat and the coffee table that was also completely stacked with books and science trinkets and other interesting things. I sat very still, careful not to disturb any of it because it all seemed alive.

Totally entranced, I watched as Daniel calmly searched for the book. His eyes sparkle and his thin frame radiates a powerful warmth. I watched his hands—refined and careful, he has those techie spiderlike fingers, and he holds things at a distance in his fingertips, away from his palms. He's pretty sure he knows where everything is and he's proud of his ordering system, too. However, on this day he was fretting because he was unable to find the book he wanted to lend me. He was mad at himself and dismayed by the fact that he loans stuff out and never gets it back. Quietly under his breath, he said, "I need a better system for tracking the loans. Someone must have borrowed that book and never returned it." Then he let out a small sharp cry, "People don't return my stuffff!"

In his late fifties, Daniel's beautiful golden boy looks have left him. He has the careworn face of an old mother. It suddenly occurred to me to ask why he didn't get a stock option at Apple. I wondered at myself for never having asked before. I had automatically aligned with Steve's telling me that, "Just because Daniel pushes a broom around when the floors need sweeping doesn't mean he deserves stock!" At the time, I had accepted the statement at face value, but by 2010 I finally had amassed enough life experience to question absolutely everything Steve had ever said.

"Oh *that*," Daniel told me. "Steve had offered me a job in marketing." His words came out soft with layers of self-knowledge beneath the simple response. Hearing this I suddenly felt emblazoned by the prospect of Daniel in marketing. It seemed like it would have been a great idea because he is so people-oriented and bright. I reacted to it with enthusiasm, "Oh my God! He did? Is *that* ever a fit!" I had never thought of it. "Steve's brilliant," I said. Then Daniel went on to tell me, "But I wasn't interested in marketing because I had something like a fever to understand the technology. I didn't want to stop learning how the computer worked. I couldn't stop!" This was even more eye opening to me. I'd never seen Daniel as having a strong, uncompromising passion for anything. He saunters, and his mind seems to have cultivated its own slim brand of equanimity, the kind that is the result of a familiarity with Buddhist thought, but somehow lacks an understanding of how much skin he has in the game. Many of my generation wanted to live the spiritual teachings, but we sometimes skipped the necessary work. The fact is, though, Daniel truly needed to understand how technology worked and his urgency to do so indicates to me that he may have been wrestling with the more profound riddles and inconsistencies in the technology itself. (The missing bite/byte, the missing piece/peace.)

"So I never pursued the marketing opportunity," Daniel told me. "I just couldn't leave off from the technology." Then he said, "Well, at least *I* have a home." He knew that I had been ill (some kind of medically undefined infection for years), virtually penniless, and living with decency only by the kindness of strangers. To this I laughed out loud, stunned that he would say such a thing to me. Then he sighed and gave up his search for the book, and made a note to "upgrade his retrieval system."

After Daniel lost out on the Apple stock because Steve thought he was undeserving, Daniel retaliated by talking to every reporter that came to town. I say "retaliated" because that's what it looked like, especially in the beginning when he was so newly burned. But then Daniel seemed to take on the role of unofficial spokesman, talking to anyone about Apple. He would explain history through his perspective, and would then, generously, I thought, direct journalists to other people. To wit, *a marketer*! In later years I've sometimes thought Daniel felt he owned Steve's history because for a while, if I ever told him something he didn't know, he'd act huffy and proprietary. But even that behavior changed. He always seemed to keep moving forward through his role and in his effort to be a person of worth.

There was day in about 2006 when I heard Daniel bragging of his association with Steve and Apple to a small group of men outside of Peet's Coffee in Palo Alto. He didn't know I was standing nearby, unable to avoid hearing all that he said. That day I saw the confusion in the full light of day that Daniel's hoarding implied to me—hoarding being the outward expression of what we cannot afford to forget . . . or remember. My jaw dropped and my body squirmed to hear his gloating because I knew he had been such a casualty of it all and didn't recognize that. When Daniel caught sight of me, he shifted effortlessly and greeted my arrival with a broad, languid smile and a bright long-drawn-out, "Well if it isn't Chrisann!"

I've truly hated Steve at times, but never for very long. Sharing a daughter with him has forced me to think about things more deeply. Steve the saint, the alien, the despot, the primitive and punishing masculine god of yore, the liar, the marionette, the shaman, the super-brilliant, super-speedy, supersensitive, obsessed narcissist, the magician amplifier, the mastermind, the cult hero, the id of the iEverything, the extraordinarily beautiful and honest genius, the broken toy under the bed, the motherless boy. It is only because of Lisa that I have felt obligated to comprehend the many broken shards of Steve's glittering brilliance—I never would have otherwise.

For all the sparkling, spacious beauty of the Apple stores, the opposite was true of one of its founders. Steve was a haunted house. There was an obvious imbalance between us—our circumstances, our life views, the things we cared about and valued. And it was beyond the psychological and legal handles of our day to bring about a balance between the two of us because his brokenness was managed and orchestrated in such an extremely masterful way. Few, if anyone, could catch up to even define what was going on, much less legally address it.

In thinking about how this polarization could have happened, I come back constantly to the reality distortion field. Because only a massive distortion of reality could seek to justify the lack of ethical accountability that was all too common in Steve, and in the world of *business as usual*.

So much is out of balance these days. And I would include the computer in that because I believe that it is out of alignment with our greatest human values. Think about it. Steve and the tech industry made the computer into one of the most seductive, affordable tools for mass use of any century—perhaps the golden calf of our day. There's no doubt that computers are incredibly useful and elegant. They increase organization, speed, and efficiency, and help us make virtual connections to people and ideas worldwide. Computers have helped us increase our productivity and creativity by magnitudes. And yet, at the risk of sounding naïve, I think it is what is inside us that makes them useful—*if* and when they are useful. I think it's important to not only look at how they free us up but also how they limit us. The computer flattens the emotional and spiritual dimensions of our lives, as it coaxes us away from real-time, face-to-face relationships with people and the natural world. I fear that one day we will finally have the science to show that generations of children have been harmed from using computers way too early and way too much.

The sobering reality is that when Apple got big Steve had a chance to change business practices in the world to create more sustainable ecological and humanistic standards for all business worldwide. But he didn't do that.

And so it is down to each one of us.

In boardrooms, cafés, governments all over the world, around dining tables in conversations with friends and especially with our children, we should be engaging in new dialogues to expand our ethical imaginations. Positive ethical interaction has a life force all its own. I think wealth should not only be measured by the market capitalization of commercial enterprise but maybe even more so by dynamic reciprocity between all people and all living systems on earth.

I feel very lucky to be Lisa's mom. She is the one who makes my heart shine. I also feel lucky because I know what my real work is, both as an artist and a mother. My work as a mother was so profoundly disregarded that I've had to go inward to where all the answers ultimately live and to acknowledge myself. From what I can see, the world is in the grip of having to work out the relationship between love and power. Between love that is not powerful enough and power that is not loving enough. Being in Steve's shadow was a call to arms for me to understand what real knowledge is. Steve never gave me money appropriate to what I did for our daughter and for him, because he never managed to understand how much I gave, so I am left with that which is priceless. How about that.

There is always more work to do. I now have the task of stepping into the world and dealing with the consequences of telling my story. But more than this, I plan on finding my way into joy—maybe even more than ever before. And Lisa, like all children, has the extraordinary job of understanding, integrating, and balancing the truth and the best of her two parents into her own one life, Since Steve and I never did work it out between us, it's a real job for her. But we both gave her many gifts and now it's her opportunity to lead a life that comes from having understood both her parents and so to move into her own calling and authority.

Lisa is a planner and she has a very good sense of right order. She can handle everything she's been given. And one of the great pleasures of my life is to watch my daughter when she putters because she processes things in such gentle and thorough ways. It's like she wheels around between heaven and earth, circling and landing, happy and intact in her perfect world of Lisa-ness. As an amalgam of her two parents, like all children, she is greater than the sum of the parts. I don't think she knows how exquisite she is or how huge her capacity and opportunities are. But she reveals it when she speaks and writes. Her ideas and sentences come out whole and as astonishing as perfect gemstones.

It's the best thing in the world to be looking forward to what she and the people of her generation will do over the next thirty to forty years.

POSTSCRIPT

On October 5, 2011, as I was driving down 280 north to Palo Alto, Lisa called to tell me that her dad had just died. Few words passed between us. There was a lot of space. I was glad her boyfriend was there with her since I couldn't be. I turned into town to meet a friend in Menlo Park. The sky overhead was covered with the darkest charcoal-gray clouds imaginable. Yet there arched between Menlo Park and Palo Alto was a breathtakingly brilliant double rainbow. It floated like a prayer flag as if in recognition and honor of Steve's death.

In Mona's book *Anywhere But Here* she writes something to the effect that, *Everyone we know before the age of twenty-five, we know for life*. Steve was the first of my peers to die. He was my only child's father, and someone, that despite it all, I truly loved. I was deeply shaken.

Lisa was with Steve the moment he died, and later that week she narrated his last moments to me. I replayed her words in my mind many times over the next months, working in finer and finer detail to take Steve's death into my heart, to fully embrace and acknowledge that he was gone. But it was like that idea of infinity that my father had shown me at the kitchen table when I was young: with every increment of allowance of Steve's death into my heart, I could only get halfway closer to what it meant to me.

I had been invited to Steve's memorial service at Stanford because I had requested to be included. But then I was uninvited because I had given *Rolling Stone* permission to print a piece about Steve and our early years together. So it was only as a result of Lisa's narration that I could see my way into my own experience of his death. I sat alone in Los Altos Hills overlooking Duveneck Ranch during the funeral and the memorial trying to fathom it all.

A few months later, I became aware that things had been written and said about me and my life with Steve that never had been checked with me. Things that were inaccurate and shameful. I felt like I had been skinned alive from the inside out. Was this Steve's reach beyond the grave? Oh clever boy! One evening I was in so much pain that I called a friend to meet me for dinner because I could not bear it alone. That night, I drank a glass of red wine and ate red meat to numb myself. My friend studied me and then said, "I don't think your pain is due to the libel. I think it is because of Steve's death." This was more than three months after he'd died. I had by this time recognized an enormous relief in myself that he was gone. Her words seemed kind but ridiculous.

The next evening, I walked around straightening my home because I could manage little else. Puttering. I was being made to look like a crazy person once again because it was easier for people to do this than to face Steve's failure to do the right thing. I felt angry and distraught, but quiet. I looked at the facts: it was going to take me *at least* another year to finish writing my own story, and I couldn't keep drinking red wine and eating meat to get through the days. And I couldn't write in this much pain, either. In a calm and calculated way my thoughts turned toward suicide. I hated this world.

Yet my mind has a habit of flipping things around to find different ways to see. I'm a problem solver. And so, without intending to, my friend's comment from the previous night came back to me. I asked myself if it could be Steve's death and not the libelous humiliation that was causing the pain. It was just an idea. I didn't expect much but once I'd posed the question, I was, to my great surprise, suddenly transported out of the acidlike pain and able to recognize my own true grief. It *was* about Steve's death and I was grieving. This was the truth. Eventually I understood that the impossible level of pain was a confusion of the two conditions, but that Steve's death was by far the stronger reality. Sorrow washed through me in waves that centered and grounded me. The truth I could live with.

When I went to bed that night I held close to my grief. I had to sleep but at the same time stay focused or I would go crazy trying to work out how I was going to deal with the libel. From within a deep emotional focus, I drifted in and out of a meditative state for about three hours. In it Steve came forward and showed me the truth of the love between us. He sort of merged into me, not as if we were one person but as if we were an intricate and complex kaleidoscope of interlocking yin and yang, fitting parts. He directed my awareness to a ball of light. It was like a brilliant sun the size of a small beach ball, hot white in the center that bled like liquid out to a rosy-, saffron-, and salmon-colored edge. In the dream we stood together at Duveneck Ranch under some trees watching the ball of light moving back and forth up a hillside like a printer stylus. It went back and forth, back and forth with a fifty-foot-wide swath as it climbed. Steve pointed out, to make sure that I saw that no matter where the ball of light was, no object cast a shadow. There wasn't a tree or a rock or even a single blade of grass that wasn't illuminated on all sides all at once, after the little sun had passed over. I studied in awe—delighted. Steve was sort of sobbing and simultaneously as sweet and happy as I had ever known him. We shared all states at once: peace and sorrow, joy, and love in the ache of truth and loss. And I kept refocusing as I rested through the hours so I could stay connected to him. Finally, after I could not focus anymore and started to fall off to sleep, I saw the ball of light move all the way up to the top of the mountain, become a setting sun, and then slip over the horizon as I finally dropped off into sleep.

Steve was right when he said he would lose his humanity in the business world. And yet the one and only true reality that we can be sure of is that despite all appearance to the contrary, everything is love. I track back to the glowing admiration I felt toward Steve at the very beginning, which is, among many things, that he had the strength to walk with who he was and would become. And though he came to lose sight of what was human and ethical all too often (and more and more as time passed), that he at one time knew the difference between who he was and the role he would play deepens my appreciation and love for him and all he carried.

ACKNOWLEDGMENTS

There are three things I never wanted to do in this life and one of them was to write a book. Nonetheless I have and without the following people, I truly could never have done it. The fact that "I" could write this book suggests anyone can do anything.

To my agent, Christine Tomasino: intelligent, funny, savvy, tireless, committed, detailed, hugely insightful, friend—a torchbearer for something bigger than words—she only stepped in when she was needed and she was needed *a lot*.

To St. Martin's Press: George Witte, Matt Baldacci, and Sally Richardson for seeing the potential and caring about this story for all the right reasons. To Brenda Copeland: my editor at St. Martin's Press; happy-go-lucky, intuitive, hilarious, genius—she got the questions right and very often went very far beyond the pale to care, meet, and to work with my content. To Laura Chasen—Brenda's assistant behind the scenes; David Stanford Burr, production editor and copy editor; James Iacobelli, cover designer; Eric Rayman, attorney; Stephanie Hargadon, publicist. I bow to all your talents with my sincerest gratitude for your expert assistance.

To Norman Seeff for granting permission for the use of your photograph of Steve for the cover.

To Ciba Shanãe, and all others who have generously shared their research and teachings with me.

To Eric Case, who just kept giving me computers as I burned through them writing drafts for over five years.

To the Suppes women: Deborah, Trisha, Anney, Christine, and Joanne, who I never had the privilege of meeting. You were pivotal in supporting, advancing, and preserving everything that was important in the development and completion of this book.

To Margo McAuliff and Rhadiante; you gave me a home to live in while I found my feet for both my health and my book.

To Jay Schaefer, Terri Beuthin, and Alan Briskin, Ph.D., for your kind and gifted assistance in the earlier edits.

To Damon Miller, M.D., for helping me keep body and soul together.

To Ruben Fuentez and Ann O'Hearn—you know what you did.

—Thank you!

INDEX